OXFORD WORLD'S CLASSICS

MARY WOLLSTONECRAFT SHELLEY
AND PERCY BYSSHE SHELLEY

History of a Six Weeks' Tour

Through a Part of France, Switzerland,
Germany, and Holland: with Letters
Descriptive of a Sail Round the Lake
of Geneva, and of the Glaciers
of Chamouni.

Edited with an Introduction and Notes by
CIAN DUFFY
ANNA MERCER

W0114020

OXFORD
UNIVERSITY PRESS

OXFORD
UNIVERSITY PRESS

Great Clarendon Street, Oxford, OX2 6DP,
United Kingdom

Oxford University Press is a department of the University of Oxford.
It furthers the University's objective of excellence in research, scholarship,
and education by publishing worldwide. Oxford is a registered trade mark of
Oxford University Press in the UK and in certain other countries

Published in the United States of America by Oxford University Press
198 Madison Avenue, New York, NY 10016, United States of America

British Library Cataloguing in Publication Data
Data available

Library of Congress Control Number: 2024946899

ISBN 9780192858276

Printed and bound in the UK by
Clays Ltd, Elcograf S.p.A.

The manufacturer's authorised representative in the EU for product safety is
Oxford University Press España S.A. of El Parque Empresarial San Fernando de Henares,
Avenida de Castilla, 2 – 28830 Madrid (www.oup.es/en or product.safety@oup.com).
OUP España S.A. also acts as importer into Spain of products made by the manufacturer.

HISTORY OF A SIX WEEKS' TOUR

MARY WOLLSTONECRAFT SHELLEY (née Godwin) was born in 1797. Her parents were William Godwin, author of *An Enquiry Concerning Political Justice* and *Caleb Williams*, and Mary Wollstonecraft, author of *Vindication of the Rights of Woman* and *Maria, or, The Wrongs of Woman*. In 1814, Mary eloped with the already-married Percy Shelley on a six weeks' tour of Western Europe, accompanied by her stepsister, Claire Clairmont. Two years later, Mary, Percy, and Claire spent the summer of 1816 in Switzerland with Lord Byron, and she married Percy in December of that year. *History of a Six Weeks' Tour*, co-written with Percy, was Mary's first publication: it describes countries torn by war and the so-called 'year without a summer', one of the most culturally productive periods in English Romanticism. Best remembered for her novels *Frankenstein* and *The Last Man*, Mary also wrote poetry, short stories, historical novels, literary biographies, translations, and more travel writing; she also compiled and published the first editions of Percy's poetry and prose. She died in 1851.

PERCY BYSSHE SHELLEY was born in 1792. He is one of the best-known poets of the English Romantic period, author of the celebrated 'Ode to the West Wind', 'Ozymandias', and 'To a Sky-Lark', of intimate love lyrics never meant for publication, and of large-scale historical and political dramas like *Prometheus Unbound, The Cenci*, and *Hellas*. When Percy met Mary Wollstonecraft Godwin in 1814, he was still relatively unknown, despite early notoriety following expulsion from Oxford University in 1811 and the publication of his inflammatory 'philosophical poem' *Queen Mab* in 1813. Percy's contributions to *History of a Six Weeks' Tour* show his interest in the legacy of the French Revolution, his appreciation for the beauty of nature, and the genesis of the ideas about imagination and cultural change he would later develop in 'A Defence of Poetry'. After Percy drowned in 1822, Mary ensured his legacy by publishing her landmark editions of *Posthumous Poems* (1824), *Poetical Works* (1839), and *Essays, Letters from Abroad, Translations and Fragments* (1840).

CIAN DUFFY is professor of English literature at Lund University, Sweden. His research examines various aspects of the intellectual life and cultural history of Europe during the Romantic period, particularly the Shelley circle, the sublime, and Romanticism in the Nordic countries. Recent publications include (ed.) *The Cambridge Companion to the Romantic Sublime* (Cambridge, 2023) and *British Romanticism and Denmark* (Edinburgh, 2022).

ANNA MERCER is senior lecturer in English literature at Cardiff University, UK. She is the author of *The Collaborative Literary Relationship of Percy Bysshe Shelley and Mary Wollstonecraft Shelley* (Routledge, 2019) as well as a range of articles on the Shelley circle and the Coleridge family. She has worked closely with Keats House Museum in Hampstead, London, since 2017, and she founded The Shelley Conference that same year.

OXFORD WORLD'S CLASSICS

For over 100 years Oxford World's Classics have brought readers closer to the world's great literature. Now with over 700 titles—from the 4,000-year-old myths of Mesopotamia to the twentieth century's greatest novels—the series makes available lesser-known as well as celebrated writing.

The pocket-sized hardbacks of the early years contained introductions by Virginia Woolf, T. S. Eliot, Graham Greene, and other literary figures which enriched the experience of reading. Today the series is recognized for its fine scholarship and reliability in texts that span world literature, drama and poetry, religion, philosophy, and politics. Each edition includes perceptive commentary and essential background information to meet the changing needs of readers.

ACKNOWLEDGEMENTS

Many people have contributed in one way or another to this edition. We would like to thank Luciana O'Flaherty and Emma Varley, at Oxford University Press, for guiding it from conception to publication. We are also indebted to previous editors of *History of a Six Weeks' Tour* for letting us stand on their shoulders: thank you Jeanne Moskal, E. B. Murray, and Anne Rouhette. For invaluable assistance with manuscript materials, thanks to Elizabeth Denlinger and her colleagues Charles Carter and Timothy Gress at the Carl H. Pforzheimer Collection of Shelley and His Circle at the New York Public Library; to Stephen Hebron and the staff at the Bodleian Library; to Fabiana Duglio at the British Library; and to Peter Findlay and Kirsty McHugh at the John Murray Archive of the National Library of Scotland. Laure Decomble at the Musée Alpin Chamonix was generous with her knowledge of historical locations and persons 'under the eye of Mont Blanc'. We are very fortunate to have 'often talked over the incidents [and] scenery' of *History of a Six Weeks' Tour* with colleagues and friends: thanks in particular to Christoph Bode, Bysshe Inigo Coffey, Nora Crook, Amanda Blake Davis, Mari Komnæs, Diego Saglia, Tess Somervell, and Patrick Vincent. Anna Mercer would like to thank Mariam Wassif for assistance regarding locations in Paris, and Rob Shakespeare and the staff at Keats House Museum, London, for supporting her work. A trip to the Keats-Shelley House in Rome, and the assistance of Ella Kilgallon, were inspirational and informative. Anna would also like to thank her students at Cardiff University for many great discussions of *History of a Six Weeks' Tour*. Cian Duffy would like to thank Lisbet Ryg Olsen, for many a 'summer of delight and beauty' in the Alps.

CONTENTS

ABBREVIATIONS

Beckford	William Beckford's marginalia in a first edition of *HSWT*, now held in The Carl H. Pforzheimer Collection of Shelley and His Circle, New York Public Library (MS S'ANA 0752). Quoted here by kind permission of The Carl H. Pforzheimer Collection of Shelley and His Circle, New York Public Library, Astor, Lenox, and Tilden Foundations.
Bieri	James Bieri, *Percy Bysshe Shelley: A Biography*, 2 vols. (Newark: University of Delaware Press, 2005).
BLJ	*Byron's Letters and Journals*, ed. Leslie A. Marchand, 12 vols. (London: John Murray, 1973).
CC Journals	*The Journals of Claire Clairmont*, ed. Marion Kingston Stocking (Cambridge, MA: Harvard University Press, 1968).
CC Revised Journal	A revision by Claire Clairmont of her first account of the six weeks' tour of 1814; reproduced in *Shelley and His Circle: Volume III*, ed. Kenneth Neil Cameron (Cambridge, MA: Harvard University Press, 1970), 324–75.
CPPBS	*The Complete Poetry of Percy Bysshe Shelley: Volume III*, ed. Neil Fraistat and Nora Crook (Baltimore: Johns Hopkins University Press, 2012).
De Beer	Gavin De Beer, 'An "Atheist" in the Alps', *Keats-Shelley Memorial Bulletin*, 9 (1958), 1–15.
Elton	Charles Isaac Elton, *An Account of Shelley's Visits to France, Switzerland, and Savoy, in the Years 1814 and 1816* (London, 1894).
Erkelenz	Michael Erkelenz, 'The Poetry of Wandering: "Mont Blanc" in "History of a Six Weeks' Tour"', *Keats–Shelley Journal*, 62 (2014), 78–101.
Essays	*Essays, Letters from Abroad, Translations and Fragments, by Percy Bysshe Shelley*, ed. Mary Wollstonecraft Shelley, 2 vols. (London, 1839).
F1818	Mary Shelley, *Frankenstein, or The Modern Prometheus*, 3 vols. (London 1818).

F1831	Mary Shelley, *Frankenstein, or The Modern Prometheus*, revised edition, 3 vols. (London, 1831).
Geneva Nbk	*The Geneva Notebook of Percy Bysshe Shelley*, ed. Michael Erkelenz, vol. 11 of *The Bodleian Shelley Manuscripts Facsimile Series*, gen. ed. Donald H. Reiman (New York: Garland, 1992).
Julie	Jean-Jacques Rousseau, *Julie, or the New Heloise: Letters of Two Lovers who Live in a Small Town at the Foot of the Alps* [1761], ed. and transl. Philip Stewart and Jean Vaché, vol. 6 of *The Collected Writings of Rousseau* (Dartmouth: University Press of New England, 1997).
Koszul	A. H. Koszul, 'Notes and Corrections to Shelley's "History of a Six Weeks' Tour" (1817)', *Modern Language Review*, vol. 2, no. 1 (October 1906), 61–2.
Moskal	*The Novels and Selected Works of Mary Shelley: Vol. III, Travel Writing*, ed. Jeanne Moskal (London: Pickering and Chatto, 1996).
Murray	*The Prose Works of Percy Bysshe Shelley*, ed. E. B. Murray, 1 vol. (Oxford: Oxford University Press, 1993).
MWS Journals	*The Journals of Mary Wollstonecraft Shelley*, ed. Paula R. Feldman and Diana Scott Kilvert (Baltimore: Johns Hopkins University Press, 1987).
MWS Letters	*The Letters of Mary Wollstonecraft Shelley*, ed. Betty T. Bennett, 3 vols. (Baltimore: Johns Hopkins University Press, 1980).
PBS Letters	*The Letters of Percy Bysshe Shelley*, ed. Frederick L. Jones, 2 vols. (Oxford: Clarendon Press, 1964).
Polidori	*The Diary of Dr. John William Polidori*, ed. William Micheal Rossetti (London: Matthews, 1911).
PoS	*The Poems of Shelley: Volume 1, 1804–1817*, ed. Geoffrey Matthews and Kelvin Everest (London: Longman, 1989).
PP1824	*Posthumous Poems of Percy Bysshe Shelley*, ed. Mary Wollstonecraft Shelley (London, 1824).
Prose	*Shelley's Prose*, ed. David Lee Clark (Albuquerque: University of New Mexico Press, 1954).
PW1839	*Poetical Works of Percy Bysshe Shelley*, ed. Mary Wollstonecraft Shelley, 4 vols. (London, 1839).

Rambles	Mary Shelley, *Rambles in Germany and Italy in 1840, 1842, and 1843*, 2 vols. (London, 1844).
Rouhette	*Histoire d'un voyage de six semaines*, ed. and transl. Anne Rouhette (Aix-en-Provence: Presse Universitaires de Provence, 2015).
SC	*Shelley and His Circle: 1772–1822*, ed. Kenneth Neil Cameron, Neil Fraistat, Donald H. Reiman, et al., 10 vols. to date (Cambridge, MA: Harvard University Press, 1961–2002).
SDN	The Scrope Davies Notebook, which contains alternative versions of 'Mont Blanc', 'Hymn to Intellectual Beauty', and other works by Percy Bysshe Shelley. Now held in the British Library (Loan MS 70/8); transcription available via The Shelley–Godwin Archive.
SPP	*Percy Bysshe Shelley: Selected Poems and Prose*, ed. Jack Donovan and Cian Duffy (London: Penguin, 2016).
Tour	Helen Maria Williams, *A Tour in Switzerland*, 2 vols. (London, 1798).
Travels	William Coxe, *Travels in Switzerland and in the Country of the Grissons*, 3 vols. (Basel, 1802).
Traveller's Guide	Henry Coxe, *The Traveller's Guide in Switzerland* (London, 1816).
Voyages	Horace-Bénédict de Saussure, *Voyages Dans Les Alpes*, 4 vols. (Neuchâtel, 1779–96).

INTRODUCTION

History of a Six Weeks' Tour through a part of France, Switzerland, Germany and Holland: with Letters Descriptive of a Sail Round the Lake of Geneva, and of the Glaciers of Chamouni (hereafter *HSWT*) is a volume of travel writing by Mary Wollstonecraft Shelley and Percy Bysshe Shelley, who are now recognized as the two of the most important writers of the English Romantic period. It was published anonymously in November 1817 and was the first occasion that writing by Mary appeared in print. It has three parts and covers two separate journeys. The six weeks' tour of the title took place between 28 July and 13 September 1814, when the 16-year-old Mary, accompanied by her stepsister Claire Clairmont, also 16, eloped with the already-married, 21-year-old Percy, travelling by sea, road, and river through countries which had been ravaged by the French Revolutionary and Napoleonic Wars. The four 'Letters' which comprise the second part of *HSWT* date from the so-called '*Frankenstein* summer' of 1816, when Mary, Percy, and Claire were again in Switzerland, and when Mary began to work on her famous novel. The first two letters describe their residence at Cologny, outside Geneva, in a little house called Maison Chapuis, where they were neighbours of Lord Byron, who had taken the nearby Villa Diodati, with his friend and doctor, John Polidori. The third describes a sailing trip made by Percy and Byron around Lake Geneva in the last week of June. And the fourth recounts a short visit to Chamonix, then one of Europe's premier tourist attractions, made by Mary, Percy, and Claire in July 1816, during which Percy began to compose his poem 'Mont Blanc', now one of his most celebrated works, which was first published as the final part of *HSWT*.

 HSWT has sometimes been considered a minor work, mainly of interest as a source of biographical and historical context for more celebrated writings dating from or influenced by these journeys: Mary's novels *Frankenstein* and *The Last Man*; Percy's poems 'Alastor', 'Hymn to Intellectual Beauty', and 'Mont Blanc', and his unfinished short story 'The Assassins' (on which Mary also collaborated); Byron's poems *Childe Harold's Pilgrimage: Canto The Third, Manfred, The Prisoner of Chillon*, and 'Darkness'; and Polidori's Gothic novel *The Vampyre*, which originated from the same ghost-story writing competition as

Frankenstein. More recent scholarship, however, has been alert to the intrinsic literary merits of *HSWT*, to its complex blend of genres and modes, to its engagement with a number of important cultural debates, and to the collaborative nature of its composition, which not only gives the lie to traditional notions of the lone 'Romantic' artist but also sheds light on the wider, lifelong collaboration between Mary and Percy.

In 1817, *HSWT* joined a literary marketplace already burgeoning with accounts of travel to Western Europe, finally accessible again after more than twenty years of war. 'When peace came', Mary recalled almost a decade later, 'when our island prison was opened to us, and our watery exit from it was declared practicable, it was the paramount wish of every English heart [...] to hasten to the continent, and to imitate our forefathers in their almost forgotten custom, of spending the greater part of their lives and fortunes in their carriages on the post-roads'.[1] *HSWT* responds to an array of recent and older writing about the scenes which it describes, notably including Jean-Jacques Rousseau's *Julie, or the New Heloise* (1761), one of the most influential and controversial novels of the late eighteenth and early nineteenth centuries, as well as various political and scientific works. As the preface makes clear, *HSWT* also exemplifies the new, 'Romantic' tendency of travel writing to foreground the response of the traveller to the places and peoples they encounter, a tendency often traced to another key influence on Mary and Percy in 1814 and 1816: *Letters Written During a Short Residence in Sweden, Norway, and Denmark* (1796), by Mary's mother, Mary Wollstonecraft. *HSWT* regularly challenges the often-conservative conventions and clichés of contemporary travel writing, but is on occasion itself markedly (if not uncharacteristically, for the time) prejudiced about foreign cultures and peoples. *HSWT* is critical of the nascent tourist industry, whilst not really registering that Mary, Percy, and Claire were themselves tourists, following, at least in 1816, what were already well-trodden routes to often-visited sites. In the early twenty-first century, *HSWT* can also be read as a record of environmental damage in the Alps in particular, registering the exponential rise in visitor numbers in the early nineteenth century, driven by new 'Romantic' attitudes to nature, and offering witness to glacial landscapes which no longer exist today in the form that Mary, Percy,

---

[1] Mary Wollstonecraft Shelley, review of *The English in Italy* (1826), *The Westminster Review*, vol. 6 (July–October 1826), pp. 325–41 (p. 325).

and Claire saw them in the summers of 1814 and 1816. *HSWT* was also composed against the backdrop of a more immediate climate emergency: 1816 had been 'the year without a summer', when temperatures much colder than average, caused by the eruption of Mount Tambora, in Indonesia, in April 1815, led to failed harvests, food shortages, and social unrest across Europe.

Composition and Publication

HSWT was co-authored by Mary and Percy, and also includes some material probably drawn from Claire's record of the 1814 journey. The published text was prepared between August and October 1817, and written out by Mary, but the collaboration out of which it grew began with the shared journal kept by Mary and Percy on their elopement journey in 1814, which survives in the Bodleian Library (MS Abinger d. 27). The earliest account of the editorial process behind *HSWT* was given by Percy in a letter of 16 December 1817 to Byron's friend, the poet Thomas Moore, who had been sent a copy of 'the little volume' by the publishers and was 'quicksighted enough' to guess the 'real authors' (*PBS Letters*, vol. 1, pp. 580 n. 4, 582–3). *HSWT*, Shelley wrote, 'is composed of two letters written to [by] me signed *S*, & some [two] other letters & the Journal signed *M*. written by Mrs. Shelley' (*PBS Letters*, vol. 1, p. 583). Percy really says no more here than can be gleaned from *HSWT* itself and in fact his letter goes on to obscure, to an extent, the actual process of composition and division of authorial roles, telling Moore that 'that the Journal was written some years ago—the style of it is almost infantine, & it was published in the idea that the Author would never be recognised' (*PBS Letters*, vol. 1, p. 583). This remark about 'the Journal', i.e. the 'six weeks' tour' portion of *HSWT*, shares some of the rhetorical defensiveness of the volume's preface, which also flags up, albeit in a more positive way, the 'youth' of the authors. But Percy's claim is also deceptive because although the original shared journal was written in 1814, the version published in *HSWT* had been very heavily revised in 1817, both by Mary and, possibly, by Percy.[2] But it is also

---

[2] Jeanne Moskal has calculated that of the approximately 8,500 words of the six weeks' tour portion of *HSWT*, 'about 1150 were selected from P.B. Shelley's entries [in the original shared journal] and reproduced, either verbatim or reworked as paraphrase' (*Moskal*, pp. 2–3).

important to remember that anonymous publications, and defensive prefaces, were far from uncommon at the time: Mary's *Frankenstein*, too, was first published without her name.

The provenance of the four letters that make up the second part of *HSWT* is equally complex. Behind Percy's seemingly straightforward account, in other words, lies a much more involved, and to an extent now indecipherable, process of composition. But statements later made by Mary in connection with her decision to include *HSWT* in her edition of *Essays, Letters from Abroad, Translations and Fragments by Percy Bysshe Shelley* (1839), lightly revised and with 'Mont Blanc' removed because she had already published it in her edition of Percy's *Posthumous Poems*, confirm that the process was essentially collaborative. Writing to Shelley's friend, the Radical magazine editor and poet Leigh Hunt, around 5 October 1839, while she was preparing *Essays*, Mary explained her hesitation over including her own work in an edition of her husband's writing: 'I mean to publish the letters appended to the 6 weeks tour—the question is whether the 6 weeks tour itself shall be printed—it was printed and corrected by Shelley though written by me—& being once published—as part of his life might well appear again' (*MWS Letters*, vol. 2, p. 325). And in *Essays* itself she emphasized Percy's role in seeing the volume through the press and attributed to him the initial impetus for the project:

'The Journal of a Six Weeks' Tour', and 'Letters from Geneva', were published many years ago by Shelley himself. The Journal is singular, from the circumstance that it was not written for publication, and was deemed too trivial for such by its author. Shelley caused it to be printed, and added to it his own letters, which contain some of the most beautiful descriptions ever written. (*Essays*, Vol. 1, pp. xx–xxi)

These remarks need to be understood, in context, as part of an edition of Percy's work and as part of Mary's wider attempt to establish and secure his reputation as a writer. And it is clear that when Mary refers to 'the Journal', she means the original shared journal of 1814 and not the revised text published in 1817. A few years later, when Mary was pitching a new volume of travel writing, her *Rambles in Germany and Italy* (1844), to her publisher Edward Moxon, she assured him that 'my 6 weeks tour brought me many compliments', evidently assuming either that he would understand the distinction

between the 'six weeks' tour' and *HSWT* or that the distinction was
in some sense pointless given the collaborative nature of the volume
(*MWS Letters*, vol. 3, p. 96).[3]

It could be argued that the composition of *HSWT* began on
28 July 1814, with the first, joint entries in Mary and Percy's shared
journal, made after they had escaped from London in the early hours
of the morning, leaving Mary's father, the political philosopher and
novelist William Godwin, furious that Percy had, as he put it, conceived 'the impious idea [...] of seducing her, playing the traitor to
me, and deserting his wife', after Godwin had refused his 'consent'.[4]
It is impossible to know whether Mary or Percy already then had the
idea that this journal of their travels would someday be worked up for
publication, but that was certainly a common practice at the time:
Wollstonecraft's *Short Residence*, for example, is based on often
heavily-redacted original letters.[5] The first mention of the project
that would become *HSWT* is a journal entry by Mary for 9 August
1817, when she noted 'write the journal of our travels' (*MWS
Journals*, p. 178). Inspiration for the book might have come from
Mary's reading that summer, which included Byron's third canto of
Childe Harold's Pilgrimage and Rousseau's *Julie*, both set largely in
the Swiss Alps, and a number of volumes of travel writing (for Mary
and Percy's shared reading list in the summer of 1817, see *MWS
Journals*, pp. 98–101). It is not clear what scope was initially envisaged
for the project, but Mary's journal entry for Wednesday, 13 August,
'write the journal of our first travels', suggests that it had by then
expanded to include material from the second, 1816 journey (*MWS
Journals*, p. 178). On Sunday, 17 August, Mary again recorded 'write'

---

[3] Mary's remark, in the same letter, that 'the six weeks' tour [was] written off hand'
should not be understood as a reflection on the quality of the former but rather as an
assurance to Moxon that she could produce *Rambles* quickly (*MWS Letters*, vol. 3, p. 96).

[4] Letter of William Godwin to John Taylor, 27 August 1814; quoted from *MWS
Journals*, p. 1.

[5] Daisy Hay argues that 'Mary Shelley understood better than most the importance of
letters in the creation of a legacy. From childhood she had watched Godwin copy and
curate his correspondence and, as Betty T. Bennett has argued, his example taught her
how to "value the personal letter as a component of public history". She had acted on this
example when she included letters by both her and Shelley in *History of a Six Weeks'
Tour* (1817).' See 'Shelley's Letters', in *The Oxford Handbook of Percy Bysshe Shelley*,
ed. Michael O'Neill and Anthony Howe, with the assistance of Madeleine Callaghan
(Oxford: Oxford University Press, 2013), 208–22 (p. 209).

and that Percy 'writes', though this was probably his epic poem *Laon and Cythna*, which would be published at the end of the year (*MWS Journals*, p. 178). A visit on 29 August by the bookseller Thomas Hookam, who Percy knew and often ordered from, and who would later co-publish *HSWT*, might also have had some influence on the shape of the project, although Mary records 'I did not see him' (see *MWS Journals*, p. 179 and n. 2).

Mary's use of the term 'write' refers not to the mere transcription for the press of entries from the shared 1814 journal, but to active selection, editing, and original composition.[6] Around 18 per cent of the 'six weeks' tour' portion of *HSWT* is based on entries made in the 1814 journal by Percy, either taken directly or very lightly revised, but Mary was also 'selective' in handling Percy's entries, using 'less than 50% of what he had originally written'.[7] Percy's journal entries tended to emphasize his response to scenes and events and hence many of the more effusive moments of the 'six weeks' tour' are based on his writing. The extent to which Percy himself was involved with the selection of his 1814 journal entries cannot be determined, but he had, at the very least, sight of them, since Mary, as already noted, told Leigh Hunt in October 1839 that the 'six weeks' tour' portion of *HSWT* 'was written by me' but 'printed and corrected by Shelley' (*MWS Letters*, vol. 2, p. 325).

Mary's rehandling of her own journal entries from 1814 was very different. These are almost entirely rewritten. Private information about health, family, and finances is minimized or excised—and even though some of the more prejudicial comments about foreign manners and customs in the 'six weeks' tour' are attributable to Mary, the *HSWT* text usually moderates her original journal entries. Mary also introduces significant new material not present in the 1814 journal. Murray estimates that as much as 70 per cent of the published text has no equivalent in the original journal and singles out 'the fine description of Lake Lucerne and environs' from the Switzerland section as one such instance, speculating that it 'could well have been

---

[6] Nora Crook has suggested that when Mary uses the term 'work' in her journals, she refers not to literary activity but to needlework or other domestic tasks. See Nora Crook, '"Work" in Mary Shelley's Journals', *The Keats–Shelley Review*, 18 (2004), 123–37.

[7] See *Moskal*, pp. 2–3 and n. 10, 7 n. 12; and *Murray*, pp. 429–30.

written by [Percy] in 1817'.[8] But there is no definitive evidence either way, and Mary's additions to the 'Germany' and 'Holland' sections in 1817 also include material quarried from her draft of *Frankenstein* and from Claire's journal of the 1814 tour. Again, the precise extent of Percy's role in this rehandling is impossible now to determine, but the first sentence of the preamble to the 'tour' suggests a thoroughly collaborative process, assuring the reader that 'few occurrences of any interest will be omitted' from the book because even though the original journal was 'not very copious', the Shelleys had 'often talked over the incidents that befel us, and attempted to describe the scenery through which we passed'.[9] During both their 1814 and 1816 journeys, Mary and Percy had also 'talked over' other works in progress. In 1814, for example, Mary acted as amanuensis on Percy's unfinished prose romance 'The Assassins'; their shared journal records various instances of 'we write' and the manuscript of the story contains material written by both Mary and Percy. During the summer of 1816 and the genesis of *Frankenstein*, their collaboration continued: that manuscript, too, contains material by both of them, with Percy adding advice and suggestions to Mary's original writing.[10]

By Thursday, 28 August 1817, Percy was attempting to secure a publisher for a volume which would certainly also include the 1816 letters. On that date, Mary wrote to him in London, saying, 'I think you took up my journal of our first travels with you if you did tell me if you have done anything with it or if you have any prospect—if you have I will go on instantly with the letters' (*MWS Letters*, vol. 1, p. 47). Percy, who was also seeing *Frankenstein* and his own poem *Laon and Cythna* through the press, obviously received some 'prospect' and by Sunday, 12 October, Mary was working on the second part of *HSWT*, recording in her journal 'write out letters from Geneva' (*MWS Journals*, p. 181). But whilst it is certain that Mary compiled the text of the four Geneva letters published in *HSWT*, that

---

[8] See *Murray*, pp. 430–1.

[9] *Moskal* (p. 3) makes this same point. Murray, arguing in a different vein, describes the whole of the preamble as 'taken over and expanded by Mary' from original journal entries made by Percy (*Murray*, p. 430).

[10] For a detailed discussion of the manuscripts for *Frankenstein* and what they reveal about its composition, see Mary Shelley, *The Frankenstein Notebooks*, 2 vols., ed. Charles Robinson (New York: Routledge, 1996).

process seems to have been rather more complex than the simple transcription that Mary's phrasing might at first glance suggest.

As noted, in his letter to Moore of 16 December 1817, Percy confirms that Mary wrote Letters I and II, which are signed '*M.*', and in her 1839 and 1845 editions of *HSWT*, Mary herself reaffirmed this by amending the signature on those letters, as well as at the end of the 'six weeks' tour section', to 'M.S.'. Betty T. Bennett suggested that they are based, at least in part, on original correspondence, no longer extant, between Mary and her stepsister, Fanny Godwin, with whom she was in fairly regular contact in 1816 (see *MWS Letters*, vol. 1, p. 19). But Mary might very well have invented them when she was preparing *HSWT* in 1817. Interestingly, Letter I contains material taken more-or-less verbatim from an actual letter sent by Percy to his friend Thomas Love Peacock on 15 May 1816, which suggests that the text published in *HSWT* is a composite of some sort. How exactly original correspondence by Percy became part of Letter I of *HSWT* presents something of a puzzle. The most likely solution is that Mary's journal for 1815–16, which is not currently extant, contained, like her 1814 journal, entries by both her and Percy, from which Percy drew his letter to Peacock in May 1816, and from which Mary drew, at least in part, Letters I and II of *HSWT* in October 1817 and any original correspondence on which they might be based. This hypothesis is further strengthened by the fact that some of the descriptions in the second Geneva letter, Letter II of *HSWT*, have close parallels in *Frankenstein*, which again suggests a common source for both texts.

The texts of the third and fourth Geneva letters in *HSWT*, which are signed S., have similarly complicated provenances and it remains unclear which sources Mary drew on when she compiled them in 1817 or to what extent Percy was involved in Mary's editorial process. Letter III, which is dated 12 July 1816, describes Percy and Byron's sailing trip around Lake Geneva from 22 to 30 June.[11] Two first-hand accounts of this trip in Percy's hand are extant: an original letter to Peacock dated 17 July 1816 and a few short fragments in the surviving parts of the notebook that Percy kept at Geneva during the summer

---

[11] For the correct dates of the tour, which are different from those given in *HSWT*, see *SC*, vol. 4, pp. 690–701.

of 1816.[12] The notebook fragments almost certainly constitute Percy's earliest account, made during the trip, and his letter to Peacock drew on these as well as on additional entries in the now missing sections of his notebook and/or perhaps copied into Mary's lost journal for 1815–16. In compiling the text of Letter III in 1817, Mary excised much of the personal material about finance and housing from Percy's original letter to Peacock, made a number of other substantive revisions, and polished the whole considerably. Whether she used as her source a copy of that letter made before it was sent, Percy's notebook, or her own journal, or some combination of these, cannot be known for sure on the basis of the available evidence. One of the more puzzling differences between Percy's original letter to Peacock and the text of Letter III which Mary prepared for *HSWT* is the date, which reads 17 July in the original and 12 July in *HSWT*. We do not know why Mary made this change, nor whether she did so deliberately or accidentally, perhaps based on some confusion in her source text—but the different dates certainly suggest that Percy's letter was not her source.[13]

Letter IV of *HSWT*, which has subsections dated 22, 24, 25, and 28 July 1816, describes an excursion made by Mary, Percy, and Claire to the village of Chamonix, about 80 kilometres away from Geneva. In this case, three accounts are extant: two brief fragments in Mary's hand in the surviving fragments of Percy's Geneva notebook; a more detailed one, partly in Percy's hand and partly in Mary's, written out at the beginning of Mary's journal for 1816–19 (see Appendix E); and Percy's original letter to Peacock, which was

[12] Percy's original letter to Peacock was only discovered in 1975, after Jones had produced his edition of *PBS Letters*. It is now in the Carl H. Pforzheimer Library (*SC*, p. 571). We have included a transcription as Appendix D. For an earlier transcription, facsimile, and detailed commentary about provenance and implications, see *SC*, vol. 7, pp. 25–49. The surviving fragments of Percy's Geneva notebook are held in the Bodleian Library (MSS Shelley adds. c. 4 and e. 16; for a facsimile and transcription, see *Geneva Nbk*).

[13] For arguments in favour of Percy's lost notebook as the source, see *Murray*, p. 441; and Richard Brinkley, 'Documenting Revision: Shelley's Lake Geneva Diary and the Dialogue with Byron in "History of a Six Weeks' Tour"', *Keats–Shelley Journal*, 39 (1990), pp. 66–82 (pp. 67–70). Donald Reiman, conversely, argues that Letter III is based on a copy of Percy's letter to Peacock, but does not address the difficulty with dates (see *SC*, vol. 7, pp. 40–1).

sent in early August 1816 when the party had returned to Geneva.[14] Mary made a copy of this letter but it is not extant (see *MWS Journal*, p. 117). The account of Chamonix and its environs given in *Frankenstein* (vol. 2, chapters 1–2) might also be considered a witness of sorts. Once again, lost notebook entries, made by Percy on the spot, probably constituted the earliest account of the journey. But beyond that, things grow much less certain. The material written by Percy in Mary's journal, and Percy's letter to Peacock, were probably quarried from his own original journal entries—and, very probably, the material in Mary's journal and her copy of Percy's letter to Peacock provided the source for the text of Letter IV. But we cannot know for sure, especially with so much of Percy's Geneva notebook now lost.

On 12 October 1817, Mary recorded in her journal not only that she was still working on the 'letters from Geneva' but also that Percy 'transcribes his poem' (*MWS Journals*, p. 181). Feldman and Scott-Kilvert, the editors of Mary's journals, assume that she refers here to Percy's poem *Laon and Cythna*, which he was working on at the time (see *MWS Journals*, p. 181 n. 3). But Mary could just as well have meant 'Mont Blanc', which was published with *HSWT* although we cannot know for sure when the decision was taken to include it (for a discussion of the composition and content of 'Mont Blanc', and its relationship to *HSWT*, see Explanatory Notes pp. 135–40). Four days later, on Thursday, 16 October, Mary wrote to Percy, who was again in London, confirming that she had sent the finished transcription to him via Hookham: 'You will have received I hope the manuscript that I sent yesterday in a parcel to Hookhams' (*MWS Letters*, vol. 1, p. 56). She adds that she is 'glad to hear that the printing goes on so well' and asks Percy to 'bring down all that you can with you', but as Murray notes, this might not be a reference to *HSWT* but to one of the other works that Percy was seeing through the press (*MWS Letters*, vol. 1, p. 56; *Murray*, p. 433). Two pages of this fair-copy manuscript survive in the Bodleian Library (MS Abinger c. 63), covering the end of the section on 'France' and the beginning of the section on 'Switzerland' from the 'six weeks' tour' part of *HSWT*

---

[14] This letter, reproduced in *PBS Letters*, vol. 1, pp. 495–502, is now in the Pierpont Morgan Library (M. 1407).

(based on the entries for 17–18 August 1814 in the original shared journal).[15]

The preface to *HSWT* has often been attributed to Percy, perhaps because he did around the same time in 1817 supply a preface for *Frankenstein*, writing in the first person to make it seem that the same individual authored both the preface and the novel. The preface to *HSWT*, however, is written in the third person and emphasizes the collaborative nature of the volume. Mary only ever claimed authorship of the 'six weeks' tour' part of *HSWT* (in subsequent editions and private correspondence). But given that she compiled the whole manuscript for publication, it seems reasonable to assume that she also had some part in the preface, perhaps drafting a text to be edited by Percy, who may have added the account of 'Mont Blanc'. It contains at least one direct echo of Percy's original letter to Peacock of 17 July 1816 (see Explanatory Notes p. 3).

HSWT was published by Hookham and Charles Ollier, another London-based bookseller and publisher who had already issued work by Leigh Hunt and who would publish all but one of the volumes of poetry that Percy subsequently brought out during his life. Exactly when is not quite clear. Advertisements in *The Morning Chronicle* (30 October) and *The Times* (1 November) newspapers suggested that *HSWT* would be published on 6 November and both papers carried announcements that it had been published 'this day' on 12 and 13 November, respectively. *The New Monthly Magazine and Universal Register* included *HSWT* on its list of 'new publications' on 1 December. Hookham deposited a copy with the stationer's office in London on 10 December, and Moore had certainly received his copy by early December. An early-mid November date therefore seems most likely, around six weeks before the publication of *Frankenstein* on 1 January 1818. The printer was Carew Henry Reynell and the book cost five shillings (the three volumes of Jane Austen's *Emma* (1816), by way of comparison, cost a guinea, or twenty-one shillings).

Several first editions of *HSWT* survive, some of which are annotated. Some illuminate the early history of the debate about authorship. A copy acquired by Keats House Museum in 2023, for

---

[15] These pages reveal further minor alterations in the final printed text: *HSWT* has more punctuation, for example, and there are a handful of word changes, such as 'filthy' beds becoming 'uncomfortable'.

instance, has 'Percy Bysshe Shelley / from Moore's Life of Byron' inscribed on the title page in an unknown hand, possibly that of the Scottish Professor of Literature and History, George Lillie Craik, whose bookplate the volume also contains. The Keats-Shelley House in Rome has a copy of a remainder edition, published in 1829 by J. Brooks of Oxford Street, which has 'by Percy B. Shelley' printed on the title page. A copy in the Huntington Library, California, has a copy with a bound-in title page reading 'by Percy Bysshe Shelley'.[16] None of these attributions were authorized by Mary or Percy—and may well have been attempts to increase the value of the book once Percy's posthumous reputation as a poet began to increase.

Sources and Themes

In 1817, a book about travel in Western Europe and the Alps was very far from a novelty. Throughout the eighteenth century, the so-called 'Grand Tour', which traditionally culminated in Rome or Naples, had been a rite-of-passage for the aristocratic and well-to-do, ostensibly educating them in foreign cultures and the remains of Classical civilization. Published accounts of individual European tours, or of commercial or ambassadorial journeys, often presented in the form of journal entries or private correspondence, were fairly common and often very popular, notable examples including Mary Wortley Montagu's *Turkish Embassy Letters* (1763), Sydney Morgan (née Owenson)'s *France* (1817), and of course Mary Wollstonecraft's *Letters written During a Short Residence*. Alongside these more personal recollections, expensive, multi-volume works, by semi-professional travel writers like John Carr, Edward Daniel Clarke, William Coxe, Mariana Starke, and Helen Maria Williams, offered authoritative accounts of pan-European routes and destinations, complete with extensive historical, socio-political, and cultural commentary. Volumes focused on particular countries or regions were also increasingly in demand, such as the guides to Switzerland published by Johann Gottfried Ebel and John Millard (writing under the pseudonym

[16] For more on this copy, see E. B. Murray, 'A Suspect Title-page of Shelley's "History of a Six Weeks' Tour"', *The Papers of the Bibliographical Society of America*, vol. 83, no. 2 (June 1989), pp. 201–6.

Henry Coxe). These are the 'more experienced and exact observers' to whom Mary and Percy refer in their preface to *HSWT*, whose work had already exhausted the 'facts' about 'scenes which are now so familiar' to the British reading public.

Travel in Europe had been significantly curtailed, especially for the British, from the outbreak of the French Revolutionary Wars in the mid-1790s until the defeat of Napoleon at Waterloo in 1815, with brief interludes during the Peace of Amiens in 1802–3 and Napoleon's first exile in 1814–15, when Mary and Percy made their six weeks' tour. Following the Battle of Waterloo, however, British travellers flocked to the mainland and wrote about their experience in greater numbers than ever before—and from a greater range of economic and social backgrounds. One of the first reviewers of *HSWT* saw the book as evidence (worrying, in the reviewer's opinion) of the growing number of aspirational middle-class tourists replacing the aristocratic travellers of the eighteenth century (see section on 'Reception and Afterlife'). The increasing proliferation of travel writing by women is another of the ways in which the genre functions as an index of broader cultural change during the Romantic period. Travel writing had often been a male pursuit in the eighteenth century, but by no means always so. In 1817 alone, however, seven English-language works of travel writing by women were published in Britain; co-authored volumes, though, especially those written by a couple, were a rarity indeed. New 'Romantic' attitudes to the natural world, too, and the increasing popularization of scientific debates, many of which are engaged in *HSWT*, meant that 'sublime' landscapes became just as important as Classical and other cultural sites on the tour of Europe: the Swiss and French Alps, for instance, once seen merely as hazardous obstacles to be overcome on the way to Italy, had become, by 1817, one of Europe's premier tourist attractions, attracting ever-greater numbers of visitors each year (see headnote to 'Mont Blanc'). When Mary, Percy, and Claire visited the famous Mer-de-Glace glacier outside Chamonix on 25 June 1816, they did so along with 'Beaucoup de Monde' ['lots of people'] (*MWS Journal*, p. 118). Byron, in his Alpine journal, was much more scathing, noting in his entry for 18 September 1816: 'I remember at Chamouni—in the very eyes of Mont Blanc—hearing another woman—English also—exclaim to her party—"did you ever see any thing more *rural*"—as if it was Highgate or Hampstead—or Brompton—or Hayes.—"*Rural*"

quotha!—Rocks—pines—torrent—Glaciers—Clouds—and
Summits of eternal snow far above them—and "*Rural!*".[17]

   The first reviewers of *HSWT* agreed that it was rather short, compared to most travel books, and didn't offer much in the way of historical or practical information about the places it covered, although
they disagreed about whether this was a strength or a weakness (see
section on 'Reception and Afterlife'). This 'simplicity', as one reviewer
called it, was partly a consequence of the manner in which *HSWT*
was compiled for publication: 'written off hand', in other words fairly
quickly, as Mary later said (*MWS Letters*, vol. 3, p. 96). But the
'unpresuming' style of *HSWT* also aligns well with the Shelleys'
insistence, in their preface, that the primary appeal of the book is
affective rather than intellectual, engaging 'sympathy' and 'feelings'
rather than 'facts' already 'familiar', and grounded in 'the enthusiasm
of youth' and 'immediate impressions', which are brought forth, as in
the writings of William Wordsworth and Jean-Jacques Rousseau, as
guarantors of authenticity and value.

   This foregrounding of the traveller's experience of the places and
peoples encountered is arguably a defining feature of 'Romantic'
travel writing. As already noted, one major influence on *HSWT*, in
this respect, was Mary Wollstonecraft's *Letters Written During a Short
Residence*, whose 'letters' (often heavily edited from the originals
to protect the details of her private life and the real reason for her
journey) blend subjective and at times highly emotive responses to
scenes and situations with rationalist social and political commentary.
Another was the wildly-popular *Canto the Third* of *Childe Harold's
Pilgrimage* (1816), by Lord Byron, the 'great poet' whom the Shelleys
say in their preface had 'clothed' many of the 'scenes beautiful in
themselves' which are described in *HSWT* 'with the freshness of
a diviner nature'—and in whose company they had spent a good deal
of the summer of 1816. *Canto the Third* continues the epic narrative
of travel through post-Napoleonic Europe by a disillusioned protagonist, who follows in Byron's own footsteps and is modelled closely
on Byron himself: not the least of the poem's many attractions for
contemporary readers was the assumption, not altogether incorrect,
that it was, essentially, autobiographical. *Canto the Third*—which

[17] Quoted from *Selected Letters and Journals*, ed. Leslie Marchand (Cambridge, MA:
Harvard University Press, 1982), pp. 126–7.

includes accounts of the battlefield at Waterloo, sailing on the Rhine, the environs of Lake Geneva, and the Alps—was composed during the spring and summer of 1816, partly against the backdrop of Byron's excursion around Lake Geneva with Percy. It both examines and embodies the affective power of the combination of spectacular landscape, cultural associations, and personal reflections, and is also influenced, at least in part, by Wordsworthian ideas about nature, as mediated to Byron by Percy, who, Byron records, 'when I was in Switzerland, used to dose me with Wordsworth physic even to nausea'.[18] Mary copied parts of the poem for Byron during the summer of 1816 and she and Percy were rereading it in the summer of 1817, with Mary recording in her journal for 28 May that doing so made her 'melancholy', presumably with memories of the previous year (*MWS Journal*, p. 171).

For all its advertised innocence, however, *HSWT* shares with Byron's poem an understanding of the role of literary and other cultural texts in creating and potentially transforming the ideological connotations of a place. In their preface, Mary and Percy signal this understanding by invoking the concept of 'classic ground', an expression fairly common in travel writing at the time, in order to describe the environs of Lake Geneva, which they describe as 'peopled with tender and glorious imaginations of the present and the past'. The phrase 'classic ground' was coined by Joseph Addison in his verse *Letter from Italy* (1701) to describe the process by which landscapes could be overwritten by cultural associations to such an extent as to seem already familiar to a traveller who had never been there before (line 12). Addison, of course, was talking about how the landscapes of modern Italy were inscribed with Classical associations: 'for here the Muse so oft her harp has strung', Addison wrote, 'that not a mountain rears its head unsung, | Renown'd in verse each shady thicket grows, | And ev'ry stream in heavenly numbers flows' (lines 13–16). As the preface to *HSWT* makes clear, by 1817, Byron's *Canto the Third* was a clear instance of how contemporary works could have similarly transformative effects, especially on landscapes like the Alps, which, from the

---

[18] See Thomas Medwin, *Conversations of Lord Byron* (London, 1824), p. 237.

perspective of foreign travellers, had a much shorter cultural
history than Italy or Greece.[19]

During the summer of 1816, though, the most prominent example
of this process—and the one to which Mary and Percy allude in their
invocation of 'classic ground' and 'peopled' landscapes in their preface to *HSWT*—was Rousseau's novel *Julie, ou la Nouvelle Héloïse:
Lettres de Deux Amans, Habitans d'une petite Ville au pied des Alpes*
[Julie, or the New Eloise: Letters from Two Lovers, Living in a small
Village at the foot of the Alps] (1761).

Along with Goethe's *Die Leiden des jungen Werthers* [The Sorrows
of Young Werther] (published in 1774 and on Mary's reading list for
1815), Rousseau's *Julie* was one of the most popular and controversial
novels of the Romantic period: at one point, it was in such demand
that copies could only be borrowed by the hour and, as with *Werther*,
many commentators were concerned about its potential impact on the
morals of young readers, and especially young women. Alluding
partly to the ill-fated medieval lovers Héloïse d'Argenteuil and Peter
Abelard, *Julie* is the story of a love affair between a young aristocrat,
Julie, and her middle-class tutor, St Preux—her eventual marriage,
her inability to forget St Preux despite living as a faithful wife, and
her death, which leaves St Preux and Julie's husband united in grief.
The novel, much of which is set around the eastern shore of Lake
Geneva and in the mountainous Upper Valais, focuses on the conflict
between love and the social norms of duty and virtue, with St Preux,
Julie, and Julie's husband all eventually coming to realize the value of
affections that transcend societal and religious conventions.

The account of Percy's visit to key sites of the novel during his tour
of Lake Geneva with Byron, in Letter III of *HSWT*, was only the
latest instance of 'the mapping' of Rousseau's work 'onto the area [...]
through successive reiterations of tourist visit and travel writing'.[20]

---

[19] Chamonix, for instance, only came to widespread public notice in Britain in the mid
eighteenth century, following the publication of William Windham and Richard Pococke's
Account of the Glacieres or Ice Alps in Savoy in 1741. 'Such was the success of [Byron's]
poem right across Europe in reconfiguring the tourist experience', says Nicola Watson,
'that for the rest of the century tourists came to look through the eyes of Byron'
('Rousseau on the Tourist Trail', in *Romanticism, Rousseau, Switzerland: New Prospects*,
ed. Angela Esterhammer, Diane Piccitto, and Patrick Vincent (London: Palgrave, 2015),
pp. 84–100 (p. 97)).

[20] Watson, 'Rousseau on the Tourist Trail', p. 84.

Percy and Byron were following in the footsteps of many others who had gone before, often with *Julie* in hand, on a pilgrimage which Rousseau himself had actually envisaged in his autobiographical *Confessions* (1782). Percy, though, was reading *Julie* for the first time during the tour and, as he admits in his original letter to Peacock of 17 July 1816, he did not read the key passages set in Meillerie until *after* he had been there (see Appendix D). But the core components of the account given in Letter III of *HSWT* are also present in Percy's original letter. He notes, like many before him, the 'inconceivable charm' of reading *Julie* on site. But he was especially struck by how Rousseau's 'powerfully bright' imagination, as embodied in *Julie*, could not only mount an effective challenge to deeply-held cultural conventions but could also transform the entire cultural significance of a place like Meillerie, making it the symbol of a progressive ethics and politics. The argument about *Julie* in *HSWT* is an early instance of the claim that Percy would, in 1821, formulate as the closing dictum of his essay 'A Defence of Poetry' and which has since become one of the most often-quoted pieces of Romantic-period literary criticism: that 'Poets are the unacknowledged legislators of the World'.[21]

Donald Reiman was the first to suggest that *HSWT* was 'carefully constructed to culminate' in Percy's poem 'Mont Blanc', which 'should be studied [...] in terms of the ideas that precede it' in the book (*SC*, vol. 7, p. 41). A number of critics have subsequently argued that Percy, inspired by the example of *Julie*, was trying in 'Mont Blanc' to reorientate the cultural significance of that mountain away from the prevailing religious and political conservatism which underpinned much contemporary tourism in Chamonix, drawing, as he did so, on state-of-the-art geological ideas (see headnote to 'Mont Blanc'). The account of Chamonix in Letter IV of *HSWT* is certainly critical of the valley's burgeoning tourist industry, albeit less so than Mary and Percy were in private correspondence. Striking, however, is the fact that *HSWT* nowhere mentions Percy's most infamous (at the time and since) response to those who, like Samuel Taylor Coleridge in his 'Hymn, before Sun-Rise, in the Vale of Chamouni' (1802), felt that the sublimity of the Alpine landscape embodied the grandeur of

---

[21] Quoted from *SPP*, p. 678.

god. During their visit to Chamonix in July 1816, in visitor books at
a number of tourist sites and hotels, Percy, writing in Greek, had
identified himself, Mary, and Claire as atheists, democrats, and philanthropists, prompting outrage and derision amongst subsequent
visitors and not a few cultural commentators.[22] A full six years later,
the final review of *HSWT* to be published during Percy's lifetime, in
April 1822, still harked back to these notorious inscriptions.

The conservative slant of Alpine tourism in 1816, and the Shelleys'
response to it in *HSWT*, also bears directly on what is arguably the
overarching concern of the entire volume: the course and legacy of
the French Revolution. On their six weeks' tour in 1814, Mary, Percy,
and Claire saw first-hand the devastation wrought by years of war
culminating in what seemed, then, like the defeat of Napoleon and
the end of the political movement begun twenty-five years earlier,
before any of them were born, with the attack on the Bastille on
14 July 1789. By the time they were again in Switzerland in the summer
of 1816, that democratic experiment had definitively ended. Following
the Battle of Waterloo, the so-called Holy Alliance—Austria, Prussia,
and Russia—was engaged in restoring old regimes across Europe,
and democratic reform in Britain seemed an increasingly distant
prospect. The big question, then, for Radicals and others on what we
would today call the political left, was how to make sense of the disastrous failure of the French Revolution and how to maintain faith in
the possibility of genuine and lasting, progressive political change. In
a letter to Byron on 8 September 1816, Percy described the French
Revolution as 'the master theme of the epoch in which we live', urging
him to write an epic poem about it (*PBS Letters*, vol. 1, p. 504). Percy
took up the challenge himself in *Laon and Cythna*, the epic poem on
which he was working whilst *HSWT* was being compiled and seen
through the press: 'methinks', Percy wrote in his long preface, 'those
who now live have survived an age of despair'.[23] Mary Shelley's
Frankenstein, similarly in progress whilst *HSWT* was being compiled,
also addresses the disastrous outcome of the Revolution: one way of
reading the course of Victor's relationship with his Creature is
as a parable for the revolutionary violence that can, and perhaps

---

[22] See Letter IV and notes. For detailed discussion of the inscriptions, their original
context, and afterlife, see *De Beer*.
[23] Quoted from *SPP*, p. 602.

inevitably will, be triggered by the failure of government to shoulder its responsibilities to the people. In addition to documenting, at first hand, the terrible consequences of such violence, *HSWT* also explores the role of Rousseau's work in the Revolution and tries to find ways of resituating short-term catastrophe within longer-scale economies of progressive change (see Explanatory Notes to Letter II).

Reception and Afterlife

HSWT did not sell particularly well. In the spring of 1820, Percy learned from the publisher, Charles Ollier, that the book had not even made enough profit to pay the printer (see *PBS Letters*, vol. 2, pp. 188, 196), and when Ollier's business folded in 1823, his remaining stock included 92 unsold copies of *HSWT*. Contemporary responses to *HSWT* were correspondingly few, but not quite so few as has sometimes been suggested. We do not know what Thomas Moore made in 1817 of the copy which he received, beyond the fact that he evidently told Percy that he had 'derived' some 'amusement' from it (see *PBS Letters*, vol. 1, p. 583). But many years later, in his *Life of Byron* (1830), Moore described *HSWT*, in perhaps a similar tone, as an 'interesting little work' and quoted some passages from Percy's account of the trip around Lake Geneva (p. 320). Another prominent contemporary cultural figure, William Beckford, author of the Gothic novel *Vathek* (1786), made a number of annotations in a copy which he owned, which now survives in the Carl H. Pforzheimer Library (MS S'ANA 0752). Many of these annotations simply mark, or comment very briefly, on specific passages, but those which are more detailed tend to be less than flattering—for example, describing the author of Letters III and IV as a 'bore', 'raving <u>mad</u> about Mountains', and 'Mont Blanc' as 'overwhelming, an avalanche of nonsense' (Beckford's annotations to specific passages are recorded in the Explanatory Notes). Edward Verall Lucas's *Life* (London, 1834) of the well-known Romantic essayist Charles Lamb records that his library also contained a first edition of *HSWT* 'with Lamb's autograph on fly-leaf' (vol. 2, p. 324). So the book clearly found some audience amongst London's literary circles.

The earliest *published* response to *HSWT* seems to have been the short notice in *The New Monthly Magazine and Universal Register* for 1 March 1818 (vol. 9, p. 154), which notes that the 'narrative' and 'correspondence' are 'written with more spirit and elegance, than most of the pompous volumes about France which have been poured forth from the press since the restoration of peace' and recommends *HSWT* particularly to readers who 'have more taste for picturesque description, than political disquisition, romantic tales, and dry speculation'. No mention is made of 'Mont Blanc'.

Later that year, longer appraisals were published in *The Eclectic Review* (May 1818, pp. 470–4) and *Blackwood's Edinburgh Magazine* (July 1818, pp. 412–16). The former describes *HSWT* as 'a rather spirited sketch' that 'contains some passages of tolerably good description, mingled with a few attempts at sublimity, not quite successful' (p. 470). But it also voices a 'strong suspicion that the *dramatis personae* are fictitious', that many of the incidents described are 'mere inventions', that the Geneva letters are designed to hint at Byron as the 'companion' of the sailing trip, and that 'Mont Blanc' has 'very much the air of being intended to pass for his Lordship's composition' (pp. 470–1). Skipping over what it calls 'a notable piece of ridiculous extravagance on p. 162', the review closes by quoting the first six lines of 'Mont Blanc' alongside the description of that poem in the preface to *HSWT*, quipping that 'how well it accomplishes this praiseworthy purpose, our readers will judge from the opening lines, at least if they can understand them' (p. 473).

The *Blackwood's* review is on the whole more favourable, albeit with a rather patronizing tone towards the 'Lady' author who 'prattles away very prettily in the true English idiom' (p. 412). Much of the review consists of quotations from the 'six weeks' tour' part of *HSWT*, which is praised for its 'simplicity' and for 'avoiding that assumed stateliness of intellect so ludicrous in your modern imbecil tourist' (p. 412). The 'poetical fervour' of the 'well-written' letters from Geneva is also noted. And a similarly equivocal estimation is offered of 'Mont Blanc': 'a little poem by the husband, which, though rather too ambitious, and at times too close an imitation of Coleridge's sublime hymn in the vale of Chamouni, is often very beautiful' (p. 416). The review closes by quoting lines 49–83, finding in them 'a darkness and confusion, as if the writer were grappling with objects above his strength' but also 'a grandeur both of thought and expression,—indubitable indications of a truly poetical mind' (p. 416).

A short notice in the *Monthly Review; Or New Literary Journal* for January 1819 (pp. 97–8) presented *HSWT* as further evidence of what the reviewer saw as a negative new trend in British travel to mainland Europe, when the 'dashing *milords* of the last age are now succeeded by a host of *roturiers* [a derogatory term for common people], who expatriate themselves for the sake of economy; or by a migratory tribe who are accused of never being satisfied with the spot on which they happen to reside' (p. 97). The reviewer condemns *HSWT* for its lack of detail about the places visited and concludes by claiming, curiously enough, that *HSWT*:

short as it is, appears to be the work of *three writers*; a lady being the author of the first and larger part, and her husband figuring in the second tour; while a travelling companion contributes a couple of epistles, and concludes by a poetical essay on Mont Blanc, which will scarcely rank him with the Scotts and Byrons of the age. (p. 98)

The Fireside Magazine for March 1819 reprinted this claim verbatim as part of its 'Summary of Reviews' (p. 115).

The only other mention of *HSWT* published during Percy's lifetime came at the end of an article on 'Southey and Byron' in *The Saturday Magazine* for 13 April 1822 (pp. 322–30). *HSWT* is brought forward in connection with Percy's 'atheist' inscriptions and as evidence of the bad company that Byron kept during the summer of 1816. *HSWT*, we are told, 'is the performance of one of the ladies whose signature graces the Album of Montalvert (viz. Shelley's *second wife*,) the daughter and namesake of Mary Wolstoncraft [*sic*], by the philosopher Godwin; and the letters, except two, are his [i.e. Percy's] own' (p. 330). A footnote then explains that the second lady from the album incident 'is Miss Clermont, another daughter of Mrs. Wolstoncraft's to another lover, and consequently half-sister to Mrs. Shelley' (p. 300). 'These', the reviewer notes snidely, 'are the parties with whom Byron lived and lives in holy communion' (p. 330).

Mary's inclusion of the 'six weeks' tour' and Geneva letters parts of *HSWT* in her editions of Percy's *Essays, Letters from Abroad, Translations and Fragments* published in 1839–40 elicited two further mentions of the book. A joint review of Mary's *Essays* and *Poetical Works of Percy Bysshe Shelley* (1839) in *The Athenæum* for 14 December 1839 (pp. 939–42) remarked that the 'six weeks' tour' portion of *HSWT*—over the inclusion of which, as we have seen, Mary hesitated—'might well have been omitted altogether, as being of the very slightest texture, telling nothing of any interest whatever, and not written by the poet', but does praise the 'spirit of poetry' in Percy's descriptions of the Lake Geneva tour and Chamonix (p. 940). And the following year, a review of *Essays* in *The Monthly Chronicle* for 5 May 1840 (pp. 179–82) describes the 'six weeks' tour' part of *HSWT* as 'possessing something of a biographical as well as descriptive interest', but suggested that Mary's inclusion of material from Percy's journals and letters, including those dating from the summer of 1816, had greater interest, providing 'reliques' of his 'prose writings, with which the world is not yet sufficiently familiar' and 'details about the poet which bring him familiarly before us' (p. 181).

Throughout the twentieth century, *HSWT* was often mined as a source of biographical and contextual information about the lives and works of the Shelley–Byron circle during the *Frankenstein* summer of 1816. One of the earliest writers to emphasize its intrinsic literary merits, however, and to recognize the possibility of reading *HSWT* as an engagement with the kinds of ideas about nature and culture that we would now call 'Romantic', was Charles Isaac Elton. A lawyer, politician, and historian, Elton is best remembered for having co-authored with his wife Mary Augusta—a collaboration Mary and Percy would no doubt have admired—a history of book collecting, including important accounts of the beginnings of the British and Bodleian libraries, called *The Great Book-Collectors* (1893). In 1894, he published *An Account of Shelley's Visits to France, Switzerland, and Savoy, in the Years 1814 and 1816, with Extracts from 'The History of a Six Weeks' Tour' and 'Letters descriptive of a Sail round the Lake of Geneva and of the Glaciers of Chamouni', first published in the year 1817*.

An attractive and expensive volume, clearly aimed at collectors and well-to-do readers, *An Account* is a curious book, something like an edition of *HSWT* by someone evidently well acquainted with Percy's life and works and familiar with the history of the places described. It has an introductory essay; a first part which basically paraphrases *HSWT* itself whilst expanding and commenting, sometimes extensively, upon the scenes and incidents described; and a second part which contains the so-called 'extracts', essentially the whole text. A harsh reader might see it almost as a parasitic volume, living off the original text, but more generously, we could also see it as an attempt

to resituate *HSWT* in the cultural history of its time.[24] Albeit
selectively so, because Elton assures the reader that he will 'have
nothing to do here with their family troubles or private affairs' (p. 15),
and his *Account* makes absolutely no reference to anything even
remotely controversial: nothing is said about the elopement, about
the Chamonix inscriptions, about rumoured goings-on at Villa Diodati
with the famous Byron, or about any of *HSWT*'s many pointedly
political observations.

Elton states in the introduction his intention to 'illustrate'
(i.e. explicate) *HSWT*, which, he says, has been 'recognised' as
'Shelley's [i.e. Percy's] publication' though Mary 'took herself a great
share in the work' (p. 1). The main interest of the book, he thinks, lies
not in 'what they actually saw' but in the 'state of mind' it reveals:

the idea that the beauty of Nature is the friend and companion of Man: the
phenomena of the universe are regarded as existing in the observer's mind,
while that mind and all that belongs to it may be viewed apart as one of the
forms presented in Nature. (p. 2)

For this, what we would now call Romantic 'idea', Elton argues, Percy
and Byron 'both owed something to Wordsworth' (p. 2). Curiously,
though, Elton says very little about the possible influence of Rousseau
(perhaps still steering clear of potentially controversial, political
topics). But he does point regularly to what he sees as correspond-
ences between the experiences described in *HSWT* and contemporary
poems by Percy and Byron, including 'Hymn to Intellectual
Beauty', 'Mont Blanc', and *Childe Harold's Pilgrimage*, as well as
a range of other literary and non-fiction works. He also proposes
a number of echoes in later writings by Percy, in minor pieces like
'To the Nile' (1818), 'The Two Spirits' (1819), and the unfinished
short story 'The Coliseum', as well as in more substantial works like
Prometheus Unbound (1820) and the portrait of Rousseau in 'The
Triumph of Life' (1822). He also comments frequently on the literary elements of *HSWT*, suggesting, for instance, that 'we should note
the classical and stately style of the opening passage [of Letter IV],

---

[24] A reviewer in *The Athenæum* for 18 August 1894 noted tartly that Elton's 'plan [...]
cannot be recommended for imitation, and, what is still more regrettable, it has been
carried out in a manner which leaves a good deal to be desired' (p. 13).

which resembles Pliny's Letters in the facility shown in moulding language into new forms' (p. 68).

Whilst Elton's *Account* does therefore anticipate some elements of a modern critical edition, the book is perhaps most successful as an enthusiastic tribute to, and invocation of, the undeniable affective charm of *HSWT*. And indeed Elton, to his credit, is fully alert to how *HSWT* contributed to shaping for subsequent generations the cultural landscape of Lake Geneva and Chamonix. 'After all', he writes, 'the "castled Rhine" will never lose the charm thrown over it by the writer of "Childe Harold"', nor Mellerie and Mont Blanc cease to be transfigured by Shelley's romantic visions' (pp. 1–2).

On 12 March 1818, four months after the publication of *HSWT*, the Shelleys and Claire left England again, this time bound for Italy, the 'Paradise of Exiles', as Percy called it in his poem 'Julian and Maddalo' (1819). Percy would never return but in the years before his death on 8 July 1822 he wrote many of the works for which he is now mainly remembered. Mary, as we have seen, took up travel writing again later in her life, when she was established as a novelist and editor of Percy's work. Her *Rambles in Germany and Italy* was also based partly on letters, including many written to Claire. Mary's preface, echoing *HSWT*, 'disclaimed any pretensions to novelty' and spoke, sometimes nostalgically, of 'spots often described', including the environs of Geneva which she first visited during the summer of 1816. One of the main reasons the Shelleys chose Geneva that summer was so that Claire could be close to Byron, with whom she had become romantically involved before he left England (we have included her first letter to him as Appendix C). Their daughter, Clara Allegra, who was born on 12 January 1817, died on 22 April 1822. Following Percy's death a few months later, Claire travelled to Austria and then to Russia, where she worked as a governess in St Petersburg and Moscow. Henry James's novella *The Aspern Papers* (1888) fictionalizes the attempt of the real-life Captain Edward Silsbee to purchase from her letters by Percy that she had kept. She died in Florence, having never published her own revised journal of the six weeks' tour of 1814.

NOTE ON THE TEXT

No manuscript of the complete text of *HSWT* is currently extant. Only two loose fair copy pages, in MWS's hand, survive in the Bodleian Library (MS Abinger c. 63). Our copy text is the first edition of 1817. We have retained the original spellings; some obvious errors by the compositor (for example, misplaced full stops) have been silently corrected. MWS included the first part of *HSWT*, and Letters III and IV from the second part, in her editions of *Essays* (1839, 1845), renaming them 'Journal of a Six Weeks' Tour' and 'Letters from Geneva', and making a number of minor changes. For a detailed collation of these variants, see *Moskal*, pp. 387–93. MWS did not include 'Mont Blanc', which she had already published in *PP1824* and *PW1839*.

SELECT BIBLIOGRAPHY

Critical Editions of HSWT

Moskal, Jeanne, *The Novels and Selected Works of Mary Shelley*, vol. 8 (London: William Pickering, 1996), pp. 1–48.

Murray, E. B., *The Prose Works of Percy Bysshe Shelley*, vol. 1 (Oxford: Clarendon Press, 1993), pp. 179–228.

Rouhette, Anne, *Histoire d'Un Voyage de Six Semaines* (Aix-en-Provence: Presse Universitaires de Provence, 2015), https://books.openedition.org/pup/9536.

Wordsworth, Jonathan, *History of a Six Weeks' Tour* (Oxford: Woodstock, 1991).

The Shelley Circle

Bennett, Betty T., *Mary Wollstonecraft Shelley: An Introduction* (Baltimore: Johns Hopkins University Press, 1998).

Bieri, James, *Percy Bysshe Shelley: A Biography*, 2 vols. (Newark: University of Delaware Press, 2005).

Cameron, Kenneth Neil, et al. (eds.), *Shelley and His Circle, 1773–1822*, 10 vols. to date (Harvard: Harvard University Press, 1961–).

Clairmont, Claire, *The Journals of Claire Clairmont*, ed. Marion Kingston Stocking (Harvard: Harvard University Press, 1968).

Holmes, Richard, *Shelley: The Pursuit* (London: Flamingo, 1995).

Mellor, Anne K., *Mary Shelley: Her Life, Her Fiction, Her Monsters* (New York: Taylor and Francis, 2012).

Reiman, Donald H. (gen. ed.), *The Bodleian Shelley Manuscripts*, 23 vols. (New York: Garland, 1986–2002).

Seymour, Miranda, *Mary Shelley* (London: John Murray, 2000).

Shelley, Mary, *The Frankenstein Notebooks*, 2 vols., ed. Charles Robinson (New York: Routledge, 1996).

Shelley, Mary, *The Novels and Selected Works of Mary Shelley*, 8 vols., gen. ed. Betty T. Bennett, Pamela Clemit, and Nora Crook (London: Pickering and Chatto, 1996).

Shelley, Mary, *The Journals of Mary Wollstonecraft Shelley*, ed. Paula R. Feldman and Diana Scott-Kilvert (Baltimore: Johns Hopkins University Press, 1987).

Shelley, Mary, *The Letters of Mary Wollstonecraft Shelley*, 3 vols., ed. Betty T. Bennett (Baltimore: Johns Hopkins University Press, 1980).

Shelley, Mary, *Collected Tales and Stories*, ed. Charles E. Robinson (Baltimore: Johns Hopkins University Press, 1976).

Shelley, Percy Bysshe, *Selected Poetry and Prose*, ed. Jack Donovan and Cian Duffy (London: Penguin, 2016).

Shelley, Percy Bysshe, *The Complete Poems of Percy Bysshe Shelley*, vol. 3, ed. Donald H. Reiman, Neil Fraistat, and Nora Crook (Baltimore: Johns Hopkins University Press, 2012).

Shelley, Percy Bysshe, *The Poems of Shelley: Volume 1, 1804–1817*, ed. Geoffrey Matthews and Kelvin Everest (London: Longman, 1989).

Shelley, Percy Bysshe, *The Letters of Percy Bysshe Shelley*, 2 vols., ed. Frederick L. Jones (Oxford: Clarendon Press, 1964).

St Clair, William, *The Godwins and the Shelleys: The Biography of a Family* (London: Faber and Faber, 1999).

Wroe, Anne, *Being Shelley* (London: Vintage, 2008).

Select Critical Studies

Bennett, Betty T., and Curran, Stuart (eds.), *Mary Shelley in Her Times* (Baltimore: Johns Hopkins University Press, 2000).

Buzard, James, *The Beaten Track: European Tourism, Literature, and the Ways to 'Culture', 1800–1918* (Oxford: Clarendon Press, 1993).

Colbert, Benjamin, *Shelley's Eye: Travel Writing and Aesthetic Vision* (London: Ashgate, 2005).

Colbert, Benjamin, 'Contemporary Notice of the Shelleys' "History of a Six Weeks' Tour": Two New Early Reviews', *Keats–Shelley Journal*, 48 (1999), pp. 22–9.

Crook, Nora, 'Pecksie and the Elf: Did the Shelleys Couple Romantically?', *Romanticism on the Net*, 18 (May 2000), https://www.erudit.org/en/journals/ron/2000-n18-ron430/005911ar/

Dekker, George G., *The Fictions of Romantic Tourism: Radcliffe, Scott, and Mary Shelley* (Stanford: Stanford University Press, 2005).

Duffy, Cian, *Shelley and the Revolutionary Sublime* (Cambridge: Cambridge University Press, 2005).

Duffy, Edward, *Rousseau in England: The Context for Shelley's Critique of the Enlightenment* (Berkeley: University of California Press, 1979).

Erkelenz, Michael, 'The Poetry of Wandering: "Mont Blanc" in "History of a Six Weeks' Tour" (1817)', *Keats–Shelley Journal*, 63 (2014), pp. 78–101.

Esterhammer, Angela, Piccitto, Diane, and Vincent, Patrick (eds.), *Romanticism, Rousseau, Switzerland: New Prospects* (London: Palgrave, 2015).

Koszul, A., 'Notes and Corrections to Shelley's "History of a Six Weeks' Tour" (1817)', *The Modern Language Review*, 2.1 (October 1906), pp. 61–2.

Lau, Beth (ed.), *Fellow Romantics: Male and Female British Writers, 1790–1835* (Farnham: Ashgate, 2009).

Mellor, Anne, *Romanticism and Gender* (London: Routledge, 1993).

Mercer, Anna, *The Collaborative Literary Relationship of Percy Bysshe Shelley and Mary Wollstonecraft Shelley* (London: Routledge, 2019).

Morton, Timothy (ed.), *The Cambridge Companion to Percy Bysshe Shelley* (Cambridge: Cambridge University Press, 2006).

Nitchie, Elizabeth, 'Mary Shelley, Traveller', *Keats–Shelley Journal*, 10 (Winter 1961), pp. 29–42.

O'Neill, Michael, and Howe, Anthony (eds.), with the assistance of Madeleine Callaghan, *The Oxford Handbook of Percy Bysshe Shelley* (Oxford: Oxford University Press, 2012).

Rossington, Michael, 'Republican Histories and Memories: The Shelleys, Switzerland and Geneva', in *Genève, lieu d'Angleterre 1725–1814/Geneva, an English Enclave 1725–1814*, ed. V. Cossy, B. Kapossy, and R. Whatmore (Geneva: Slatkine, 2009), pp. 307–25.

Rossington, Michael, 'Rousseau and Tacitus: Republican Inflections in the Shelleys' *History of a Six Weeks' Tour*', *European Romantic Review*, 19/4 (2008), pp. 321–33.

Rouhette, Anne, ' "S." ou "M."? Voyage et auctorialité dans *Histoire d'un voyage de six semaines*', *Viatica*, 3 (2016), https://revues-msh.uca.fr/viatica/index.php?id=556.

Rouhette, Anne, 'Apogée ou appendice? La place du "Mont Blanc" et du Mont Blanc dans *Histoire d'un voyage de six semaines*, de Mary et Percy Bysshe Shelley (1817)', *Viatica*, 2 (2015), https://revues-msh.uca.fr/viatica/index.php?id=506.

Schor, Esther (ed.), *The Cambridge Companion to Mary Shelley* (Cambridge: Cambridge University Press, 2003).

Further Reading in Oxford World's Classics

Byron, George Gordon, Lord, *The Major Works*, ed. Jerome J. McGann (Oxford: Oxford University Press, 2008).

Polidori, John, *The Vampyre and Other Tales of the Macabre*, ed. Chris Baldick and Robert Morrison (Oxford: Oxford University Press, 2008).

Shelley, Percy Bysshe, *The Major Works*, ed. Zachary Leader and Michael O'Neill (Oxford: Oxford University Press, 2009).

Shelley, Mary Wollstonecraft, *Frankenstein: The 1818 Text*, ed. Nick Groom (Oxford: Oxford University Press, 2019).

Shelley, Mary Wollstonecraft, *The Last Man*, ed. Morton Paley (Oxford: Oxford University Press, 2008).

Shelley, Mary Wollstonecraft, *Valperga: Or, The Life and Adventures of Castruccio, Prince of Lucca*, ed. Michael Rossington (Oxford: Oxford University Press, 2000).

Wollstonecraft, Mary, *Letters Written during a Short Residence in Sweden, Norway, and Denmark*, ed. Tonne Brekke and Jon Mee (Oxford: Oxford University Press, 2009).

Online Resources

The Shelley–Godwin Archive (http://shelleygodwinarchive.org)

Carl H. Pforzheimer Collection of Shelley and His Circle (https://archives.nypl.org/cps/)

Bodleian Library Shelley Manuscripts and Relics (https://archives.bodleian.ox.ac.uk/repositories/2/resources/767)

A SELECTED CHRONOLOGY
OF THE SHELLEYS

1789 The storming of the Bastille prison in Paris (14 July) and beginning of the French Revolution. William Blake publishes *Songs of Innocence*.

1790 Edmund Burke publishes *Reflections on the Revolution in France*. Mary Wollstonecraft publishes *A Vindication of the Rights of Men*.

1791 Thomas Paine publishes *The Rights of Man*.

1792 PBS born 4 August, at Field Place, Sussex. In France, the newly established National Convention abolishes the monarchy and declares a republic. Mary Wollstonecraft publishes *A Vindication of the Rights of Woman*.

1793 Execution of Louis XVI of France and Marie Antoinette. Start of the Revolutionary 'Terror' in Paris. Britain declares war on France. William Godwin publishes *An Enquiry Concerning Political Justice*. Charlotte Smith publishes *The Emigrants*. Germaine De Staël publishes *Corinne, or Italy*. Blake publishes *Songs of Experience*.

1794 London Treason Trials of radicals including Thomas Hardy, John Horne Tooke, and John Thelwall (all acquitted). Suspension of habeas corpus in England (again in 1799, 1801, and 1803). Godwin publishes *Things as They Are; or, The Adventures of Caleb Williams*. Ann Radcliffe publishes *The Mysteries of Udolpho*.

1796 Napoleon leads his army over the Alps into northern Italy and defeats the Austrians. Wollstonecraft publishes *Letters Written During a Short Residence in Sweden, Norway, and Denmark*.

1797 Wollstonecraft marries Godwin at St Pancras Old Church in London. Their daughter, MWS, born 30 August in Somers Town, London. Wollstonecraft dies from blood poisoning 10 September, as a result of complications during MWS's birth. Napoleon becomes overall commander of the French army. Ann Radcliffe publishes *The Italian*.

1798 Rebellion in Ireland by the United Irishmen, led by Wolfe Tone. Nelson defeats the French navy at the Battle of the Nile. France invades Switzerland. Godwin publishes *Memoirs of the Author of A Vindication of the Rights of Woman* and Wollstonecraft's incomplete novel *Maria; or the Wrongs of Woman*. William Wordsworth and Samuel Taylor Coleridge publish *Lyrical Ballads, with A Few Other Poems*. CC born 27 April near Bristol.

1799   Napoleon returns to France and is made First Consul for Life.

1800   Act of Union of Great Britain and Ireland. Napoleon defeats the Austrians at Marengo.

1801   William Godwin marries Mary Jane Clairmont, CC's mother.

1802   PBS attends Syon House Academy, in Isleworth. The Peace of Amiens ends the French Revolutionary Wars between Britain and France.

1803   Start of the Napoleonic Wars.

1804   PBS attends Eton College. Napoleon becomes Emperor of France.

1805   Godwin's Juvenile Library opens at 4 Skinner Street, London. Britain defeats the French and Spanish navies at the Battle of Trafalgar; Nelson is fatally wounded. Napoleon defeats the Austrians and Russians at Austerlitz.

1806   Deaths of William Pitt and Charles James Fox. PBS's uncle is made a baronet. Death of Charlotte Smith. Sydney Morgan publishes *The Wild Irish Girl*.

1807   Abolition of the Slave Trade in the British Empire. Smith's *Beachy Head and Other Poems* published posthumously. Wordsworth publishes *Poems, in Two Volumes*.

1810   PBS attends University College, Oxford. Publishes two Gothic novels, *Zastrozzi* and *St. Irvyne*, and a collection of poetry *Posthumous Fragments of Margaret Nicholson*. Riots in London following the imprisonment of Francis Burdett, who had called for reform of the House of Commons.

1811   PBS and Thomas Hogg are expelled from Oxford for publishing *The Necessity of Atheism*. PBS marries Harriet Westbrook in Edinburgh. The newlyweds travel to the Lake District, where PBS meets Robert Southey, future Poet Laureate. George III of England is declared insane; his son, the future George IV, becomes Prince Regent. Luddite Rebellion. Jane Austen publishes *Sense and Sensibility*.

1812   PBS and Harriet visit Dublin, where PBS publishes *An Address to the Irish People* and *Proposals for an Association of Philanthropists*. They travel to Wales and Devon before settling in Tremadoc. MWS sent to stay with the Baxter family in Dundee. PBS meets William Godwin in London; MWS possibly present at dinner with Godwin, PBS, and Harriet. Lord Byron publishes the first two cantos of *Childe Harold's Pilgrimage*. Napoleon invades Russia and, having reached Moscow, is eventually forced to retreat.

1813   PBS and Harriet move from Wales to Ireland and then London; their daughter, Ianthe, born 23 June. PBS's poem *Queen Mab* is privately printed and distributed. The radical journalist and poet, Leigh Hunt, is imprisoned for libel. Austen publishes *Pride and Prejudice*. Byron publishes *The Giaour*, the first of his so-called 'Turkish Tales'.

1814 PBS publishes *A Refutation of Deism*. The Armies of the Sixth Coalition invade France, capturing Paris at the end of March. Napoleon abdicates and is exiled to Elba. Louis XVIII becomes king of France. The first Treaty of Paris restores the French borders of 1792. Start of the Congress of Vienna. PBS and MWS meet in London and fall in love; together with CC, PBS and MWS (now pregnant) elope on their 'six weeks' tour' in August–September. They return to London penniless. Charles, PBS's son with Harriet, born 30 November. Byron publishes *The Corsair*. Wordsworth publishes *The Excursion*.

1815 PBS's grandfather dies 5 January. A financial settlement eventually enables PBS to pay his debts and grants him an income of £1,000 per annum. PBS's daughter with MWS is born and dies prematurely. Napoleon returns from exile in March, beginning the Hundred Days campaign; he is finally defeated at the Battle of Waterloo on 18 June. Eruption of Mount Tambora in Indonesia which will trigger cold weather, crop failures and food shortages in the following 'year without a summer'. PBS and MWS settle at Bishopsgate, near Windsor Great Park.

1816 PBS and MWS have a son, William, born 24 January. PBS publishes *Alastor [. . .] and Other Poems*. Byron leaves England in April. PBS, MWS, and CC go to Geneva in May, where they meet Byron and his travelling companion, John Polidori. PBS corresponds with Thomas Love Peacock, describing excursions around Lake Geneva and Chamonix, and composes 'Hymn to Intellectual Beauty' and 'Mont Blanc'. MWS begins work on *Frankenstein*. They return to England in September, settling at Bath. Fanny Imlay, MWS's half-sister, dies by suicide 9 October. Harriet Shelley dies by suicide 2 December. PBS and MWS marry at St Mildred's, London, 30 December; Godwin attends. Byron publishes *Childe Harold's Pilgrimage: Canto the Third*. Coleridge publishes *Christabel and Other Poems*.

1817 Allegra, CC's daughter with Byron, born 12 January. The Shelleys and CC move to Marlow, Buckinghamshire. PBS meets John Keats and publishes *Proposals for Putting Reform to the Vote*. The Court of Chancery denies PBS custody of his children with Harriet. MWS completes *Frankenstein* in May. MWS and PBS compile *History of a Six Weeks' Tour*, which is published in November. Clara Shelley born 2 September. PBS writes *Laon and Cythna*, which is printed and immediately withdrawn; it is reissued, with some passages excised, as *The Revolt of Islam*. The so-called Gagging Acts restrict freedom of expression and assembly in Britain. Deaths of Jane Austen and Princess Charlotte, the latter prompting PBS's *Address to the People on the Death of the Princess Charlotte*. Byron publishes *Manfred*. Coleridge publishes *Biographia Literaria*. Thomas Moore publishes *Lalla Rookh: An Oriental Romance*.

1818 *Frankenstein* is published. PBS writes *Rosalind and Helen*. On 12 March, the Shelleys and CC leave England for Italy, travelling around much of the north and as far south as Naples before settling in Este, near Venice, in August. PBS writes 'Lines Written Among the Euganean Hills', translates Plato's *Symposium*, and starts working on *Prometheus Unbound* and 'Julian and Maddalo'. Clara Shelley dies 24 September. Austen's *Northanger Abbey* and *Persuasion* are published posthumously. Keats publishes *Endymion*.

1819 The Shelleys move to Rome. William Shelley dies 7 June. The Shelleys move to Livorno. PBS writes *The Cenci*. MWS begins her novella *Mathilda* (published in 1959). The 'Peterloo Massacre' in Manchester prompts PBS's *Mask of Anarchy* (published 1832); he completes *Prometheus Unbound* and writes 'Ode to the West Wind' and 'Peter Bell the Third'. The Shelleys move to Florence where their son, Percy Florence, is born 12 November. PBS writes 'A Philosophical View of Reform'. The 'Six Acts' further repress freedom of speech and assembly in Britain. Byron publishes *Don Juan* Cantos I–II. Wordsworth publishes *Peter Bell*.

1820 MWS begins *Valperga*. PBS writes 'The Sensitive-Plant', 'Ode to Liberty', 'Ode to Naples', 'To a Sky-Lark, 'Letter to Maria Gisborne', 'The Witch of Atlas', and 'Oedipus Tyrannus'. *Prometheus [...] With Other Poems* published. CC moves to Florence. The Shelleys move to Pisa. PBS meets Emilia Viviani. PBS and MWS meet the Greek exile and future revolutionary leader, Alexandros Mavrokordatos. The Cato Street Conspiracy. George III dies; George IV made king. Revolution in Naples. Constitutional monarchy established in Spain. Keats publishes *Lamia, Isabella, The Eve of St. Agnes, and Other Poems*.

1821 PBS writes *Epipsychidion*, addressed to Emilia Viviani and published anonymously; 'A Defence of Poetry'; and *Hellas*, inspired by the outbreak of the Greek War of Independence. MWS writes mythological dramas *Prosperine* and *Midas*, to which PBS contributes some songs; finishes *Valperga*. Death of Keats, for whom PBS writes *Adonais*. Deaths of Napoleon and Polidori. PBS and MWS meet Edward and Jane Williams. Byron moves to Pisa, publishes *Cain* and *Don Juan* Cantos III–V. Laetitia Elizabeth Landon (L.E.L.) publishes *The Fate of Adelaide*.

1822 PBS writes lyric poetry for Jane Williams. Edward Trelawny joins the Shelleys, CC, and Byron at Pisa. *Hellas* published. Allegra Byron dies 20 April. The Shelleys, CC, and the Williamses move to Casa Magni, San Terenzo. PBS begins 'The Triumph of Life'. MWS has near-fatal miscarriage in June; PBS saves her life. PBS, Williams, and Charles Vivian drown 8 July when their boat sinks during a storm. Leigh Hunt arrives in Italy. MWS starts to plan a posthumous collection of PBS's poems.

1823 PBS's ashes buried in the Protestant Cemetery, Rome. MWS publishes *Valperga*, writes a poem about PBS's death called 'The Choice'. MWS is denied financial support by PBS's father. She returns to England. Richard Brinsley Peake's *Presumption; or the Fate of Frankenstein* opens at the English Opera House; MWS attends a performance with Godwin and publishes a second edition of *Frankenstein*, with 'Mary W. Shelley' named as author. MWS granted £100 per annum by PBS's family to support her only surviving child, Percy Florence. Byron publishes *Don Juan* Cantos XII–XIV. Death of Ann Radcliffe.

1824 MWS begins *The Last Man*, publishes short stories in *The London Magazine* and her edition *Posthumous Poems of Percy Bysshe Shelley*. PBS's father threatens to stop MWS's allowance if she continues to edit and publish PBS's work. Byron publishes *Don Juan* Cantos XV–XVI, dies 19 April at Missolonghi. PBS's cousin, Thomas Medwin, publishes *Conversations of Lord Byron*. Landon publishes *The Improvisatrice and Other Poems*.

1826 MWS publishes *The Last Man*. PBS's first son with Harriet dies on 14 September, making Percy Florence heir to the Shelley baronetcy. William Hazlitt publishes *The Spirit of the Age*.

1827 MWS begins *The Fortunes of Perkin Warbeck*. PBS's father increases Percy Florence's annual allowance to £250 (rising to £300 in 1829). Death of William Blake. John Clare publishes *The Shepherd's Calendar*.

1830 MWS publishes *The Fortunes of Perkin Warbeck*. Death of George IV and accession of William IV.

1831 MWS publishes a third, revised and corrected edition of *Frankenstein*. Trelawny publishes *Adventures of a Younger Son*, helped by MWS.

1832 The Reform Act is passed by the British Parliament.

1834 Death of Coleridge.

1835 MWS publishes *Lodore*.

1836 Godwin dies 7 April.

1837 MWS publishes *Falkner*. Percy Florence goes up to Cambridge. Death of William IV and accession of Queen Victoria.

1839 MWS publishes her four-volume edition of *The Poetical Works of Percy Bysshe Shelley*, with a preface and notes; and an edition of PBS's *Essays, Letters from Abroad, Translations and Fragments*, which includes 'Journal of a Six Weeks' Tour' and 'Letters from Geneva' from *HSWT*.

1840 MWS travels in Europe, revisiting Geneva and other scenes from
−3   *HSWT*.

1844 PBS's father dies 24 April; MWS and Percy Florence inherit his estate. MWS publishes *Rambles in Germany and Italy*.

1845 MWS publishes a corrected version of *Essays*; it includes a lightly revised text of *HSWT*.

1847 Medwin publishes *The Life of Percy Bysshe Shelley*.

1850 Death of William Wordsworth.

1851 MWS dies of a brain tumour 1 February at her final home in Chester Square, London; she is buried in St Peter's, Bournemouth; Godwin and Wollstonecraft are reinterred there.

1858 Trelawny publishes *Recollections of the Last Days of Shelley and Byron*; reissued in 1878 as *Records of Byron, Shelley and the Author* (ed. William Michael Rossetti).

1870 William Michael Rossetti publishes an edition of *The Poetical Works of Percy Bysshe Shelley*.

1876 Harry Buxton Forman publishes an edition of *The Poetical Works of Shelley*.

1879 CC dies 19 March in Florence.

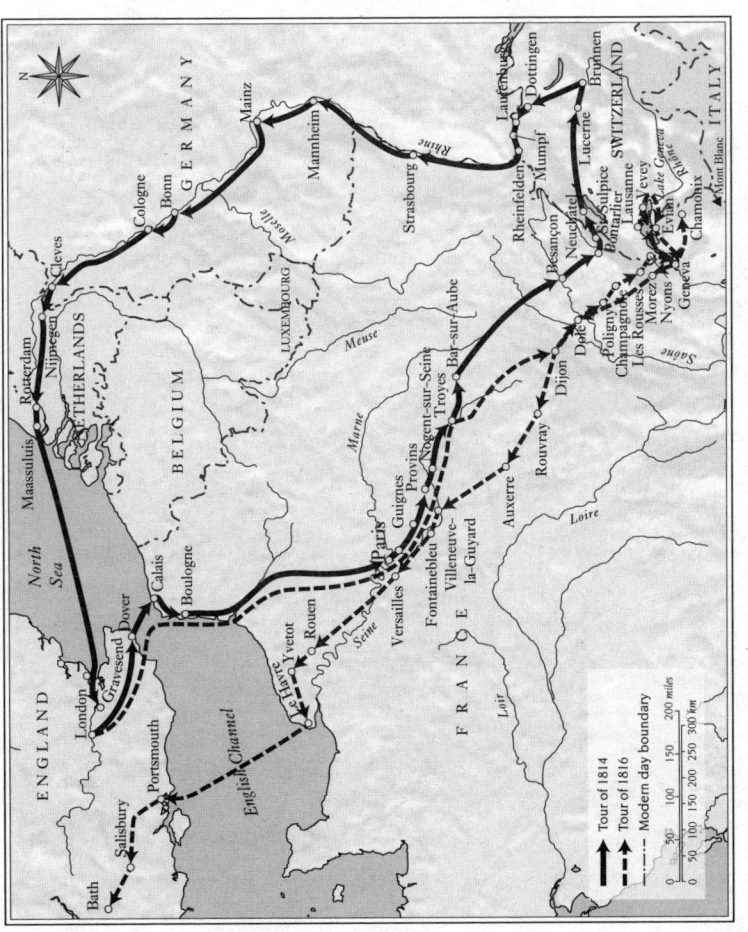

MAP 1   The two tours of Mary, Percy, and Claire across Europe in July–September 1814 and May–September 1816.

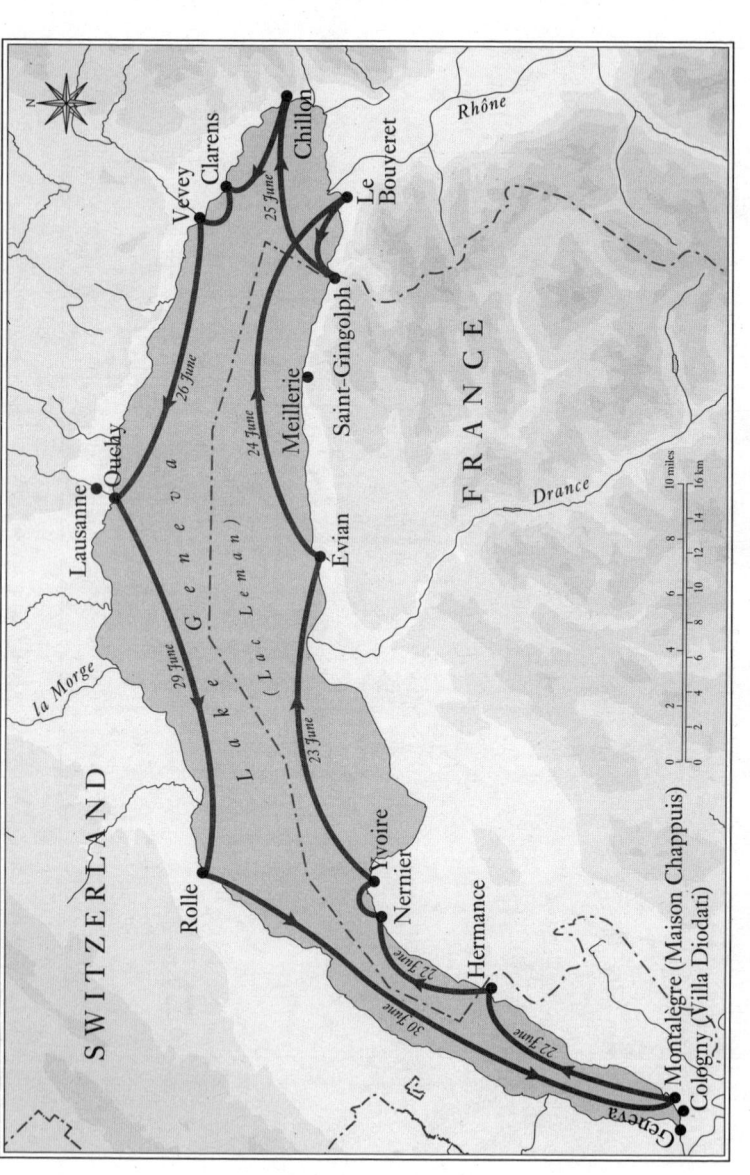

MAP 2 Percy and Lord Byron's tour of Lake Geneva, 22–30 June 1816.

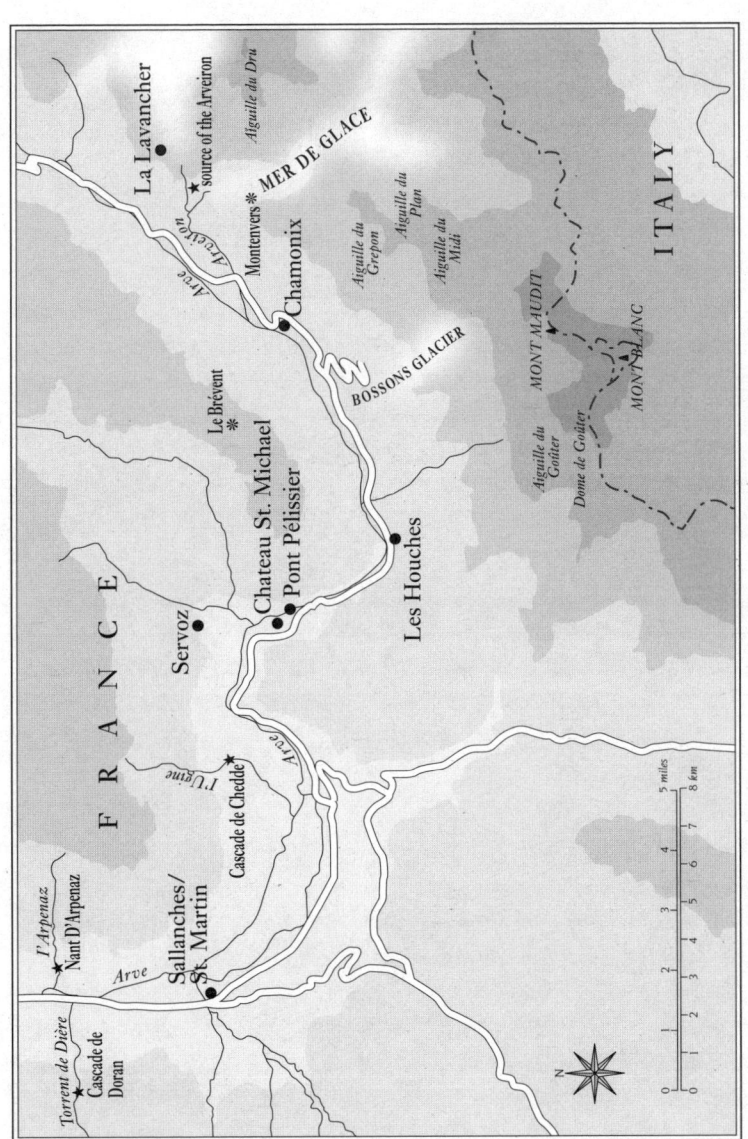

MAP 3 Mary, Percy, and Claire's visit to Chamonix–Mont Blanc, 22–26 July 1816.

History
of
a Six Weeks' Tour

Through

A Part of France, Switzerland, Germany, and Holland: with Letters

Descriptive of a Sail Round the Lake of Geneva, and of The Glaciers of Chamouni.

LONDON:
PUBLISHED BY T. HOOKHAM, JUN.
OLD BOND STREET;
AND C. AND J. OLLIER,
WELBECK STREET.
1817.

Reynell, Printer, 45, Broad-street,
Golden-square.

PREFACE.°

NOTHING can be more unpresuming than this little volume. It contains the account of some desultory visits by a party of young people to scenes which are now so familiar to our countrymen, that few facts relating to them can be expected to have escaped the many more experienced and exact observers, who have sent their journals to the press. In fact, they have done little else than arrange the few materials which an imperfect journal, and two or three letters to their friends in England afforded. They regret, since their little History is to be offered to the public, that these materials were not more copious and complete. This is a just topic of censure to those who are less inclined to be amused than to condemn. Those whose youth has been past as their's (with what success it imports not) in pursuing, like the swallow, the inconstant summer of delight and beauty which invests this visible world,° will perhaps find some entertainment in following the author, with her husband and sister,° on foot, through part of France and Switzerland, and in sailing with her down the castled Rhine, through scenes beautiful in themselves, but which, since she visited them, a great Poet has clothed with the freshness of a diviner nature.° They will be interested to hear of one who has visited Mellerie, and Clarens, and Chillon, and Vevai—classic ground, peopled with tender and glorious imaginations of the present and the past.°

They have perhaps never talked with one° who has beheld in the enthusiasm of youth the glaciers, and the lakes, and the forests, and the fountains of the mighty Alps. Such will perhaps forgive the imperfections of their narrative for the sympathy which the adventures and feelings which it recounts, and a curiosity respecting scenes already rendered interesting and illustrious, may excite.

The Poem,° entitled "Mont Blanc," is written by the author of the two letters from Chamouni and Vevai. It was composed under the immediate impression of the deep and powerful feelings excited by the objects which it attempts to describe; and as an undisciplined overflowing of the soul,° rests its claim to approbation on an attempt to imitate the untameable wildness and inaccessible solemnity from which those feelings sprang.

IT is now nearly three years since this Journey took place, and the journal I then kept was not very copious; but I have so often talked over the incidents that befel us, and attempted to describe the scenery through which we passed, that I think few occurrences of any interest will be omitted.

We left London July 28th, 1814, on a hotter day than has been known in this climate for many years. I am not a good traveller, and this heat agreed very ill with me, till, on arriving at Dover, I was refreshed by a sea-bath.° As we very much wished to cross the channel with all possible speed, we would not wait for the packet° of the following day (it being then about four in the afternoon) but hiring a small boat, resolved to make the passage the same evening, the seamen promising us a voyage of two hours.

The evening was most beautiful; there was but little wind, and the sails flapped in the flagging breeze: the moon rose, and night came on, and with the night a slow, heavy swell, and a fresh breeze, which soon produced a sea so violent as to toss the boat very much.° I was dreadfully sea-sick,° and as is usually my custom when thus affected, I slept during the greater part of the night, awaking only from time to time to ask where we were, and to receive the dismal answer each time—"Not quite half way."°

The wind was violent and contrary; if we could not reach Calais, the sailors proposed making for Boulogne. They promised° only two hours' sail from shore, yet hour after hour passed, and we were still far distant, when the moon sunk in the red and stormy horizon, and the fast-flashing lightning became pale in the breaking day.

We were proceeding slowly against the wind, when suddenly a thunder squall struck the sail, and the waves rushed into the boat: even the sailors acknowledged that our situation was perilous; but they succeeded in reefing the sail;°—the wind was now changed, and we drove before the gale directly to Calais. As we entered the harbour I awoke from a comfortless sleep, and saw the sun rise broad, red, and cloudless over the pier.

FRANCE.

EXHAUSTED with sickness and fatigue, I walked over the sands with my companions to the hotel. I heard for the first time the confused buzz of voices speaking a different language from that to which I had been accustomed; and saw a costume very unlike that worn on the opposite side of the channel; the women with high caps and short jackets; the men with earrings; ladies walking about with high bonnets or *coiffures*° lodged on the top of the head, the hair dragged up underneath, without any stray curls to decorate the temples or cheeks.° There is, however, something very pleasing in the manners and appearance of the people of Calais, that prepossesses you in their favour. A national reflection might occur, that when Edward III. took Calais, he turned out the old inhabitants, and peopled it almost entirely with our own countrymen; but unfortunately the manners are not English.°

We remained during that day and the greater part of the next at Calais: we had been obliged to leave our boxes the night before at the English custom-house,° and it was arranged that they should go by the packet of the following day, which, detained by contrary wind, did not arrive until night. S*** and I walked among the fortifications on the outside of the town; they consisted of fields where the hay was making. The aspect of the country was rural and pleasant.

On the 30th of July, about three in the afternoon, we left Calais, in a cabriolet drawn by three horses.° To persons who had never before seen any thing but a spruce English chaise and post-boy,° there was something irresistibly ludicrous in our equipage. A cabriolet is shaped somewhat like a post-chaise, except that it has only two wheels, and consequently there are no doors at the sides; the front is let down to admit the passengers. The three horses were placed abreast, the tallest in the middle, who was rendered more formidable by the addition of an unintelligible article of harness, resembling a pair of wooden wings fastened to his shoulders; the harnesses were of rope; and the postillion, a queer, upright little fellow with a long pigtail, *craquèed*° his whip, and clattered on, while an old forlorn shepherd with a cocked hat gazed on us as we passed.

The roads are excellent, but the heat was intense, and I suffered greatly from it. We slept at Boulogne the first night, where there was an ugly but remarkably good-tempered femme de chambre.° This made us for the first time remark the difference which exists between this class of persons in France and in England. In the latter country they are prudish, and if they become in the least degree familiar they are impudent. The lower orders in France have the easiness and politeness of the most well-bred English; they treat you unaffectedly as their equal, and consequently there is no scope for insolence.

We had ordered horses to be ready during the night, but we were too fatigued to make use of them. The man insisted on being paid for the whole post.° *Ah! Madame*, said the femme-de-chambre, *pensez-y; c'est pour de dommager les pauvres chevaux d'avoir perdues leur douce sommeil.*° A joke from an English chamber-maid would have been quite another thing.

The first appearance that struck our English eyes was the want of enclosures; but the fields were flourishing with a plentiful harvest.° We observed no vines on this side of Paris.

The weather still continued very hot, and travelling produced a very bad effect upon my health; my companions were induced by this circumstance to hasten the journey as much as possible; and accordingly we did not rest the following night, and the next day, about two, arrived in Paris.

In this city there are no hotels where you can reside as long or as short a time as you please, and we were obliged to engage apartments at an hotel for a week.° They were dear, and not very pleasant. As usual in France, the principal apartment was a bedchamber; there was another closet with a bed, and an anti-chamber, which we used as a sitting-room.

The heat of the weather was excessive, so that we were unable to walk except in the afternoon. On the first evening we walked to the gardens of the Thuilleries;° they are formal, in the French fashion, the trees cut into shapes, and without grass. I think the Boulevards infinitely more pleasant. This street nearly surrounds Paris, and is eight miles in extent; it is very wide, and planted on either side with trees.° At one end is a superb cascade° which refreshes the senses by its continual splashing: near this stands the gate of St. Denis,° a beautiful piece of sculpture. I do not know how it may at present be disfigured by the Gothic barbarism° of the conquerors of France, who were not contented with retaking the spoils of Napoleon, but with impotent° malice, destroyed the monuments of their own defeat. When I saw this gate, it was in its splendour, and made you imagine that the days of Roman greatness were transported to Paris.

After remaining a week in Paris, we received a small remittance that set us free from a kind of imprisonment there which we found very irksome. But how should we proceed? After talking over and rejecting many plans, we fixed on one eccentric enough, but which, from its romance,° was very pleasing to us. In England we could not have put it in execution without sustaining continual insult and impertinence: the French are far more tolerant of the vagaries of their neighbours. We resolved to walk through France;° but as I was too weak for any considerable distance, and my sister could not be supposed to be able to walk as far as S*** each day, we determined to purchase an ass, to carry our portmanteau° and one of us by turns.

Early, therefore, on Monday, August 8th, S*** and C*** went to the ass market, and purchased an ass, and the rest of the day, until four in the afternoon, was spent in preparations for our departure;° during which, Madame L'Hôte° paid us a visit, and attempted to dissuade us from our design. She represented to us that a large army had been recently disbanded,° that the soldiers and officers wandered idle about the country, and that *les Dames seroient certainement enlevèes.*° But we were proof against her arguments, and packing up a few necessaries, leaving the rest to go by the diligence,° we departed in a fiacre° from the door of the hotel, our little ass following.

We dismissed the coach at the barrier. It was dusk, and the ass seemed totally unable to bear one of us, appearing to sink under the portmanteau, although it was small and light. We were, however, merry enough, and thought the leagues short.° We arrived at Charenton° about ten.

Charenton is prettily situated in a valley, through which the Seine flows, winding among banks variegated with trees. On looking at this scene, C*** exclaimed, "Oh! this is beautiful enough; let us live here." This was her exclamation on every new scene,° and as each surpassed the one before, she cried, "I am glad we did not stay at Charenton, but let us live here."

Finding our ass useless, we sold it before we proceeded on our journey, and bought a mule, for ten Napoleons.° About nine o'clock we departed. We were clad in black silk.° I rode on the mule, which carried also our portmanteau; S*** and C*** followed, bringing a small basket of provisions. At about one we arrived at Gros Bois,° where, under the shade of trees, we ate our bread and fruit, and drank our wine, thinking of Don Quixote and Sancho.°

The country through which we passed was highly cultivated, but uninteresting; the horizon scarcely ever extended beyond the circumference of a few fields, bright and waving with the golden harvest. We met several travellers; but our mode, although novel, did not appear to excite any curiosity or remark. This night we slept at Guignes, in

the same room and beds in which Napoleon and some of his Generals°
had rested during the late war. The little old woman of the place was
highly gratified in having this little story to tell, and spoke in warm
praise of the Empress Josephine and Marie Louise,° who had at different times passed on that road.

As we continued our route, Provins was the first place that struck
us with interest. It was our stage of rest for the night; we approached
it at sunset. After° having gained the summit of a hill, the prospect of
the town opened upon us as it lay in the valley below; a rocky hill rose
abruptly on one side, on the top of which stood a ruined citadel with
extensive walls and towers; lower down, but beyond, was the cathedral,° and the whole formed a scene for painting.° After having travelled for two days through a country perfectly without interest, it was
a delicious relief for the eye to dwell again on some irregularities and
beauty of country. Our fare° at Provins was coarse, and our beds
uncomfortable, but the remembrance of this prospect made us contented and happy.

We now approached scenes that reminded us of what we had nearly
forgotten, that France had lately been the country in which great and
extraordinary events had taken place. Nogent,° a town we entered
about noon the following day, had been entirely desolated by the
Cossacs.° Nothing could be more entire than the ruin which these
barbarians had spread as they advanced; perhaps they remembered
Moscow and the destruction of the Russian villages;° but we were
now in France, and the distress of the inhabitants, whose houses had
been burned, their cattle killed, and all their wealth destroyed, has
given a sting to my detestation of war, which none can feel who have
not travelled through a country pillaged and wasted by this plague,
which, in his pride, man inflicts upon his fellow.

We quitted the great route soon after we had left Nogent, to strike
across the country to Troyes. About° six in the evening we arrived at
St. Aubin, a lovely village embosomed in trees; but on a nearer view
we found the cottages roofless, the rafters black, and the walls dilapidated;—a few inhabitants remained. We asked for milk—they had
none to give; all their cows had been taken by the Cossacs. We had still
some leagues to travel that night, but we found that they were not post
leagues, but the measurement of the inhabitants, and nearly double
the distance. The road lay over a desart plain, and as night advanced
we were often in danger of losing the track of wheels, which was our

only guide. Night closed in, and we suddenly lost all trace of the road; but a few trees, indistinctly seen, seemed to indicate the position of a village. About ten we arrived at Trois Maisons,° where, after a supper on milk and sour bread, we retired to rest on wretched beds: but sleep is seldom denied, except to the indolent, and after the day's fatigue, although my bed was nothing more than a sheet spread upon straw, I slept soundly until the morning was considerably advanced.°

S*** had hurt his ancle° so considerably the preceding evening, that he was obliged, during the whole of the following day's journey, to ride on our mule. Nothing could be more barren and wretched than the track through which we now passed; the ground was chalky and uncovered even by grass, and where there had been any attempts made towards cultivation, the straggling ears of corn discovered more plainly the barren nature of the soil. Thousands of insects, which were of the same white colour as the road, infested our path; the sky was cloudless, and the sun darted its rays upon us, reflected back by the earth, until I nearly fainted under the heat. A village appeared at a distance, cheering us with a prospect of rest. It gave us new strength to proceed; but it was a wretched place, and afforded us but little relief. It had been once large and populous, but now the houses were roofless, and the ruins that lay scattered about, the gardens covered with the white dust of the torn cottages, the black burnt beams, and squalid looks of the inhabitants, presented in every direction the melancholy aspect of devastation. One house, a *cabarêt*,° alone remained; we were here offered plenty of milk, stinking bacon, sour bread, and a few vegetables, which we were to dress° for ourselves.

As we prepared our dinner in a place, so filthy that the sight of it alone was sufficient to destroy our appetite, the people of the village collected around us, squalid with dirt, their countenances expressing every thing that is disgusting and brutal. They seemed indeed entirely detached from the rest of the world, and ignorant of all that was passing in it. There is much less communication between the various towns of France than in England. The use of passports° may easily account for this: these people did not know that Napoleon was deposed,° and when we asked why they did not rebuild their cottages, they replied, that they were afraid that the Cossacs would destroy them again upon their return. Echemine° (the name of this village) is in every respect the most disgusting place° I ever met with.

Two leagues beyond, on the same road, we came to the village of Pavilion,° so unlike Echemine, that we might have fancied ourselves in another quarter of the globe; here every thing denoted cleanliness and hospitality; many of the cottages were destroyed, but the inhabitants were employed in repairing them. What could occasion so great a difference?

Still our road lay over this track of uncultivated country, and our eyes were fatigued by observing nothing but a white expanse of ground, where no bramble or stunted shrub adorned its barrenness. Towards evening we reached a small plantation of vines, it appeared like one of those islands of verdure that are met with in the midst of the sands of Lybia,° but the grapes were not yet ripe. S*** was totally incapable of walking, and C*** and I were very tired before we arrived at Troyes.

We rested° here for the night, and devoted the following day to a consideration of the manner in which we should proceed. S***'s sprain rendered our pedestrianism impossible. We accordingly sold our mule, and bought an open *voiture*° that went on four wheels, for five Napoleons,° and hired a man with a mule for eight more, to convey us to Neufchâtel° in six days.

The suburbs of Troyes were destroyed, and the town itself dirty and uninviting. I remained at the inn writing,° while S*** and C*** arranged this bargain and visited the cathedral of the town; and the next morning we departed in our *voiture* for Neufchâtel. A curious instance of French vanity occurred on leaving this town. Our *voiturier*° pointed to the plain around, and mentioned, that it had been the scene of a battle between the Russians and the French. "In which the Russians gained the victory?"—"Ah no, Madame," replied the man, "the French are never beaten." "But how was it then," we asked, "that the Russians had entered Troyes soon after?"—"Oh, after having been defeated, they took a circuitous route, and thus entered the town."

Vandeuvres° is a pleasant town, at which we rested during the hours of noon. We walked in the grounds of a nobleman, laid out in the English taste, and terminated in a pretty wood; it was a scene that reminded us of our native country. As we left Vandeuvres the aspect of the country suddenly changed; abrupt hills, covered with vineyards, intermixed with trees, enclosed a narrow valley, the channel of the Aube. The view was interspersed by green meadows, groves of poplar and white willow, and spires of village churches, which the Cossacs had yet spared. Many villages, ruined by the war, occupied the most romantic spots.

In the evening we arrived at Bar-sur-Aube, a beautiful town, placed at the opening of the vale where the hills terminate abruptly. We climbed the highest of these,° but scarce had we reached the top, when a mist descended upon every thing, and the rain began to fall: we were wet through before we could reach our inn. It was evening,° and the laden clouds made the darkness almost as deep as that of midnight; but in the west an unusually brilliant and fiery redness occupied an opening in the vapours, and added to the interest of our little expedition: the cottage lights were reflected in the tranquil river, and the dark hills behind, dimly seen, resembled vast and frowning mountains.°

As we quitted Bar-sur-Aube, we at the same time bade a short farewel to hills. Passing through the towns of Chaumont,° Langres° (which was situated on a hill, and surrounded by ancient fortifications), Champlitte,° and Gray, we travelled for nearly three days through plains, where the country gently undulated, and relieved the eye from a perpetual flat, without exciting any peculiar interest. Gentle rivers, their banks ornamented by a few trees, stole through these plains, and a thousand beautiful summer insects skimmed over the streams. The third day was a day of rain, and the first that had taken place during our journey. We were soon wet through, and were glad to stop at a little inn to dry ourselves. The reception we received here was very unprepossessing, the people still kept their seats round the fire, and seemed very unwilling to make way for the dripping guests. In the afternoon, however, the weather became fine, and at about six in the evening we entered Besançon.

Hills had appeared in the distance during the whole day, and we had advanced gradually towards them, but were unprepared for the scene° that broke upon us as we passed the gate of this city. On quitting the walls, the road wound underneath a high precipice; on the other side the hills rose more gradually, and the green valley that intervened between them was watered by a pleasant river;° before us arose an amphitheatre of hills covered with vines, but irregular and rocky. The last gate of the town was cut through the precipitous rock that arose on one side, and in that place jutted into the road.

This approach to mountain scenery filled us with delight;° it was otherwise with our *voiturier*: he came from the plains of Troyes, and these hills so utterly scared him, that he in some degree lost his reason.° After winding through the valley, we began to ascend the mountains which were its boundary: we left our *voiture*, and walked on, delighted with every new view that broke upon us.

When we had ascended the hills for about a mile and a half, we found our *voiturier* at the door of a wretched inn, having taken the mule from the *voiture*, and obstinately determined to remain for the night at this miserable village of Mort.° We could only submit, for he was deaf to all we could urge, and to our remonstrances only replied, *Je ne puis pas.*°

Our beds were too uncomfortable to allow a thought of sleeping in them: we could only procure one room, and our hostess gave us to understand that our *voiturier* was to occupy the same apartment. It was of little consequence, as we had previously resolved not to enter the beds. The evening was fine, and after the rain the air was perfumed by many delicious scents. We climbed to a rocky seat on the hill that overlooked the village, where we remained until sunset. The night was passed by the kitchen fire in a wretched manner, striving to catch a few moments of sleep, which were denied to us. At three in the morning we pursued our journey.

Our road led to the summit of the hills that environ Besançon. From the top° of one of these we saw the whole expanse of the valley filled with a white undulating mist, which was pierced like islands by the piny mountains. The sun had just risen, and a ray of red light lay upon the waves of this fluctuating vapour. To the west, opposite the sun, it seemed driven by the light against the rocks in immense masses of foaming cloud, until it became lost in the distance, mixing its tints with the fleecy sky.

Our *voiturier* insisted on remaining two hours at the village of Noè, although we were unable to procure any dinner, and wished to go on to the next stage. I have already said, that the hills scared his senses, and he had become disobliging, sullen, and stupid. While he waited° we walked to the neighbouring wood: it was a fine forest, carpeted beautifully with moss, and in various places overhung by rocks, in whose crevices young pines had taken root, and spread their branches for shade to those below; the noon heat was intense, and we were glad to shelter ourselves from it in the shady retreats of this lovely forest.

On our return to the village we found, to our extreme surprise, that the *voiturier* had departed nearly an hour before, leaving word that he expected to meet us on the road. S***'s sprain rendered him incapable of much exertion; but there was no remedy, and we proceeded on foot to Maison Neuve, an *auberge*,° four miles and a half distant.

At Maison Neuve the man had left word that he should proceed to Pontalier,° the frontier town of France, six leagues distant, and that if we did not arrive that night, he should the next morning leave the *voiture* at an inn, and return with the mule to Troyes. We were astonished at the impudence of this message, but the boy of the inn comforted us by saying, that by going on a horse by a cross road, where the *voiture* could not venture, he could easily overtake and intercept the *voiturier*, and accordingly we dispatched him, walking slowly after. We waited at the next inn for dinner, and in about two hours the boy returned. The man promised to wait for us at an *auberge* two leagues further on. S***'s ancle had become very painful, but we could procure no conveyance, and as the sun was nearly setting, we were obliged to hasten on. The evening was most beautiful, and the scenery lovely enough to beguile us of our fatigue: the horned moon° hung in the light of sunset, that threw a glow of unusual depth of redness over the piny mountains and the dark deep vallies they enclosed; at intervals in the woods were beautiful lawns interspersed with picturesque clumps of trees, and dark pines overshadowed our road.

In about two hours we arrived at the promised termination of our journey, but the *voiturier* was not there: after the boy had left him, he again pursued his journey towards Pontalier. We were enabled, however, to procure here a rude kind of cart, and in this manner arrived late at Pontalier, where we found our conductor, who blundered out many falsehoods for excuses; and thus ended the adventures of that day.

SWITZERLAND.

ON passing the French barrier, a surprising difference may be observed between the opposite nations that inhabit either side. The Swiss cottages are much cleaner and neater, and the inhabitants exhibit the same contrast.° The Swiss women wear a great deal of white linen, and their whole dress is always perfectly clean. This superior cleanliness is chiefly produced by the difference of religion: travellers in Germany remark the same contrast between the protestant and catholic towns, although they be but a few leagues separate.

The scenery° of this day's journey was divine, exhibiting piny mountains, barren rocks, and spots of verdure surpassing imagination. After descending for nearly a league between lofty rocks, covered with pines, and interspersed with green glades, where the grass is short, and soft, and beautifully verdant, we arrived at the village of St. Sulpice.°

The mule had latterly become very lame, and the man so disobliging, that we determined to engage a horse for the remainder of the way. Our *voiturier* had anticipated us, without in the least intimating his intention: he had determined to leave us at this village, and taken measures to that effect. The man we now engaged was a Swiss,° a cottager of the better class, who was proud of his mountains and his country. Pointing to the glades that were interspersed among the woods, he informed us that they were very beautiful, and were excellent pasture; that the cows thrived there, and consequently produced excellent milk, from which the best cheese and butter in the world were made.

The mountains after St. Sulpice became loftier and more beautiful.° We passed through a narrow valley between two ranges of mountains, clothed with forests, at the bottom of which flowed a river, from whose narrow bed on either side the boundaries of the vale arose precipitously. The road lay about half way up the mountain, which formed one of the sides, and we saw the overhanging rocks above us and below, enormous pines, and the river, not to be perceived but from its reflection of the light of heaven, far beneath. The mountains of this beautiful ravine are so little asunder, that in time of war with France an iron chain° is thrown across it. Two leagues° from Neufchâtel we saw the Alps: range after range of black mountains are seen extending one before the other, and far behind all, towering above every feature of the scene, the snowy Alps. They were an hundred miles distant, but reach so high in the heavens, that they look like those accumulated clouds of dazzling white that arrange themselves on the horizon during summer. Their immensity staggers the imagination, and so far surpasses all conception, that it requires an effort of the understanding to believe that they indeed form a part of the earth.

From this point we descended to Neufchâtel, which is situated in a narrow plain, between the mountains and its immense lake,° and presents no additional aspect of peculiar interest.

We remained the following day at this town, occupied in a consideration of the step it would now be advisable for us to take. The money we had brought with us from Paris was nearly exhausted, but we obtained about £38. in silver upon discount° from one of the bankers of the city, and with this we resolved to journey towards the lake of Uri,° and seek in that romantic and interesting country some cottage where we might dwell in peace and solitude. Such were our dreams, which we should probably have realized, had it not been for the deficiency of that indispensible article money, which obliged us to return to England.

A Swiss, whom S*** met at the postoffice,° kindly interested himself in our affairs, and assisted us to hire a *voiture* to convey us to Lucerne, the principal town of the lake of that name, which is connected with the lake of Uri. The journey to this place occupied rather more than two days.° The country was flat and dull, and, excepting that we now and then caught a glimpse of the divine Alps, there was nothing in it to interest us.° Lucerne promised better things, and as soon as we arrived (August 23d) we hired a boat,° with which we proposed to coast the lake until we should meet with some suitable habitation, or perhaps, even going to Altorf,° cross Mont St. Gothard, and seek in the warm climate of the country to the south of the Alps an air more salubrious, and a temperature better fitted for the precarious state of S***'s health,° than the bleak region to the north. The lake of Lucerne is encompassed on all sides by high mountains that rise abruptly from the water;—sometimes their bare fronts descend perpendicularly and cast a black shade upon the waves;—sometimes they are covered with thick wood, whose dark foliage is interspersed by the brown bare crags on which the trees have taken root. In every part where a glade shews itself in the forest it appears cultivated, and cottages peep from among the woods. The most luxuriant islands, rocky and covered with moss, and bending trees, are sprinkled over the lake. Most of these are decorated by the figure of a saint in wretched waxwork.

The direction of this lake extends at first from east to west, then turning a right angle, it lies from north to south; this latter part is distinguished in name from the other, and is called the lake of Uri. The former part is also nearly divided midway, where the jutting land almost meets, and its craggy sides cast a deep shadow on the little strait through which you pass. The summits of several of the mountains that enclose the lake to the south are covered by eternal glaciers; of one of these, opposite Brunen,° they tell the story of a priest and his mistress,° who, flying from persecution, inhabited a cottage at the foot of the snows. One winter night an avelanche overwhelmed them, but their plaintive voices are still heard in stormy nights, calling for succour from the peasants.

Brunen is situated on the northern side of the angle which the lake makes, forming the extremity of the lake of Lucerne. Here we rested for the night, and dismissed our boatmen. Nothing could be more magnificent than the view from this spot. The high mountains encompassed us, darkening the waters; at a distance on the shores of Uri we could perceive the chapel of Tell,° and this was the village where he matured the conspiracy which was to overthrow the tyrant of his country; and indeed this lovely lake, these sublime mountains, and wild forests, seemed a fit cradle for a mind aspiring to high adventure and heroic deeds.° Yet we saw no glimpse of his spirit in his present countrymen. The Swiss appeared to us then, and experience has confirmed our opinion, a people slow of comprehension and of action; but habit has made them unfit for slavery, and they would, I have little doubt, make a brave defence against any invader of their freedom.

Such were our reflections, and we remained until late in the evening on the shores of the lake conversing, enjoying the rising breeze, and contemplating with feelings of exquisite delight the divine objects that surrounded us.

The following day was spent in a consideration of our circumstances, and in contemplation of the scene around us. A furious *vent d'Italie*° (south wind) tore up the lake, making immense waves, and carrying the water in a whirlwind high in the air, when it fell like heavy rain into the lake. The waves broke with a tremendous noise on the rocky shores. This conflict continued during the whole day, but it became calmer towards the evening. S*** and I walked on the banks, and sitting on a rude pier, S*** read aloud the account of the Siege of Jerusalem from Tacitus.°

In the mean time we endeavoured to find an habitation, but could only procure two unfurnished rooms in an ugly big house, called the Chateau.° These we hired at a guinea a month, had beds moved into them, and the next day took possession. But it was a wretched place, with no comfort or convenience. It was with difficulty that we could get any food prepared: as it was cold and rainy, we ordered a fire—they lighted an immense stove which occupied a corner of the room; it was long before it heated, and when hot, the warmth was so unwholesome, that we were obliged to throw open our windows to prevent a kind of suffocation; added to this, there was but one person in Brunen who could speak French, a barbarous kind of German being the language of this part of Switzerland. It was with difficulty, therefore, that we could get our most ordinary wants supplied.

These immediate inconveniences led us to a more serious consideration of our situation. The £28. which we possessed, was all the money that we could count upon with any certainty, until the following December.° S***'s presence in London was absolutely necessary for the procuring any further supply. What were we to do? we should soon be reduced to absolute want. Thus, after balancing the various topics that offered themselves for discussion, we resolved to return to England.°

Having formed this resolution, we had not a moment for delay: our little store was sensibly decreasing, and £28. could hardly appear sufficient for so long a journey. It had cost us sixty to cross France from Paris to Neufchâtel; but we now resolved on a more economical mode of travelling. Water conveyances are always the cheapest, and fortunately we were so situated, that by taking advantage of the rivers of the Reuss and Rhine, we could reach England without travelling a league on land. This was our plan; we should travel eight hundred miles, and was this possible for so small a sum? but there was no other alternative, and indeed S*** only knew° how very little we had to depend upon.

We departed the next morning for the town of Lucerne. It rained violently during the first part of our voyage, but towards its conclusion the sky became clear, and the sun-beams dried and cheered us. We saw again, and for the last time, the rocky shores of this beautiful lake, its verdant isles, and snow-capt mountains.

We landed at Lucerne, and remained in that town the following night, and the next morning (August 28th) departed in the *diligence par-eau*° for Loffenburgh,° a town on the Rhine, where the falls of that river prevented the same vessel from proceeding any further. Our companions in this voyage were of the meanest class, smoked prodigiously, and were exceedingly disgusting. After having landed for refreshment in the middle of the day, we found, on our return to the boat, that our former seats were occupied; we took others, when the original possessors angrily, and almost with violence, insisted upon our leaving them. Their brutal rudeness to us, who did not understand their language, provoked S*** to knock one of the foremost down: he did not return the blow, but continued his vociferations until the boatmen interfered, and provided us with other seats.

The Reuss is exceedingly rapid,° and we descended several falls, one of more than eight feet. There is something very delicious in the sensation, when at one moment you are at the top of a fall of water, and before the second has expired you are at the bottom, still rushing on with the impulse which the descent has given. The waters of the Rhone are blue, those of the Reuss are of a deep green.° I should think that there must be something in the beds of these rivers, and that the accidents of the banks and sky cannot alone cause this difference.

Sleeping at Dettingen,° we arrived the next morning at Loffenburgh, where we engaged a small canoe to convey us to Mumph.° I give these boats this Indian appellation,° as they were of the rudest construction—long, narrow, and flat-bottomed: they consisted merely of straight pieces of deal board, unpainted, and nailed together with so little care, that the water constantly poured in at the crevices, and the boat perpetually required emptying. The river was rapid, and sped swiftly, breaking as it passed on innumerable rocks just covered by the water: it was a sight of some dread to see our frail boat winding among the eddies of the rocks, which it was death to touch, and when the slightest inclination on one side would instantly have overset it.

We could not procure a boat at Mumph, and we thought ourselves lucky in meeting with a return *cabriolet* to Rheinfelden; but our good fortune was of short duration: about a league from Mumph the *cabriolet* broke down, and we were obliged to proceed on foot.° Fortunately we were overtaken by some Swiss soldiers, who were discharged and returning home, who carried our box for us as far as Rheinfelden,° when we were directed to proceed a league farther to a village, where boats were commonly hired. Here, although not without some difficulty, we procured a boat for Basle,° and proceeded down a swift river, while evening came on, and the air was bleak and comfortless. Our voyage was, however, short, and we arrived at the place of our destination by six in the evening.

GERMANY.

BEFORE we slept, S*** had made a bargain for a boat to carry us to Mayence,° and the next morning, bidding adieu to Switzerland, we embarked in a boat laden with merchandize, but where we had no fellow-passengers to disturb our tranquillity by their vulgarity and rudeness. The wind was violently against us, but the stream, aided by a slight exertion from the rowers, carried us on; the sun shone pleasantly, S*** read aloud to us Mary Wollstonecraft's Letters from Norway,° and we passed our time delightfully.°

The evening was such as to find few parallels in beauty; as it approached, the banks which had hitherto been flat and uninteresting, became exceedingly beautiful. Suddenly° the river grew narrow, and the boat dashed with inconceivable rapidity round the base of a rocky hill covered with pines; a ruined tower, with its desolated windows, stood on the summit of another hill that jutted into the river; beyond, the sunset was illuminating the distant mountains and clouds, casting the reflection of its rich and purple hues on the agitated river. The brilliance and contrasts of the colours on the circling whirlpools of the stream, was an appearance entirely new and most beautiful; the shades grew darker as the sun descended below the horizon, and after we had landed, as we walked to our inn round a beautiful bay, the full moon arose with divine splendour, casting its silver light on the before-purpled waves.

The following morning we pursued our journey in a slight canoe, in which every motion was accompanied with danger; but the stream had lost much of its rapidity, and was no longer impeded by rocks, the banks were low, and covered with willows. We passed Strasburgh,° and the next morning it was proposed to us that we should proceed in the *diligence par-eau*, as the navigation would become dangerous for our small boat.

There were only four passengers besides ourselves, three of these were students° of the Strasburgh university: Schwitz, a rather handsome, good tempered young man; Hoff, a kind of shapeless animal, with a heavy, ugly, German face; and Schneider, who was nearly an ideot, and on whom his companions were always playing a thousand tricks: the remaining passengers were a woman, and an infant.

The country was uninteresting, but we enjoyed fine weather, and slept in the boat in the open air without any inconvenience. We saw on the shores few objects that called forth our attention, if I except the town of Manheim,° which was strikingly neat and clean. It was situated at about a mile from the river, and the road to it was planted on each side with beautiful acacias. The last part of this voyage was performed close under land, as the wind was so violently against us, that even with all the force of a rapid current in our favour, we were hardly permitted to proceed. We were told (and not without reason) that we ought to congratulate ourselves on having exchanged our canoe for this boat, as the river was now of considerable width, and tossed by the wind into large waves. The same morning a boat, containing fifteen persons, in attempting to cross the water, had upset in the middle of the river, and every one in it perished. We saw the boat turned over, floating down the stream. This was a melancholy sight, yet ludicrously commented on by the *batalier*;° almost the whole stock of whose French consisted in the word *seulement*. When we asked him what had happened, he answered, laying particular emphasis on this favourite dissyllable, *C'est seulement un bateau, qui etoit seulement renversèe, et tous les peuples sont seulement noyès.*°

Mayence is one of the best fortified towns in Germany. The river, which is broad and rapid, guards it to the east, and the hills for three leagues around exhibit signs of fortifications. The town itself is old, the streets narrow, and the houses high: the cathedral and towers of the town still bear marks of the bombardment which took place in the revolutionary war.°

We took our place in the *diligence par-eau* for Cologne,° and the next morning (September 4th) departed. This conveyance appeared much more like a mercantile° English affair than any we had before seen; it was shaped like a steam-boat,° with a cabin and a high deck. Most of our companions chose to remain in the cabin; this was fortunate for us, since nothing could be more horribly disgusting than the lower order of smoking, drinking Germans who travelled with us; they swaggered and talked, and what was hideous to English eyes, kissed one another:° there were, however, two or three merchants of a better class, who appeared well-informed and polite.

The part of the Rhine down which we now glided, is that so beautifully described by Lord Byron in his third canto of *Childe Harold.*° We read these verses with delight, as they conjured before us these lovely scenes with the truth and vividness of painting, and with the exquisite addition of glowing language and a warm imagination. We were carried down by a dangerously rapid current, and saw on either side of us hills covered with vines and trees, craggy cliffs crowned by desolate towers, and wooded islands, where picturesque ruins peeped from behind the foliage, and cast the shadows of their forms on the troubled waters, which distorted without deforming them. We heard the songs of the vintagers, and if surrounded by disgusting Germans, the sight was not so replete with enjoyment as I now fancy it to have been; yet memory, taking all the dark shades from the picture, presents this part of the Rhine to my remembrance as the loveliest paradise on earth.

We had sufficient leisure for the enjoyment of these scenes,° for the boatmen, neither rowing nor steering, suffered us to be carried down by the stream, and the boat turned round and round as it descended.

While I speak with disgust of the Germans who travelled with us, I should in justice to these borderers° record, that at one of the inns here we saw the only pretty woman we met with in the course of our travels. She is what I should conceive to be a truly German beauty; grey eyes, slightly tinged with brown, and expressive of uncommon sweetness and frankness. She had lately recovered from a fever, and this added to the interest of her countenance, by adorning it with an appearance of extreme delicacy.°

On the following day we left the hills of the Rhine, and found that, for the remainder of our journey, we should move sluggishly through the flats of Holland: the river also winds extremely; so that, after calculating our resources, we resolved to finish our journey in a land diligence. Our water conveyance remained that night at Bonn, and that we might lose no time, we proceeded post the same night to Cologne, where we arrived late; for the rate of travelling in Germany seldom exceeds a mile and a half an hour.

Cologne appeared an immense town, as we drove through street after street to arrive at our inn. Before, we slept, we secured places in the diligence, which was to depart next morning for Clêves.°

Nothing in the world can be more wretched than travelling in this German diligence: the coach is clumsy and comfortless, and we proceeded so slowly, stopping so often, that it appeared as if we should never arrive at our journey's end. We were allowed two hours for dinner, and two more were wasted in the evening while the coach was being changed. We were then requested, as the diligence had a greater demand for places than it could supply, to proceed in a *cabriolet* which was provided for us. We readily consented, as we hoped to travel faster than in the heavy diligence; but this was not permitted, and we jogged on all night behind this cumbrous machine. In the morning when we stopped, and for a moment indulged a hope that we had arrived at Clêves, which was at the distance of five leagues from our last night's stage; but we had only advanced three leagues in seven or eight hours, and had yet eight miles to perform. However, we first rested about three hours at this stage, where we could not obtain breakfast or any convenience, and at about eight o'clock we again departed, and with slow, although far from easy travelling, faint with hunger and fatigue, we arrived by noon at Clêves.

HOLLAND.

TIRED by the slow pace of the diligence, we resolved to post the remainder of the way.° We had now, however, left Germany, and travelled at about the same rate as an English post-chaise. The country was entirely flat, and the roads so sandy, that the horses proceeded with difficulty. The only ornaments of this country are the turf fortifications that surround the towns. At Nimeguen we passed the flying bridge, mentioned in the letters of Lady Mary Montague.° We had intended to travel all night, but at Triel,° where we arrived at about ten o'clock, we were assured that no post-boy was to be found who would proceed at so late an hour, on account of the robbers who infested the roads. This was an obvious imposition; but as we could procure neither horses nor driver, we were obliged to sleep here.

During the whole of the following day° the road lay between canals, which intersect this country in every direction. The roads were excellent, but the Dutch have contrived as many inconveniences as possible. In our journey of the day before, we had passed by a windmill, which was so situated with regard to the road, that it was only by keeping close to the opposite side, and passing quickly, that we could avoid the sweep of its sails.

The roads between the canals were only wide enough to admit of one carriage, so that when we encountered another we were obliged sometimes to back for half a mile, until we should come to one of the drawbridges which led to the fields, on which one of the *cabriolets* was rolled, while the other passed. But they have another practice, which is still more annoying: the flax° when cut is put to soak under the mud of the canals, and then placed to dry against the trees which are planted on either side of the road; the stench that it exhales, when the beams of the sun draw out the moisture, is scarcely endurable. We saw many enormous frogs and toads in the canals; and the only sight which refreshed the eye by its beauty was the delicious verdure of the fields, where the grass was as rich and green as that of England, an appearance not common on the continent.

Rotterdam is remarkably clean: the Dutch even wash the outside brickwork of their houses. We remained here one day, and met with a man in a very unfortunate condition:° he had been born in Holland, and had spent so much of his life between England, France, and Germany, that he had acquired a slight knowledge of the language of each country, and spoke all very imperfectly. He said that he understood English best, but he was nearly unable to express himself in that.

On the evening of the 8th of August° we sailed from Rotterdam, but contrary winds obliged us to remain nearly two days at Marsluys,° a town about two leagues from Rotterdam. Here our last guinea was expended, and we reflected with wonder that we had travelled eight hundred miles for less than thirty pounds, passing through lovely scenes, and enjoying the beauteous Rhine, and all the brilliant shews of earth and sky,° perhaps more, travelling as we did, in an open boat, than if we had been shut up in a carriage, and passed on the road under the hills.

The captain of our vessel was an Englishman, and had been a king's pilot.° The bar of the Rhine° a little below Marsluys is so dangerous, that without a very favourable breeze none of the Dutch vessels dare attempt its passage; but although the wind was a very few points in our favour, our captain resolved to sail, and although half repentant before he had accomplished his undertaking, he was glad and proud when, triumphing over the timorous Dutchmen, the bar was crossed, and the vessel safe in the open sea. It was in truth an enterprise of some peril; a heavy gale had prevailed during the night, and although it had abated since the morning, the breakers at the bar were still exceedingly high. Through some delay, which had arisen from the ship having got a-ground in the harbour, we arrived half an hour after the appointed time. The breakers were tremendous, and we were informed that there was the space of only two feet between the bottom of the vessel and the sands. The waves, which broke against the sides of the ship with a terrible shock, were quite perpendicular, and even sometimes overhanging in the abrupt smoothness of their sides. Shoals of enormous porpoises were sporting with the utmost composure amidst the troubled waters.

We safely past this danger, and after a navigation unexpectedly short, arrived at Gravesend on the morning of the 13th of September, the third day after our departure from Marsluys.°

M.

LETTERS.

LETTERS

WRITTEN

DURING A RESIDENCE OF THREE MONTHS IN THE ENVIRONS OF GENEVA,

In the Summer of the Year 1816.

LETTER I.

Hôtel de Secheron,° Geneva,
May 17, 1816.

WE arrived at Paris on the 8th of this month, and were detained two days for the purpose of obtaining the various signatures necessary to our passports, the French government having become much more circumspect since the escape of Lavalette.° We had no letters of introduction, or any friend in that city, and were therefore confined to our hotel, where we were obliged to hire apartments for the week, although when we first arrived we expected to be detained one night only; for in Paris there are no houses where you can be accommodated with apartments by the day.

The manners of the French° are interesting, although less attractive, at least to Englishmen, than before the last invasion of the Allies:° the discontent and sullenness of their minds perpetually betrays itself. Nor is it wonderful that they should regard the subjects of a government which fills their country with hostile garrisons, and sustains a detested dynasty on the throne, with an acrimony and indignation of which that government alone is the proper object. This feeling is honourable to the French, and encouraging to all those of every nation in Europe who have a fellow feeling with the oppressed, and who cherish an unconquerable hope that the cause of liberty must at length prevail.

Our route after Paris, as far as Troyes, lay through the same uninteresting tract of country which we had traversed on foot nearly two

years before, but on quitting Troyes we left the road leading to
Neufchâtel,° to follow that which was to conduct us to Geneva. We
entered Dijon on the third evening after our departure from Paris,
and passing through Dôle,° arrived at Poligny. This town is built at
the foot of Jura,° which rises abruptly from a plain of vast extent. The
rocks of the mountain overhang the houses. Some difficulty in procuring horses detained us here until the evening closed in, when we
proceeded, by the light of a stormy moon, to Champagnolles,° a little
village situated in the depth of the mountains. The road was serpen-
tine and exceedingly steep, and was overhung on one side by half
distinguished precipices, whilst the other was a gulph, filled by the
darkness of the driving clouds. The dashing of the invisible mountain
streams announced to us that we had quitted the plains of France, as
we slowly ascended, amidst a violent storm of wind and rain, to
Champagnolles, where we arrived at twelve o'clock, the fourth night
after our departure from Paris.

The next morning we proceeded, still ascending among the ravines
and vallies of the mountain. The scenery perpetually grows more
wonderful and sublime: pine forests of impenetrable thickness,
and untrodden, nay, inaccessible expanse° spread on every side.
Sometimes the dark woods descending, follow the route into the vallies, the distorted trees struggling with knotted roots between the
most barren clefts; sometimes the road winds high into the regions of
frost, and then the forests become scattered, and the branches of the
trees are loaded with snow, and half of the enormous pines themselves
buried in the wavy drifts. The spring, as the inhabitants informed us,
was unusually late, and indeed the cold was excessive;° as we ascended
the mountains, the same clouds which rained on us in the vallies
poured forth large flakes of snow thick and fast. The sun occasionally
shone through these showers, and illuminated the magnificent ravines
of the mountains, whose gigantic pines were some laden with snow,
some wreathed round by the lines of scattered and lingering vapour;
others darting their dark spires into the sunny sky, brilliantly clear
and azure.

As the evening advanced, and we ascended higher, the snow, which
we had beheld whitening the overhanging rocks, now encroached
upon our road, and it snowed fast as we entered the village of Les
Rousses, where we were threatened by the apparent necessity of passing the night in a bad inn and dirty beds. For from that place there are

two roads to Geneva; one by Nion,° in the Swiss territory, where the
mountain route is shorter, and comparatively easy at that time of the
year, when the road is for several leagues covered with snow of an
enormous depth; the other road lay through Gex, and was too circuitous and dangerous to be attempted at so late an hour in the day. Our
passport,° however, was for Gex, and we were told that we could not
change its destination; but all these police laws, so severe in themselves, are to be softened by bribery, and this difficulty was at length
overcome.° We hired four horses, and ten men to support the carriage, and departed from Les Rousses at six in the evening, when the
sun had already far descended, and the snow pelting against the windows of our carriage, assisted the coming darkness to deprive us of
the view of the lake of Geneva and the far distant Alps.

The prospect around, however, was sufficiently sublime to com-
mand our attention—never was scene more awfully desolate. The
trees in these regions are incredibly large, and stand in scattered
clumps over the white wilderness; the vast expanse of snow was che-
quered only by these gigantic pines, and the poles that marked our
road: no river or rock-encircled lawn relieved the eye, by adding the
picturesque to the sublime.° The natural silence of that uninhabited
desert° contrasted strangely with the voices of the men who conducted us, who, with animated tones and gestures, called to one
another in a *patois*° composed of French and Italian, creating disturb-
ance, where but for them, there was none.

To what a different scene are we now arrived! To the warm sunshine and to the humming of sun-loving insects. From the windows
of our hotel we see the lovely lake, blue as the heavens which it reflects,
and sparkling with golden beams. The opposite shore is sloping, and
covered with vines, which however do not so early in the season add
to the beauty of the prospect. Gentlemens' seats° are scattered over
these banks, behind which rise the various ridges of black mountains,
and towering far above, in the midst of its snowy Alps, the majestic
Mont Blanc, highest and queen of all.° Such is the view reflected by
the lake; it is a bright summer scene without any of that sacred solitude and deep seclusion° that delighted us at Lucerne.

We have not yet found out any very agreeable walks, but you know
our attachment to water excursions. We have hired a boat, and every
evening at about six o'clock we sail on the lake, which is delightful,
whether we glide over a glassy surface or are speeded along by a strong

wind. The waves of this lake never afflict me with that sickness° that deprives me of all enjoyment in a sea voyage; on the contrary, the tossing of our boat raises my spirits and inspires me with unusual hilarity. Twilight here is of short duration, but we at present enjoy the benefit of an increasing moon, and seldom return until ten o'clock, when, as we approach the shore, we are saluted by the delightful scent of flowers and new mown grass, and the chirp of the grasshoppers, and the song of the evening birds.

We do not enter into society here, yet our time passes swiftly and delightfully. We read Latin and Italian° during the heats of noon, and when the sun declines we walk in the garden of the hotel, looking at the rabbits, relieving fallen cockchaffers,° and watching the motions of a myriad of lizards, who inhabit a southern wall of the garden.° You know that we have just escaped from the gloom of winter and of London; and coming to this delightful spot during this divine weather, I feel as happy as a new-fledged bird, and hardly care what twig I fly to, so that I may try my new-found wings. A more experienced bird may be more difficult in its choice of a bower; but in my present temper of mind, the budding flowers, the fresh grass of spring, and the happy creatures about me that live and enjoy these pleasures, are quite enough to afford me exquisite delight, even though clouds should shut out Mont Blanc from my sight. Adieu!

M.°

LETTER II.

COLIGNY — GENEVA — PLAINPALAIS.

Campagne C******, near Coligny,°
1st June.

You will perceive from my date that we have changed our residence since my last letter. We now inhabit a little cottage on the opposite shore of the lake, and have exchanged the view of Mont Blanc and her snowy *aiguilles*° for the dark frowning Jura, behind whose range we every evening see the sun sink, and darkness approaches our valley from behind the Alps, which are then tinged by that glowing rose-like hue° which is observed in England to attend on the clouds of an autumnal sky when day-light is almost gone. The lake is at our feet, and a little harbour contains our boat, in which we still enjoy our evening excursions on the water.° Unfortunately we do not now enjoy those brilliant skies that hailed us on our first arrival to this country. An almost perpetual rain confines us principally to the house; but when the sun bursts forth it is with a splendour and heat unknown in England. The thunder storms that visit us are grander and more terrific than I have ever seen before. We watch them as they approach from the opposite side of the lake, observing the lightning play among the clouds in various parts of the heavens, and dart in jagged figures upon the piny heights of Jura, dark with the shadow of the overhanging cloud, while perhaps the sun is shining cheerily upon us. One night we *enjoyed* a finer storm° than I had ever before beheld. The lake was lit up—the pines on Jura made visible, and all the scene illuminated for an instant, when a pitchy blackness succeeded, and the thunder came in frightful bursts over our heads amid the darkness.

But while I still dwell on the country around Geneva, you will expect me to say something of the town itself: there is nothing, however, in it that can repay you for the trouble of walking over its rough stones. The houses are high, the streets narrow, many of them on the ascent, and no public building of any beauty to attract your eye, or any architecture to gratify your taste. The town is surrounded by a wall, the three gates of which are shut exactly at ten o'clock, when no bribery (as in France) can open them. To the south of the town is the promenade of the Genevese, a grassy plain planted with a few trees, and called Plainpalais.° Here a small obelisk is erected to the glory of Rousseau, and here (such is the mutability of human life) the magistrates, the successors of those who exiled him from his native country, were shot by the populace during that revolution, which his writings mainly contributed to mature, and which, notwithstanding the temporary bloodshed and injustice with which it was polluted, has produced enduring benefits to mankind, which all the chicanery of statesmen, nor even the great conspiracy of kings, can entirely render vain.° From respect to the memory of their predecessors, none of the present magistrates ever walk in Plainpalais. Another Sunday recreation for the citizens is an excursion to the top of Mont Salêve.° This hill is within a league of the town, and rises perpendicularly from the cultivated plain. It is ascended on the other side, and I should judge from its situation that your toil is rewarded by a delightful view of the course of the Rhone and Arve,° and of the shores of the lake. We have not yet visited it.

There is more equality of classes here than in England.° This occasions a greater freedom and refinement of manners among the lower orders than we meet with in our own country. I fancy the haughty English ladies are greatly disgusted with this consequence of republican institutions, for the Genevese servants complain very much, of their *scolding*, an exercise of the tongue, I believe, perfectly unknown here. The peasants of Switzerland may not however emulate the vivacity and grace of the French. They are more cleanly, but they are slow and inapt.° I know a girl of twenty, who although she had lived all her life among vineyards, could not inform me during what month the vintage took place, and I discovered she was utterly ignorant of the order in which the months succeed to one another. She would not have been surprised if I had talked of the burning sun and delicious fruits of December, or of the frosts of July. Yet she is by no means deficient in understanding.

The Genevese are also much inclined to puritanism.° It is true that from habit they dance on a Sunday, but as soon as the French government was abolished° in the town, the magistrates ordered the theatre to be closed, and measures were taken to pull down the building.

We have latterly enjoyed fine weather, and nothing is more pleasant than to listen to the evening song of the vine-dressers. They are all women, and most of them have harmonious although masculine voices. The theme of their ballads consists of shepherds, love, flocks, and the sons of kings who fall in love with beautiful shepherdesses. Their tunes are monotonous, but it is sweet to hear them in the stillness of evening, while we are enjoying the sight of the setting sun, either from the hill behind our house or from the lake.

Such are our pleasures here, which would be greatly increased if the season had been more favourable, for they chiefly consist in such enjoyments as sunshine and gentle breezes bestow. We have not yet made any excursion in the environs of the town, but we have planned several, when you shall again hear of us; and we will endeavour, by the magic of words, to transport the ethereal part of you to the neighbourhood of the Alps, and mountain streams, and forests, which, while they clothe the former, darken the latter with their vast shadows. Adieu!

M.°

LETTER III.

MELLTERIE—CLAREN—SCHILLON—VEVAI—LAUSANNE.°

Montalegre,° near Coligni, Geneva,
July 12th.°

IT is nearly a fortnight since I have returned from Vevai. This journey
has been on every account delightful, but most especially, because then
I first knew the divine beauty of Rousseau's imagination, as it exhibits
itself in Julie.° It is inconceivable what an enchantment the scene itself
lends to those delineations, from which its own most touching charm
arises.° But I will give you an abstract of our voyage, which lasted eight
days, and if you have a map of Switzerland, you can follow me.

We left Montalegre at half past two on the 23d of June.° The lake
was calm, and after three hours of rowing we arrived at Hermance,
a beautiful little village, containing a ruined tower,° built, the villagers
say, by Julius Cæsar. There were three other towers similar to it, which
the Genevese destroyed for their own fortifications in 1560.° We got
into the tower by a kind of window. The walls are immensely solid,
and the stone of which it is built so hard, that it yet retained the mark
of chisels. The boatmen said, that this tower was once three times
higher than it is now. There are two staircases in the thickness of the
walls, one of which is entirely demolished, and the other half ruined,
and only accessible by a ladder. The town itself, now an inconsider-
able village inhabited by a few fishermen, was built by a Queen of
Burgundy,° and reduced to its present state by the inhabitants of
Berne,° who burnt and ravaged every thing they could find.

Leaving Hermance, we arrived at sunset at the village of Nerni.°
After looking at our lodgings, which were gloomy and dirty, we walked
out by the side of the lake. It was beautiful to see the vast expanse of
these purple and misty waters broken by the craggy islets near to its
slant and "beached margin."° There were many fish sporting in the
lake, and multitudes were collected close to the rocks to catch the flies
which inhabited them.

On returning to the village, we sat on a wall beside the lake, looking at some children who were playing at a game like ninepins.° The children here appeared in an extraordinary way deformed and diseased. Most of them were crooked, and with enlarged throats;° but one little boy had such exquisite grace in his mien° and motions, as I never before saw equalled in a child. His countenance was beautiful for the expression with which it overflowed. There was a mixture of pride and gentleness in his eyes and lips, the indications of sensibility, which his education will probably pervert to misery or seduce to crime;° but there was more of gentleness than of pride, and it seemed that the pride was tamed from its original wildness by the habitual exercise of milder feelings. My companion° gave him a piece of money, which he took without speaking, with a sweet smile of easy thankfulness, and then with an unembarrassed air turned to his play. All this might scarcely be;° but the imagination surely could not forbear to breathe into the most inanimate forms some likeness of its own visions, on such a serene and glowing evening, in this remote and romantic village, beside the calm lake that bore us hither.

On returning to our inn, we found that the servant had arranged our rooms, and deprived them of the greater portion of their former disconsolate appearance. They reminded my companion of Greece: it was five years, he said, since he had slept in such beds.° The influence of the recollections excited by this circumstance on our conversation gradually faded, and I retired to rest with no unpleasant sensations, thinking of our journey tomorrow, and of the pleasure of recounting the little adventures of it when we return.

The next morning we passed Yvoire, a scattered village with an ancient castle, whose houses are interspersed with trees, and which stands at a little distance from Nerni, on the promontory which bounds a deep bay, some miles in extent. So soon as we arrived at this promontory, the lake began to assume an aspect of wilder magnificence. The mountains of Savoy, whose summits were bright with snow, descended in broken slopes to the lake: on high, the rocks were dark with pine forests, which become deeper and more immense, until the ice and snow mingle with the points of naked rock that pierce the blue air; but below, groves of walnut, chesnut, and oak, with openings of lawny fields, attested the milder climate.

As soon as we had passed the opposite promontory, we saw the river Drance,° which descends from between a chasm in the mountains, and makes a plain near the lake, intersected by its divided streams. Thousands of *besolets*,° beautiful water-birds, like sea-gulls, but smaller, with purple on their backs, take their station on the shallows, where its waters mingle with the lake. As we approached Evian, the mountains descended more precipitously to the lake, and masses of intermingled wood and rock overhung its shining spire.

We arrived at this town about seven o'clock, after a day which involved more rapid changes of atmosphere than I ever recollect to have observed before. The morning was cold and wet; then an easterly wind, and the clouds hard and high; then thunder showers, and wind shifting to every quarter; then a warm blast from the south, and summer clouds hanging over the peaks, with bright blue sky between. About half an hour after we had arrived at Evian, a few flashes of lightning came from a dark cloud, directly over head, and continued after the cloud had dispersed. "Diespiter, per pura tonantes egit equos:"° a phenomenon which certainly had no influence on me, corresponding with that which it produced on Horace.

The appearance of the inhabitants of Evian is more wretched, diseased and poor, than I ever recollect to have seen. The contrast indeed between the subjects of the King of Sardinia° and the citizens of the independent republics of Switzerland, affords a powerful illustration of the blighting mischiefs of despotism, within the space of a few miles. They have mineral waters here, *eaux savonneuses*,° they call them. In the evening we had some difficulty about our passports, but so soon as the syndic° heard my companion's rank and name, he apologized for the circumstance. The inn was good. During our voyage, on the distant height of a hill, covered with pine-forests, we saw a ruined castle, which reminded me of those on the Rhine.

We left Evian on the following morning, with a wind of such violence as to permit but one sail to be carried. The waves also were exceedingly high, and our boat so heavily laden, that there appeared to be some danger. We arrived however safe at Mellerie, after passing with great speed mighty forests which overhung the lake, and lawns of exquisite verdure, and mountains with bare and icy points, which rose immediately from the summit of the rocks, whose bases were echoing to the waves.

We here heard that the Empress Maria Louisa° had slept at Mellerie, before the present inn was built, and when the accommodations were those of the most wretched village, in remembrance of

St. Preux.° How beautiful it is to find that the common sentiments of human nature can attach themselves to those who are the most removed from its duties and its enjoyments, when Genius pleads for their admission at the gate of Power. To own them was becoming in the Empress, and confirms the affectionate praise contained in the regret of a great and enlightened nation. A Bourbon dared not even to have remembered Rousseau.° She owed this power to that democracy which her husband's dynasty outraged, and of which it was however in some sort the representative among the nations of the earth.° This little incident shews at once how unfit and how impossible it is for the ancient system of opinions, or for any power built upon a conspiracy to revive them, permanently to subsist among mankind. We dined there, and had some honey, the best I have ever tasted, the very essence of the mountain flowers, and as fragrant.° Probably the village derives its name from this production.° Mellerie is the well known scene of St. Preux's visionary exile;° but Mellerie is indeed inchanted ground, were Rousseau no magician. Groves of pine, chesnut, and walnut overshadow it; magnificent and unbounded forests to which England affords no parallel. In the midst of these woods are dells of lawny expanse, inconceivably verdant, adorned with a thousand of the rarest flowers and odourous with thyme.

The lake appeared somewhat calmer as we left Mellerie,° sailing close to the banks, whose magnificence augmented with the turn of every promontory. But we congratulated ourselves too soon: the wind gradually increased in violence, until it blew tremendously; and as it came from the remotest extremity of the lake, produced waves of a frightful height, and covered the whole surface with a chaos of foam. One of our boatmen, who was a dreadfully stupid fellow, persisted in holding the sail at a time when the boat was on the point of being driven under water by the hurricane. On discovering his error, he let it entirely go, and the boat for a moment refused to obey the helm; in addition, the rudder was so broken as to render the management of it very difficult; one wave fell in, and then another. My companion, an excellent swimmer, took off his coat, I did the same, and we sat with our arms crossed, every instant expecting to be swamped. The sail was however again held, the boat obeyed the helm, and still in imminent peril from the immensity of the waves, we arrived in a few minutes at a sheltered port, in the village of St. Gingoux.

I felt in this near prospect of death a mixture of sensations, among which terror entered, though but subordinately. My feelings would have been less painful had I been alone; but I know that my companion would have attempted to save me, and I was overcome with humiliation, when I thought that his life might have been risked to preserve mine. When we arrived at St. Gingoux, the inhabitants, who stood on the shore, unaccustomed to see a vessel as frail as our's, and fearing to venture at all on such a sea, exchanged looks of wonder and congratulation with our boatmen, who, as well as ourselves, were well pleased to set foot on shore.

St. Gingoux is even more beautiful than Mellerie; the mountains are higher, and their loftiest points of elevation descend more abruptly to the lake. On high, the aerial summits still cherish great depths of snow in their ravines, and in the paths of their unseen torrents. One of the highest of these is called Roche de St. Julien,° beneath whose pinnacles the forests become deeper and more extensive; the chesnut gives a peculiarity to the scene, which is most beautiful, and will make a picture in my memory, distinct from all other mountain scenes which I have ever before visited.

As we arrived here early, we took a *voiture* to visit the mouth of the Rhone. We went between the mountains and the lake, under groves of mighty chesnut trees, beside perpetual streams, which are nourished by the snows above, and form stalactites° on the rocks, over which they fall. We saw an immense chesnut tree, which had been overthrown° by the hurricane of the morning. The place where the Rhone joins the lake was marked by a line of tremendous breakers; the river is as rapid as when it leaves the lake, but is muddy and dark. We went about a league farther on the road to La Valais,° and stopped at a castle called La Tour de Bouverie,° which seems to be the frontier of Switzerland and Savoy, as we were asked for our passports, on the supposition of our proceeding to Italy.

On one side of the road was the immense Roche de St. Julien, which overhung it; through the gateway of the castle we saw the snowy mountains of La Valais, clothed in clouds, and on the other side was the willowy plain of the Rhone, in a character of striking contrast with the rest of the scene, bounded by the dark mountains that overhang Clarens, Vevai, and the lake that rolls between. In the midst of the plain rises a little isolated hill, on which the white spire of a church peeps from among the tufted chesnut woods.

We returned to St. Gingoux before sun-set, and I passed the evening in reading Julie.

As my companion rises late,° I had time before breakfast, on the ensuing morning, to hunt the waterfalls of the river° that fall into the lake at St. Gingoux. The stream is indeed, from the declivity over which it falls, only a succession of waterfalls, which roar over the rocks with a perpetual sound,° and suspend their unceasing spray on the leaves and flowers that overhang and adorn its savage banks. The path that conducted along this river sometimes avoided the precipices of its shores, by leading through meadows; sometimes threaded the base of the perpendicular and caverned rocks. I gathered in these meadows a nosegay° of such flowers as I never saw in England, and which I thought more beautiful for that rarity.

On my return, after breakfast, we sailed for Clarens, determining first to see the three mouths of the Rhone, and then the castle of Chillon;° the day was fine, and the water calm. We passed from the blue waters of the lake over the stream of the Rhone, which is rapid even at a great distance from its confluence with the lake; the turbid waters mixed with those of the lake, but mixed with them unwillingly. *(See Nouvelle Heloise, Lettre* 17, *Part* 4.°*)* I read Julie all day; an overflowing, as it now seems, surrounded by the scenes which it has so wonderfully peopled, of sublimest genius, and more than human sensibility. Mellerie, the Castle of Chillon, Clarens, the mountains of La Valais and Savoy, present themselves to the imagination as monuments of things that were once familiar, and of beings that were once dear to it. They were created indeed by one mind, but a mind so powerfully bright as to cast a shade of falsehood on the records that are called reality.°

We passed on to the Castle of Chillon, and visited its dungeons and towers. These prisons are excavated below the lake; the principal dungeon is supported by seven columns,° whose branching capitals support the roof. Close to the very walls, the lake is 800 feet deep; iron rings are fastened to these columns, and on them were engraven a multitude of names, partly those of visitors, and partly doubtless of the prisoners, of whom now no memory remains, and who thus beguiled a solitude which they have long ceased to feel. One date was as ancient as 1670. At the commencement of the Reformation, and indeed long after that period, this dungeon was the receptacle of those who shook, or who denied the system of idolatry, from the effects of which mankind is even now slowly emerging.

Close to this long and lofty dungeon was a narrow cell, and beyond it one larger and far more lofty and dark, supported upon two unornamented arches. Across one of these arches was a beam, now black and rotten, on which prisoners were hung in secret. I never saw a monument more terrible of that cold and inhuman tyranny, which it has been the delight of man to exercise over man. It was indeed one of those many tremendous fulfilments which render the "pernicies humani generis" of the great Tacitus,° so solemn and irrefragable° a prophecy. The gendarme,° who conducted us over this castle, told us that there was an opening to the lake, by means of a secret spring, connected with which the whole dungeon might be filled with water before the prisoners could possibly escape!

We proceeded with a contrary wind to Clarens, against a heavy swell. I never felt more strongly than on landing at Clarens, that the spirit of old times had deserted its once cherished habitation. A thousand times, thought I, have Julia and St. Preux walked on this terrassed road, looking towards these mountains which I now behold; nay, treading on the ground where I now tread. From the window of our lodging our landlady pointed out "le bosquet de Julie."° At least the inhabitants of this village are impressed with an idea, that the persons of that romance had actual existence.° In the evening we walked thither. It is indeed Julia's wood. The hay was making under the trees; the trees themselves were aged, but vigorous, and interspersed with younger ones, which are destined to be their successors, and in future years, when we are dead, to afford a shade to future worshippers of nature, who love the memory of that tenderness and peace of which this was the imaginary abode. We walked forward among the vineyards, whose narrow terraces overlook this affecting scene. Why did the cold maxims of the world compel me at this moment to repress the tears of melancholy transport which it would have been so sweet to indulge, immeasurably, even until the darkness of night had swallowed up the objects which excited them?

I forgot to remark, what indeed my companion remarked to me, that our danger from the storm took place precisely in the spot° where Julie and her lover were nearly overset, and where St. Preux was tempted to plunge with her into the lake.

On the following day we went to see the castle of Clarens, a square strong house, with very few windows, surrounded by a double terrace that overlooks the valley, or rather the plain of Clarens. The road which conducted to it wound up the steep ascent through woods of walnut and chesnut. We gathered roses on the terrace, in the feeling that they might be the posterity of some planted by Julia's hand. We sent their dead and withered leaves to the absent.

We went again to "the bosquet de Julie," and found that the precise spot was now utterly obliterated, and a heap of stones marked the place where the little chapel had once stood. Whilst we were execrating the author of this brutal folly,° our guide informed us that the land belonged to the convent of St. Bernard, and that this outrage had been committed by their orders. I knew before, that if avarice could harden the hearts of men, a system of prescriptive religion has an influence far more inimical to natural sensibility. I know that an isolated man is sometimes restrained by shame from outraging the venerable feelings arising out of the memory of genius, which once made nature even lovelier than itself; but associated man holds it as the very sacrament of his union to forswear all delicacy, all benevolence, all remorse, all that is true, or tender, or sublime.

We sailed from Clarens to Vevai. Vevai is a town more beautiful in its simplicity than any I have ever seen. Its market-place, a spacious square interspersed with trees, looks directly upon the mountains of Savoy and La Valais, the lake, and the valley of the Rhone. It was at Vevai° that Rousseau conceived the design of Julie.

From Vevai we came to Ouchy, a village near Lausanne. The coasts of the Pays de Vaud,° though full of villages and vineyards, present an aspect of tranquillity and peculiar beauty which well compensates for the solitude which I am accustomed to admire. The hills are very high and rocky, crowned and interspersed with woods. Water-falls echo from the cliffs, and shine afar. In one place we saw the traces of two rocks of immense size, which had fallen from the mountain behind. One of these lodged in a room where a young woman was sleeping, without injuring her. The vineyards were utterly destroyed in its path, and the earth torn up.

The rain detained us two days at Ouchy. We however visited Lausanne, and saw Gibbon's house.° We were shewn the decayed summer-house where he finished his History, and the old acacias on the terrace, from which he saw Mont Blanc, after having written the last sentence. There is something grand and even touching in the regret which he expresses at the completion of his task. It was conceived amid the ruins of the Capitol.° The sudden departure of his cherished and accustomed toil must have left him, like the death of a dear friend, sad and solitary.

My companion gathered some acacia leaves° to preserve in remembrance of him. I refrained from doing so, fearing to outrage the greater and more sacred name of Rousseau; the contemplation of whose imperishable creations had left no vacancy in my heart for mortal things. Gibbon had a cold and unimpassioned spirit.° I never felt more inclination to rail at the prejudices which cling to such a thing, than now that Julie and Clarens, Lausanne and the Roman Empire, compelled me to a contrast between Rousseau and Gibbon.

When we returned, in the only interval of sunshine during the day, I walked on the pier which the lake was lashing with its waves. A rainbow spanned the lake, or rather rested one extremity of its arch upon the water, and the other at the foot of the mountains of Savoy. Some white houses, I know not if they were those of Mellerie, shone through the yellow fire.°

On Saturday the 30th of June° we quitted Ouchy, and after two days of pleasant sailing arrived on Sunday evening° at Montalegre.

S.

LETTER IV.

TO T. P. ESQ.

ST. MARTIN°—SERVOZ—CHAMOUNI—MONTANVERT—
MONT BLANC.

Hôtel de Londres,° Chamouni,
July 22d, 1816.

WHILST you, my friend, are engaged in securing a home for us,° we are wandering in search of recollections to embellish it. I do not err in conceiving that you are interested in details of all that is majestic or beautiful in nature; but how shall I describe to you the scenes by which I am now surrounded? To exhaust the epithets° which express the astonishment and the admiration—the very excess of satisfied astonishment, where expectation scarcely acknowledged any boundary, is this, to impress upon your mind the images which fill mine now even till it overflow? I too have read the raptures of travellers; I will be warned by their example; I will simply detail to you all that I can relate, or all that, if related, would enable you to conceive of what we have done or seen since the morning of the 20th, when we left Geneva.

We commenced our intended journey to Chamouni at half-past eight in the morning. We passed through the champain country,° which extends from Mont Salêve to the base of the higher Alps. The country is sufficiently fertile, covered with corn fields and orchards, and intersected by sudden acclivities with flat summits. The day was cloudless and excessively hot, the Alps were perpetually in sight, and as we advanced, the mountains, which form their outskirts, closed in around us. We passed a bridge over a stream, which discharges itself into the Arve. The Arve itself, much swollen by the rains, flows constantly to the right of the road.

As we approached Bonneville° through an avenue composed of a beautiful species of drooping poplar, we observed that the corn fields on each side were covered with inundation. Bonneville is a neat little town, with no conspicuous peculiarity, except the white towers of the prison, an extensive building overlooking the town. At Bonneville the Alps commence, one of which, clothed by forests, rises almost immediately from the opposite bank of the Arve.

From Bonneville to Cluses the road conducts through a spacious and fertile plain, surrounded on all sides by mountains, covered like those of Mellerie with forests of intermingled pine and chesnut. At Cluses the road turns suddenly to the right, following the Arve along the chasm, which it seems to have hollowed for itself among the perpendicular mountains. The scene assumes here a more savage and colossal character: the valley becomes narrow, affording no more space than is sufficient for the river and the road. The pines descend to the banks, imitating with their irregular spires, the pyramidal crags which lift themselves far above the regions of forest into the deep azure of the sky, and among the white dazzling clouds. The scene, at the distance of half a mile from Cluses, differs from that of Matlock° in little else than in the immensity of its proportions, and in its untameable, inaccessible solitude, inhabited only by the goats which we saw browsing on the rocks.

Near Maglans,° within a league of each other, we saw two waterfalls.° They were no more than mountain rivulets, but the height from which they fell, at least of *twelve* hundred feet, made them assume a character inconsistent with the smallness of their stream. The first fell from the overhanging brow of a black precipice on an enormous rock, precisely resembling some colossal Egyptian statue of a female deity.° It struck the head of the visionary image, and gracefully dividing there, fell from it in folds of foam more like to cloud than water, imitating a veil of the most exquisite woof.° It then united, concealing the lower part of the statue, and hiding itself in a winding of its channel, burst into a deeper fall, and crossed our route in its path towards the Arve.

The other waterfall was more continuous and larger. The violence with which it fell made it look more like some shape which an exhalation had assumed, than like water, for it streamed beyond the mountain, which appeared dark behind it, as it might have appeared behind an evanescent cloud.

The character of the scenery continued the same until we arrived at St. Martin (called in the maps Sallanches) the mountains perpetually becoming more elevated, exhibiting at every turn of the road more craggy summits, loftier and wider extent of forests, darker and more deep recesses.

The following morning we proceeded from St. Martin on mules to Chamouni, accompanied by two guides. We proceeded, as we had done the preceding day, along the valley of the Arve, a valley surrounded on all sides by immense mountains, whose rugged precipices are intermixed on high with dazzling snow. Their bases were still covered with the eternal forests, which perpetually grew darker and more profound as we approached the inner regions of the mountains.

On arriving at a small village, at the distance of a league from St. Martin, we dismounted from our mules, and were conducted by our guides to view a cascade.° We beheld an immense body of water fall two hundred and fifty feet, dashing from rock to rock, and casting a spray which formed a mist around it, in the midst of which hung a multitude of sunbows, which faded or became unspeakably vivid, as the inconstant sun shone through the clouds. When we approached near to it, the rain of the spray reached us, and our clothes were wetted by the quick-falling but minute particles of water. The cataract fell from above into a deep craggy chasm at our feet, where, changing its character to that of a mountain stream, it pursued its course towards the Arve, roaring over the rocks that impeded its progress.

As we proceeded, our route still lay through the valley, or rather, as it had now become, the vast ravine, which is at once the couch and the creation of the terrible Arve.° We ascended, winding between mountains whose immensity staggers the imagination. We crossed the path of a torrent, which three days since had descended from the thawing snow, and torn the road away.

We dined at Servoz, a little village, where there are lead and copper mines, and where we saw a cabinet of natural curiosities, like those of Keswick and Bethgelert.° We saw in this cabinet some chamois' horns,° and the horns of an exceedingly rare animal called the bouquetin,° which inhabits the desarts of snow to the south of Mont Blanc: it is an animal of the stag kind; its horns weigh at least twenty-seven English pounds. It is inconceivable how so small an animal could support so inordinate a weight. The horns are of a very peculiar conformation, being broad, massy, and pointed at the ends, and surrounded with a number of rings, which are supposed to afford an indication of its age: there were seventeen rings on the largest of these horns.

From Servoz three leagues remain to Chamouni.—Mont Blanc was before us—the Alps, with their innumerable glaciers on high all around, closing in the complicated windings of the single vale—forests inexpressibly beautiful, but majestic in their beauty—intermingled beech and pine, and oak, overshadowed our road, or receded, whilst lawns of such verdure as I have never seen before occupied these openings, and gradually became darker in their recesses. Mont Blanc was before us, but it was covered with cloud; its base, furrowed with dreadful gaps, was seen above. Pinnacles of snow intolerably bright, part of the chain connected with Mont Blanc, shone through the clouds at intervals on high.° I never knew—I never imagined what mountains were before. The immensity of these aerial summits excited, when they suddenly burst upon the sight, a sentiment of extatic wonder, not unallied to madness.° And remember this was all one scene, it all pressed home to our regard and our imagination. Though it embraced a vast extent of space, the snowy pyramids which shot into the bright blue sky seemed to overhang our path; the ravine, clothed with gigantic pines, and black with its depth below, so deep that the very roaring of the untameable Arve, which rolled through it, could not be heard above—all was as much our own, as if we had been the creators of such impressions in the minds of others as now occupied our own.° Nature was the poet,° whose harmony held our spirits more breathless than that of the divinest.

As we entered the valley of Chamouni (which in fact may be considered as a continuation of those which we have followed from Bonneville and Cluses) clouds hung upon the mountains at the distance perhaps of 6000 feet from the earth, but so as effectually to conceal not only Mont Blanc, but the other *aiguilles*,° as they call them here, attached and subordinate to it. We were travelling along the valley, when suddenly we heard a sound as of the burst of smothered thunder rolling above; yet there was something earthly in the sound, that told us it could not be thunder. Our guide hastily pointed out to us a part of the mountain opposite, from whence the sound came. It was an avalanche. We saw the smoke of its path among the rocks, and continued to hear at intervals the bursting of its fall. It fell on the bed of a torrent, which it displaced, and presently we saw its tawny-coloured waters also spread themselves over the ravine, which was their couch.

We did not, as we intended, visit the *Glacier de Boisson*° to-day, although it descends within a few minutes' walk of the road, wishing to survey it at least when unfatigued. We saw this glacier which comes close to the fertile plain, as we passed, its surface was broken into a thousand unaccountable figures: conical and pyramidical crystalizations,°

more than fifty feet in height, rise from its surface, and precipices of ice, of dazzling splendour, overhang the woods and meadows of the vale. This glacier winds upwards from the valley, until it joins the masses of frost from which it was produced above, winding through its own ravine like a bright belt flung over the black region of pines. There is more in all these scenes than mere magnitude of proportion: there is a majesty of outline; there is an awful grace in the very colours which invest these wonderful shapes—a charm which is peculiar to them, quite distinct even from the reality of their unutterable greatness.

July 24.

Yesterday morning we went to the source of the Arveiron.° It is about a league from this village; the river rolls forth impetuously from an arch of ice, and spreads itself in many streams over a vast space of the valley, ravaged and laid bare by its inundations. The glacier by which its waters are nourished, overhangs this cavern and the plain, and the forests of pine which surround it, with terrible precipices of solid ice. On the other side rises the immense glacier of Montanvert,° fifty miles in extent, occupying a chasm among mountains of inconceivable height, and of forms so pointed and abrupt, that they seem to pierce the sky. From this glacier we saw as we sat on a rock, close to one of the streams of the Arveiron, masses of ice detach themselves from on high, and rush with a loud dull noise into the vale. The violence of their fall turned them into powder, which flowed over the rocks in imitation of waterfalls, whose ravines they usurped and filled.

In the evening I went with Ducrée,° my guide, the only tolerable person I have seen in this country, to visit the glacier of Boisson. This glacier, like that of Montanvert, comes close to the vale, overhanging the green meadows and the dark woods with the dazzling whiteness of its precipices and pinnacles, which are like spires of radiant crystal, covered with a net-work of frosted silver. These glaciers flow perpetually into the valley, ravaging in their slow but irresistible progress the pastures and the forests which surround them, performing a work of desolation in ages, which a river of lava might accomplish in an hour, but far more irretrievably;° for where the ice has once descended, the hardiest plant refuses to grow; if even, as in some extraordinary instances, it should recede after its progress has once commenced. The glaciers perpetually move onward, at the rate of a foot each day, with a motion that commences at the spot where, on the boundaries of perpetual congelation, they are produced by the freezing of the waters which arise from the partial melting of the eternal snows. They drag with them from the regions whence they derive their origin, all the ruins of the mountain, enormous rocks, and immense accumulations of sand and stones. These are driven onwards by the irresistible stream of solid ice; and when they arrive at a declivity of the mountain, sufficiently rapid, roll down, scattering ruin. I saw one of these rocks which had descended in the spring, (winter here is the season of silence and safety) which measured forty feet in every direction.

The verge of a glacier, like that of Boisson, presents the most vivid image of desolation that it is possible to conceive. No one dares to approach it; for the enormous pinnacles of ice which perpetually fall, are perpetually reproduced. The pines of the forest, which bound it at one extremity, are overthrown and shattered to a wide extent at its base. There is something inexpressibly dreadful in the aspect of the few branchless trunks, which, nearest to the ice rifts, still stand in the uprooted soil. The meadows perish, overwhelmed with sand and stones. Within this last year, these glaciers have advanced three hundred feet into the valley. Saussure, the naturalist, says, that they have their periods of increase and decay: the people of the country hold an opinion entirely different; but as I judge, more probable.° It is agreed by all, that the snow on the summit of Mont Blanc and the neighbouring mountains perpetually augments, and that ice, in the form of glaciers, subsists without melting in the valley of Chamouni during its transient and variable summer. If the snow which produces this glacier must augment, and the heat of the valley is no obstacle to the perpetual existence of such masses of ice as have already descended into it, the consequence is obvious; the glaciers must augment and will subsist, at least until they have overflowed this vale.

I will not pursue Buffon's sublime but gloomy theory°—that this globe which we inhabit will at some future period be changed into a mass of frost by the encroachments of the polar ice, and of that produced on the most elevated points of the earth. Do you, who assert the supremacy of Ahriman,° imagine him throned among these desolating snows, among these palaces of death and frost, so sculptured in this their terrible magnificence by the adamantine hand of necessity,° and that he casts around him, as the first essays of his final usurpation, avalanches, torrents, rocks, and thunders, and above all these deadly glaciers, at once the proof and symbols of his reign;—add to this, the degradation of the human species—who in these regions are half deformed or idiotic, and most of whom are deprived of any thing that can excite interest or admiration. This is a part of the subject more mournful and less sublime; but such as neither the poet nor the philosopher should disdain to regard.

This morning we departed, on the promise of a fine day, to visit the glacier of Montanvert.° In that part where it fills a slanting valley, it is called the Sea of Ice. This valley, is 950 toises, or 7600 feet° above the level of the sea. We had not proceeded far before the rain began to fall, but we persisted until we had accomplished more than half of our journey, when we returned, wet through.

Chamouni, July 25th.

We have returned from visiting the glacier of Montanvert, or as it is called, the Sea of Ice, a scene in truth of dizzying wonder.° The path that winds to it along the side of a mountain, now clothed with pines, now intersected with snowy hollows, is wide and steep. The cabin of Montanvert° is three leagues from Chamouni, half of which distance is performed on mules, not so sure footed, but that on the first day the one which I rode fell in what the guides call a *mauvais pas*,° so that I narrowly escaped being precipitated down the mountain. We passed over a hollow covered with snow, down which vast stones are accustomed to roll. One had fallen the preceding day, a little time after we had returned: our guides desired us to pass quickly, for it is said that sometimes the least sound will accelerate their descent. We arrived at Montanvert, however, safe.

On all sides precipitous mountains, the abodes of unrelenting frost, surround this vale: their sides are banked up with ice and snow, broken, heaped high, and exhibiting terrific chasms. The summits are sharp and naked pinnacles, whose overhanging steepness will not even permit snow to rest upon them. Lines of dazzling ice occupy here and there their perpendicular rifts, and shine through the driving vapours with inexpressible brilliance: they pierce the clouds like things not belonging to this earth. The vale itself is filled with a mass of undulating ice, and has an ascent sufficiently gradual even to the remotest abysses of these horrible desarts. It is only half a league (about two miles) in breadth, and seems much less. It exhibits an appearance as if frost had suddenly bound up the waves and whirlpools of a mighty torrent.° We walked some distance upon its surface. The waves are elevated about 12 or 15 feet from the surface of the mass, which is intersected by long gaps of unfathomable depth, the ice of whose sides is more beautifully azure than the sky. In these regions every thing changes, and is in motion.° This vast mass of ice has one general progress, which ceases neither day nor night; it breaks and bursts for ever:° some undulations sink while others rise; it is never the same. The echo of rocks, or of the ice and snow which fall from their overhanging precipices, or roll from their aerial summits, scarcely ceases for one moment. One would think that Mont Blanc, like the god of the Stoics,° was a vast animal, and that the frozen blood for ever circulated through his stony veins.

We dined (M***, C***,° and I) on the grass, in the open air, surrounded by this scene. The air is piercing and clear. We returned down the mountain, sometimes encompassed by the driving vapours, sometimes cheered by the sunbeams, and arrived at our inn by seven o'clock.

Montalegre, July 28th.

The next morning we returned through the rain to St. Martin. The scenery had lost something of its immensity, thick clouds hanging over the highest mountains; but visitings of sunset intervened between the showers, and the blue sky shone between the accumulated clouds of snowy whiteness which brought them; the dazzling mountains sometimes glittered through a chasm of the clouds above our heads, and all the charm of its grandeur remained. We repassed *Pont Pellisier*,° a wooden bridge over the Arve, and the ravine of the Arve. We repassed the pine forests which overhang the defile, the chateau of St. Michel,° a haunted ruin, built on the edge of a precipice, and shadowed over by the eternal forest. We repassed the vale of Servoz, a vale more beautiful, because more luxuriant, than that of Chamouni. Mont Blanc forms one of the sides of this vale also, and the other is inclosed by an irregular amphitheatre of enormous mountains, one of which is in ruins, and fell fifty years ago into the higher part of the valley:° the smoke of its fall was seen in Piedmont, and people went from Turin to investigate whether a volcano had not burst forth among the Alps. It continued falling many days, spreading, with the shock and thunder of its ruin, consternation into the neighbouring vales. In the evening we arrived at St. Martin. The next day we wound through the valley, which I have described before, and arrived in the evening at our home.

We have bought some specimens of minerals and plants, and two or three crystal seals, at Mont Blanc, to preserve the remembrance of having approached it. There is a cabinet of *Histoire Naturelle* at Chamouni,° just as at Keswick, Matlock, and Clifton;° the proprietor of which is the very vilest specimen of that vile species of quack that, together with the whole army of aubergistes° and guides, and indeed the entire mass of the population, subsist on the weakness and credulity of travellers as leaches subsist on the sick.° The most interesting of my purchases is a large collection of all the seeds of rare alpine plants, with their names written upon the outside of the papers that contain them. These I mean to colonize in my garden in England, and to permit you to make what choice you please from them. They are companions which the Celandine—the classic Celandine, need not despise; they are as wild and more daring than he, and will tell him tales of things even as touching and sublime as the gaze of a vernal poet.°

Did I tell you that there are troops of wolves° among these mountains? In the winter they descend into the vallies, which the snow occupies six months of the year, and devour every thing that they can find out of doors. A wolf is more powerful than the fiercest and strongest dog. There are no bears in these regions. We heard, when we were at Lucerne, that they were occasionally found in the forests which surround that lake. Adieu.

S.

LINES

WRITTEN IN THE VALE OF CHAMOUNI.

MONT BLANC.

LINES WRITTEN IN THE VALE OF CHAMOUNI.

I.

THE everlasting universe of things
Flows through the mind, and rolls its rapid waves,°
Now dark—now glittering—now reflecting gloom—
Now lending splendour, where from secret springs
The source of human thought its tribute brings
Of waters,—with a sound but half its own,
Such as a feeble brook will oft assume
In the wild woods, among the mountains lone,
Where waterfalls around it leap for ever,
Where woods and winds contend, and a vast river
Over its rocks ceaselessly bursts and raves.°

II.

Thus thou, Ravine of Arve—dark, deep Ravine—°
Thou many-coloured, many-voiced vale,
Over whose pines, and crags, and caverns sail
Fast cloud shadows and sunbeams: awful scene,
Where Power in likeness of the Arve comes down°
From the ice gulphs that gird his secret throne,
Bursting through these dark mountains like the flame
Of lightning thro' the tempest;—thou dost lie,
Thy giant brood of pines around thee clinging,
Children of elder time, in whose devotion
The chainless winds still come and ever came
To drink their odours, and their mighty swinging
To hear—an old and solemn harmony;
Thine earthly rainbows stretched across the sweep

Of the ethereal waterfall, whose veil
Robes some unsculptured image; the strange sleep°
Which when the voices of the desart fail
Wraps all in its own deep eternity;—
Thy caverns echoing to the Arve's commotion,
A loud, lone sound no other sound can tame;
Thou art pervaded with that ceaseless motion,
Thou art the path of that unresting sound—
Dizzy Ravine! and when I gaze on thee°
I seem as in a trance sublime and strange
To muse on my own separate phantasy,
My own, my human mind, which passively
Now renders and receives fast influencings,
Holding an unremitting interchange
With the clear universe of things around;°
One legion of wild thoughts, whose wandering wings°
Now float above thy darkness, and now rest
Where that or thou art no unbidden guest,
In the still cave of the witch Poesy,°
Seeking among the shadows that pass by,°
Ghosts of all things that are, some shade of thee,
Some phantom, some faint image; till the breast
From which they fled recalls them, thou art there!

III.

Some say that gleams of a remoter world
Visit the soul in sleep,—that death is slumber,
And that its shapes the busy thoughts outnumber
Of those who wake and live.—I look on high;
Has some unknown omnipotence unfurled
The veil of life and death? or do I lie
In dream, and does the mightier world of sleep
Spread far around and inaccessibly
Its circles? For the very spirit fails,
Driven like a homeless cloud from steep to steep
That vanishes among the viewless gales!°
Far, far above, piercing the infinite sky,

Mont Blanc appears,—still, snowy, and serene—
Its subject mountains their unearthly forms°
Pile around it, ice and rock; broad vales between
Of frozen floods, unfathomable deeps,
Blue as the overhanging heaven, that spread
And wind among the accumulated steeps;
A desart peopled by the storms alone,
Save when the eagle brings some hunter's bone,
And the wolf tracts her there—how hideously°
Its shapes are heaped around! rude, bare, and high,
Ghastly, and scarred, and riven.—Is this the scene
Where the old Earthquake-dæmon taught her young
Ruin? Were these their toys? or did a sea
Of fire, envelope once this silent snow?
None can reply—all seems eternal now.°
The wilderness has a mysterious tongue
Which teaches awful doubt, or faith so mild,
So solemn, so serene, that man may be
But for such faith with nature reconciled;°
Thou hast a voice, great Mountain, to repeal
Large codes of fraud and woe; not understood°
By all, but which the wise, and great, and good°
Interpret, or make felt, or deeply feel.

IV.

The fields, the lakes, the forests, and the streams,
Ocean, and all the living things that dwell
Within the dædal earth; lightning, and rain,°
Earthquake, and fiery flood, and hurricane,
The torpor of the year when feeble dreams°
Visit the hidden buds, or dreamless sleep
Holds every future leaf and flower;—the bound
With which from that detested trance they leap;
The works and ways of man, their death and birth,
And that of him and all that his may be;
All things that move and breathe with toil and sound
Are born and die; revolve, subside and swell.

Power dwells apart in its tranquillity
Remote, serene, and inaccessible:°
And *this*, the naked countenance of earth,°
On which I gaze, even these primeval mountains
Teach the adverting mind. The glaciers creep°
Like snakes that watch their prey, from their far fountains,°
Slow rolling on; there, many a precipice,
Frost and the Sun in scorn of mortal power
Have piled: dome, pyramid, and pinnacle,°
A city of death, distinct with many a tower°
And wall impregnable of beaming ice.
Yet not a city, but a flood of ruin
Is there, that from the boundaries of the sky
Rolls its perpetual stream; vast pines are strewing
Its destined path, or in the mangled soil
Branchless and shattered stand; the rocks, drawn down
From yon remotest waste, have overthrown
The limits of the dead and living world,
Never to be reclaimed. The dwelling-place
Of insects, beasts, and birds, becomes its spoil;
Their food and their retreat for ever gone,
So much of life and joy is lost. The race
Of man, flies far in dread; his work and dwelling
Vanish, like smoke before the tempest's stream,
And their place is not known. Below, vast caves°
Shine in the rushing torrents' restless gleam,
Which from those secret chasms in tumult welling
Meet in the vale, and one majestic River,°
The breath and blood of distant lands, for ever
Rolls its loud waters to the ocean waves,
Breathes its swift vapours to the circling air.

V.

Mont Blanc yet gleams on high:—the power is there,
The still and solemn power of many sights,
And many sounds, and much of life and death.°
In the calm darkness of the moonless nights,

In the lone glare of day, the snows descend
Upon that Mountain; none beholds them there,
Nor when the flakes burn in the sinking sun,
Or the star-beams dart through them:—Winds contend
Silently there, and heap the snow with breath
Rapid and strong, but silently! Its home
The voiceless lightning in these solitudes°
Keeps innocently, and like vapour broods
Over the snow. The secret strength of things
Which governs thought, and to the infinite dome
Of heaven is as a law, inhabits thee!
And what were thou, and earth, and stars, and sea,
If to the human mind's imaginings
Silence and solitude were vacancy?°

June 23, 1816.
Reynell, Printer, 45, Broad-street,
Golden-square.

APPENDIX A

EXTRACT FROM MARY AND PERCY'S JOURNAL FOR 29–31 AUGUST 1814

This extract from Mary and Percy's shared journal entry for 29–31 August 1814 is part of their account of sailing down the Rhine. It is characteristic of the shared journal in that it features writing by both Mary and Percy and shows instances of personal material (Mary's birthday, and earlier, her frustration—'Mary groans') which was excised when Mary was compiling the text for publication in *HSWT*. The extract also shows how Mary expanded Percy's descriptive passages from the original journal when she was preparing *HSWT*. This extract can also be compared with Claire's journal entries for the same days, given here as Appendix B. Italics indicate Percy's hand. Punctuation, line breaks, and the spelling of place names follow the original holograph. Percy's reference to an overnight stay in 'Shaufhauc' constitutes a puzzle. Probably he meant Schœnau, south-west of Strasbourg. Claire refers to the same place as 'Shoff Hock' (see *CC Journals*, p. 34). Text from Bodleian Library MS Abinger d. 27. ff.15r–16r. Transcription created and reproduced with permission of Bodleian Libraries, University of Oxford, with thanks to Stephen Hebron; the transcription has been informed by the version published in *MWS Journals*, pp. 21–2.

> ~~Wed~~ Monday 29. —
> *We set out from Dettingen at 6. alone.*
> *We stop at Loffenburgh & engage a*
> *boat for Mumph. The boat is small*
> *& frail; it requires much attention to*
> *prevent an overset. At Mumph we*
> *cannot procure a boat for Rheinfelt.*
> *We proceed in a return voiture. it*
> *breaks down a mile from the town.* ~~a~~
> some kind Swiss convey our little luggage
> for us and we walk to Rheimfelden. Unable
> to procure a boat we walk a ¼ of a ~~mile~~ league
> further where after being threatened with
> the evil of sleeping at this nasty village
> we get a boat and arrive at Basel at 6
> cold & comfortless. Shelley makes a bargain
> that night very kindlily helped by a stupid

bookseller. We get the stove heated and
procure supper – Beds very uncomfor
table – Mary groans –

Tuesday 30 Germany
It is Marys birth day, we do not solemnize
this day in comfort. We expect to be
not happier but more at our ease
before the year passes.
We leave Basle in the boat that we
had engaged. The wind is violently
against us. we stop at Shaufhauc
& sleep there. The Rhine is violently
rapid to-day ~~Wednesday 31~~ *& although*
interrupted by no rocks is swoln
with high waves. It is full of little
islands green and beautiful. Before
we arrived at Shaufhauc the river
became suddenly narrow, & the boat
dashed with inconceivable rapidity round
the base of a rocky hill covered with
pines. A ruined tower, with its deso
lated windows stood on the summit of
another hill that jutted into the river.
beyond the sunset was ~~the~~ *illumining*
the mountains & the clouds, &
casting the reflection of its hues on the
agitated river. The brilliance & contrasts
of the shades & colourings on the circling
whirl pools of the stream was an appearance
entirely new & most beautiful

Wednesday 31
Pursue our voyage in the slight canoe that
accompanied our boat. Shelley reads aloud
the letters from Norway. Arrive at Stras
burgh, buy provision & proceed. Evening
comes on. Shelley finishes Mary a fiction
We sleep at a little village beyond Strasburg

APPENDIX B

EXTRACT FROM CLAIRE CLAIRMONT'S JOURNAL FOR AUGUST 1814

A sample entry (30 August) from Claire's original journal of the 1814 tour. Claire records what the group was reading, comments on the dramatic landscape and wildlife (a 'sea-mew' is a seagull) and notes personal details such as Mary's seventeenth birthday. On f. 1 of the journal—the inside front cover—there are some pencil sketches by Percy, and the final pages of this notebook also contain notes by Percy (ff. 103b–106b); like Mary's journal, this was a shared writing space. Punctuation and line breaks are shown as in the original holograph, with square brackets indicating damage to the manuscript, and so where full words must be inferred. Text from BL Ashley MS 394, ff. 23v–26r. Transcription created and reproduced with permission of the British Library, with thanks to Fabiana Duglio; the transcription has been informed by the version published in *CC Journals*, 33–4.

> August
> Tuesday Aug 30th. Rise at five – Break-
> fast – Go down to the Quay – Do not
> [g]et on board till ½ past seven – The
> [m]orning cold & cloudy – now & then
> [ra]in – The Rhine begins to get broad
> a few leagues from Basle – Its banks
> are very beautiful – Verdantly slopin
> =g down to meet ~~the~~ its waves & covered
> with young willows – Islands ~~no~~
> rise on the surface of the water
>
> August
> they are numerous & covered with
> groves – We saw a sea-mew & wonder[ed]
> much how came in a place so m[any]
> miles from the sea – We stopt for abou[t]
> an hour on a small green hill to d[ine]
> as we had taken provisions – I gathered
> some of the most beautiful grass I
> ever beheld – The Wind had been against

us the whole day & was violent – The
Clouds fleeted fast away & the Sun
broke forth in the Afternoon –

August
on both sides of the Rhine there was in
the distance two high ridges of black
Hills – ~~the b~~ About four o'clock we
[la]nded at Brisaac a town in Baden –
[the] Watermen said they could not proceed
[w]ith so strong a wind against us – We
were afraid we should be obliged to delay
our journey & sleep here but in about
an hour they came with the news that
the wind was changed & we hastened on
Board – Shelley reads aloud the Letters
from Norway – This is one of my

August
very favourite Books – The language is so ~~ve~~
very flowing & Eloquent & it is altogether a
beautiful Poem – We witnessed one of the
finest Sun sets – The West was a long
continued strip of yellow dying away with
a lovely pink which again mellowed it
=self imperceptibly into an amazing horiz[on]
of the deepest purple – The Rhine was
extremely rapid – The Waves borrowed the
divine colours of the sky – Never were tints
so numerous or so perpetually varied – The
undulating motion of the waves rolling
ever one over the other produced the same

August
effect as if snakes were creeping perpetu
ally onwards – I now thought of Coleridge's
[A]ncient Mariner – "Beyond the shadow of
[the] ship – I watched the water snakes" – I am
[c]onvinced that the descriptions contained in
more
[th]at Poem are copied from Nature than
^

one is at first aware of – The Rhine appe
-ared narrow here for it ~~was~~ is covered with

islands which produce the same effect as
if you were passing through a narrow defile.
The Shore on the Right were black hills –
now rocky – then woody & sometimes gently

    August

declined into glassy slopes – We passed a ruined
castle situated on the top of a black Hill.
The ruins suited with the scene – Every
thing seemed declining – the Sun had hi[d]
his beams – the trees were gaining a dar[k]
hue & the mountains were receeding.
We slept at Schoff Hock – M's birthday – 167.

APPENDIX C

LETTER FROM CLAIRE CLAIRMONT
TO LORD BYRON OF SPRING 1816

A letter from Claire to Lord Byron, written in London in March or April 1816. Claire alludes to the relationship between 'creator' and 'creation', anticipating ideas discussed in Mary's *Frankenstein* (1818). Claire's subsequent love affair with Byron would be the primary reason Geneva was selected as a destination in 1816, and as such her interaction with the poet prompted the group gathering at Villa Diodati with the Shelleys and Polidori. Punctuation and line breaks are shown as in the original holograph. Text: National Library of Scotland, Murray Coll. MS 43419 f. 1r–1v. Transcription created and reproduced with permission of the John Murray Archive, National Library of Scotland, with thanks to Peter Findlay and Kirsty McHugh; the transcription has been informed by the version published by Marion Kingston Stocking (ed.) in *The Clairmont Correspondence*, vol. 1 (Baltimore: The Johns Hopkins University Press, 1995), 24–5.

An utter stranger takes the liberty of addressing you. It is earnestly
requested that for one moment you pardon the intrusion, & laying
aside every remembrance of who & what you are, listen with a friendly
ear. A moment of passion, or an impulse of pride often destroys our
own happiness & that of others. If in this case your refusal shall not
affect yourself, yet you are not aware how much it will injure
another. It is not charity I demand, for of that I stand in no need:
I imply by that you should think kindly & gently of this letter, that
if I seem impertinent you should pardon it for a while, & that you
should wait patiently till I am emboldened by you to disclose myself.

I tremble with fear at the fate of this letter. I cannot blame
if it shall be received by you as an imprudent imposture. There
are cases where virtue may stoop to assume the garb of folly; it
is for the piercing eye of genius to discover her disguise, do you
then give me credit for something better than this letter may
seem to portend. Mine is a delicate case; my feet are on the
edge of a precipice; Hope flying on forward wings beckons me
to follow her & rather than resign this cherished creature, I jump
through at the peril of my Life.

It may seem a strange assertion, but it is not the less
true that I place my happiness in your hands. I wish to give

you a suspicion without at first disclosing myself; because
it would be a cruel addition to all I otherwise endure to become
the object of your contempt & the ridicule of others.

If you feel your indignation rising, if you feel tempted
to read no more, or to cast with levity into the fire, what has
been written by me with so much fearful inquietude, check
your hand: my folly may be great, but the Creator ought not
to destroy his Creature. If you shall condescend to answer
the following question you will at least be rewarded by
the gratitude I shall feel.

If a woman, whose reputation has yet remained
unstained, if without either guardian or husband to control
she should throw herself upon your mercy, if with a beating
heart she should confess the love she has borne you many
years, if she should secure to you secrecy & safety, if she should
return your kindness with fond affection & unbounded devotion
could you betray her, or would you be silent as the grave?

I am not given to many words. Either you will or you
will not. Do not decide hastily, & yet I must entreat your
answer without delay, not only because I hate to be tortured
~~to~~ by suspense, but because my departure a short way out
of town is unavoidable & I would know your reply ere I go. Address
me, as E. Trefusis, 21. Foley Place, Mary le Bonne.

APPENDIX D

LETTER FROM PERCY SHELLEY TO THOMAS LOVE PEACOCK OF 17 JULY 1816

PBS's original letter of 17 July 1816 to Thomas Love Peacock, which describes the sailing expedition around Lake Geneva with Lord Byron. The letter was found in 1975 (for a detailed discussion of provenance, see *SC*, vol. 7, pp. 37–9) and is now held in the Carl H. Pforzheimer Collection of the New York Public Library. It contains a number of details not present in the version published as Letter III of *HSWT*. Comparison of the two texts therefore sheds considerable light on the way in which original journals and correspondence were revised in preparing *HSWT* for the press: both through the omission of private material and through the revision and expansion (and, in some cases, condensing) of loco-descriptive and reflective passages. Text from Pforz MS PBS0275, reproduced by kind permission of The Carl H. Pforzheimer Collection of Shelley and His Circle, New York Public Library, Astor, Lenox, and Tilden Foundations. The transcription has been informed by the version published in *SC*, vol. 7, pp. 25–35. We have retained PBS's original spelling and punctuation including dashes of various lengths and varying numbers of points to signal pauses; we have used carets (^^) to indicate words written in above the line; <?> indicates material difficult or impossible to read.

Montalegre Pres de
Geneva, July 17. 1816.

My dear Peacock

My opinion of the necessity of turning to one spot of earth & calling it my home & of the excellence & usefulness of the sentiments arising out of this attachment has at length produced in me the resolution of acquiring this possession. You are the only man I know who have sufficient regard for me to take an interest in the fulfilment of this design, & whose tastes conform sufficiently to mine to engage me to confide the execution of it to your discretion.—I do not trouble you with apologies for making no bones in giving you this commission.—I require only <u>rural</u> excursions.. walks & circuitous wanderings. some slight negotiations about the letting of a home. The superintandance of a disorderly garden—some <u>palings</u> to be mended some books to be removed & set up. –

I wish you would get all my books & all my furniture from Bishopgate, & all other effects apportioning to me.—I have written to No 26 Marchmont

Street to send all that belongs to me there, to you. I have written also to Longdill to give up possession of the house on the 3^d of August.—When you have possessed yourself of all my affairs, I wish you to look out for a home for me & Mary & William & the kitten (who is now in pension in Marchmont Street).

– I wish you to get an unfurnished house with as good a garden as may be, near the forest, & to take a lease on it for 14 or 21 years.. The house must not be too small. I wish the situation to resemble as nearly as possible that of Bishopgate; & should think that Sunning Hill or Winkfield Plain or the neighbourhood of Virginia Water would allow some possibilities.—Homes are now exceedingly cheap & plentiful.—But I intrust the whole of this affair entirely to your own discretion.

I shall hear from you of course as to what you have done on this subject, & shall not delay to remit you whatever expenses you may find it necessary to incur. Perhaps however you had better sell the useless part of the Bishopgate furniture. I mean that odious curtain &^{c}– Will you write to Longdill, & tell him that you are authorised on my part to go over the inventory with Lady Lumley's people on the 3^d of August if they please; & to make whatever arrangement may be requisite.

I should be content with the Bishopgate house, dear as it is, if Lady Lumley would make the sale of it a post obit transaction.—I merely suggest this, that, if you see any possibility of proposing such an arrangement with effect, you might do it. –

My present intention is to return to England & to make that most excellent of nations my perpetual resting place. I think it exceedingly probable that we shall return next spring.. perhaps before, perhaps after.. but certainly we shall return. On the motives & on the consequences of this journey I reserve much explanation for some future winter walk or summer expedition. Thus much alone is certain that before we return we shall have in a short space of time seen & heard & felt a multiplicity of things which will haunt our talk, & make us a little better worth knowing than we were before our departure. If possible, we think of descending the Danube in a boat of visiting Constantinople & Athens, then Rome & the Tuscan cities & returning by the South of France; always following great rivers; The Danube, the Po, the Rhone, the Garonne. Rivers are not like roads the work of the hands of men. They imitate mind which wanders at will over the pathless deserts, & flows thro natures loneliest recesses which are inaccessible to any thing besides. They have the viler advantage also of affording a cheaper mode of conveyance. This eastern scheme is one which has but just now seised on our imaginations; I fear that the detail of execution will destroy it like all other wild & beautiful visions. But at all events you will hear from us wherever we are or to whatever adventures destiny forces us.—Tell me in return all English news.—What has become of my poem? I hope it has already sheltered itself in the bosom of its mother Oblivion, from whose embraces no one could have so barbarous as to [???] to tear it except me.—Tell me of the political state of England. Its literature. of which when I speak, Coleridge is in my thoughts.—Yourself, lastly, your own employments, your historical labours, the success of your Headlong Hall of which I hear every day merited & indeed extravagant praise.

I had written thus far when your letter to Mary dated the 8th arrived. What you say of Bishopgate of course modifies that part of this letter which relates to it. I confess I did not learn the destined ruin without some pain. But it is well for me perhaps that a situation requiring so large an expenditure should be placed beyond my hopes. You must shelter my roofless Penates, dedicate some new temple to them, & perform the functions of a priest in my absence. They are innocent deities, & their worship is neither sanguinary nor absurd. Leave Mammon & Jehovah to those who delight in wickedness & slavery, their altars are stained with blood or polluted with gold the price of blood. But the shrines of the penates are good wood fires, or window frames intertwined with creeping plants; [*sic*] thier hymns are the purring of kittens, the hissing of kettles, long talks over the past & the dead, the laugh of children, the warm wind of summer filling the quiet house, & the pelting storm of winter struggling in vain for entrance. In talking of the Penates now, will you not liken me to Julius Caesar dedicating a temple to liberty?

As I have said in the former part of my letter I trust entirely to your discretion on the subject of the house. Certainly the forest engages my preference, because of the sylvan nature of the place & the beasts with which it is filled. But I am not insensible to the beauties of the Thames, & any extraordinary eligibility in the situation you mention in your letter would overbalance our habitual affection for the neighbourhood of Bishopgate.—Its proximity to the spot which you have chosen is an argument with us in favour of the Thames.—Recollect however that we are now choosing a fixed, settled, eternal home, & as such its internal qualities will affect us more constantly than those which consist in the surrounding scenery, which whatever the it may be at first, will shortly be worth no more than the colours ^with^ which our own habits shall invest it. I am glad that circumstances do not permit the choice to be my own. I shall abide by yours as by others abide by the necessity of thier birth. I confide the whole concern to your discretion.

Mary has told you that we see a good deal of Lord Byron, & that I projected a jo voyage to Vevai with him. Lord Byron is an exceedingly interesting person, & as such, is it not to be regretted that he is a slave to the vilest & most vulgar prejudices, & as mad as the winds? I do not mean to say that he is a Christian, or that his ordinary conduct is devoid of prudence. But in the course of an intimacy of two months, & an observation the most minute I see reason to regret the union of great genius, & things which make genius useless. For a short time I shall see no more of Lord Byron, a circumstance I cannot avoid regretting as he has shewn me great kindness, & as I had some hope that an intercourse with me would operate to weaken those superstitions of rank & wealth & revenge & servility to opinion with which he, in common with other men, is so poisonously imbued. It is nearly a fortnight since I have returned from Vevai. This journey was on every account delightful, but most especially because then I first knew the divine beauty of Rousseau's imagination as it exhibits itself in Julie. It is inconcievable what a charm the scene itself lends to those delineations from which its own most touching charm arises. But I will give you an abstract of our voyage which lasted eight days, if you have a map of La Suisse you can follow me.

1st day. We left Montalagre with Lord B. his servant, & two bateliers. At Hermance we saw a ruined tower, one of four which the Genevese had demolished for their fortifications in 1560. The marks of the chisels of Caesar's liberticide legions yet remain on the wall. I wondered at the massy structure, cursed its builder, & departed. This night we slept at Nerni, and sat on the wall in the twilight watching the children at play; most of the children (this is Savoy, the King of Sardinia's dominion) were exceedingly deformed and ugly very unlike those of Switzerland. One child however was far more beautiful than I had ever seen. He was a boy of ten years old a model of grace both for mein & motions, & with a countenance overflowing with such expression as made it more beautiful than any mere combination of lineaments however exquisite.—Lord Byron, a new convert to Wordsworth, reminded me of the Highland girl.

2nd day. We passed the promontory of Ivoire, which bounds the western side of the bay of Thonon, this bay is sheltered by an amphiatre of mountains (for the plain ends here) luxuriantly covered with interminable forests of chesnut & walnut & pine ... the ~~pines~~ ^forest of pines^ becomes~~s~~ darker & more immense until the ice & snow mingle with the points of naked rock that pierce the blue air. We pass the mouth of the river drance which descends from between a chasm in the mountains & makes a plain near the lake intersected by its divided streams. Thousands of besolets, beautiful water birds take their station where its waters mingle with the lake. Besolets are birds like seagulls but smaller & with purple on thier backs. As we approached Evian the mountains came nearer to the lake & masses of wood & mountain overhung its shining spire. The day was changeable & wild. Gusts of wind—sudden showers—then a warm south wind with summer clouds hanging thier white volumes below the mountain tops with intervals of sky dazzlingly blue. When we arrived at Evian flashes of lightning & thunderpeals suddenly came on, & continued after a black cloud which brought them had dispersed. "Diespiter per pura tonantes egit equos." a phenomenon I never witnessed before.

3^d day. I must tell you now that our boat is English, very like, but somewhat larger ~~that of~~ that with which we ascended the Thames. It is rigged with four sails & is exceedingly manageable & convenient.—When we left Evian the wind was violent & we sailed right with it towards the end of the lake. The boat was heavily laden, the sea very high, & there appeared to be some danger of swamping. We arrived however safely at Mellerie after passing with inconcievable speed woody rocks immediately overhanging the lake & piney mountains with bare & icy summits which rose almost at once from the rocks whose base was echoing to the surge– Mellerie is the well known scene of St Preux's visionary exile. I had not yet read enough of Julie to enjoy the scene as I do by retrospect. but Mellerie is indeed enchanted ground, were Rousseau no magician. Groves of chestnuts overshadow it, magnificent & extensive forests to which England affords no parallell. The grandeur & beauty of this scene augments with the turn of every promontory. Loftier points of elevation descend still closer to the lake, & on high the aerial mountains cherish vast depths of snow in their ravines & the paths of their winter torrents. The rocks ~~open~~ & forest open in parts & leave interstices of lawney expanse covered with moss & odorous with thyme. thousands of delightful flowers unknown in England cover these lawns. It makes a distinct picture in my memory from all other mountain scenes which I have ever visited until now.—We went from Mellerie to St Gingoux, & were overtaken by a tremendous storm which made the waves at least 15 feet high. We all prepared for ^a^ swamp as it was impossible to keep the smallest sail & the water began to break over the head. Contrary to all chances we arrived safe at St Gingoux, all the inhabitants of which town were watching on the shore to see who had ventured in so perilous a sea & who exchanged looks of wonder & congratulation with our conductors. On the shore we found an immense chesnut tree which had been overthrown just before by the storm. At Mellerie we eat bread & honey . . . the honey the best I ever tasted—the very essence of the mountain flowers—& as fragrant. The Empress Marie Louise had slept at ~~Rous~~ Mellerie from veneration to the recollections of Julie before the present inn was built & when the accommodations were what we found at Nerni; as bad as those of Greece Lord B says. In the evening we went to see the Rhone enter the lake among its pines & willows—strange mixture! We went hither through chesnut woods beneath mighty mountains & turning to the right proceeded as far as the Tour de Beaverie, separating La Suisse & Savoie. We saw the snowy mountains of La Valais, & the gigantic couch of the Rhone thro the portcullised gateway & returned.

Day 4th. We left St Gingoux & crossed the lake leaving Villeneuve an old wretched town to the right & landed at the Chateau de Chillon. The waters of the Rhone mixed with the blue lake turbidly (Julie letter 17 part 4) I read Julie all day. I forgot its prejudices—it is an overflowing of sublimest genius & more than mortal sensibility.—It ought to be read amongst its own scenes which it has so wonderfully peopled. Mellerie, Chillon¹ Clarens the mountains of La Valais & Savoy are monuments of the being of Rousseau. like the valley path of a mighty river—whose waters are indeed exhausted but which has made a chasm among the mountains that will endure forever. The feelings excited by this Romance have suited my creed, which strongly inclines to immaterialism.

– The beings who inhabit this romance, were created indeed by one mind—but a mind so powerfully bright as to cast a shade of falsehood on the records that are called reality.²

—I must leave Rousseau for a while—We saw the Castle of Chillon; it is an old castle built on a rock by the Lake which close to the very walls is 800 feet perpendicular deep.—The dungeons of this castle are excavated below the lake & have outlets which connect with it by the means of which it could be let in upon the prisoners by the sudden opening of the sluice. The large dungeon is supported on several carved columns whose outbranching capitals support the roof A narrow cell is near it, & beyond one larger & far more [*sic*] loft & quite dark supported by three unornamented arches Across one of these arches was a beam now black & rotten on which prisoners were hung in secret.—a terrible monument was this castle altogether of the tyranny of that loathsome superstition which the great Tacitus so prophetically announced as the pernicies humani generis. There at the reformation thousands pined to death for religious disbelief. The exterior of the Castle is not at all remarkable, & only constructed for strength. From Chillon we went to Clarens. I never felt more strongly than on landing at Clarens that the spirit of old times had deserted its once cherished habitation. A thousand times I said have Julie & St Preux walked on this terrassed road looking on the scene which now I see . . . nay treading the very ground

¹ PBS inserted a small x above this word, presumably directing Peacock to the more detailed description of Chillon below, which is marked with another x.
² In the original MS, this and the next sentence are marked by a vertical line in the left-hand margin.

which I now tread.—All the people at Clarens are convinced of the existence of these creations of Rousseau. Our landlady pointed out the "bosquet
de Julie. In the evening we walked hither. the hay was making under the
trees.—All breathed the spirit of Rousseau—the trees were aged but vigorous ~~but~~ & interspersed with younger ones which were destined to succeed them & when we are dead to afford a shade to future worshippers of
nature. I forgot to remark that our danger took place precisely in the spot
where Julie & her lover were in a similar peril, & where he was tempted
after many years of absence to plunge with her into the lake.

day 5th We walked about & went to the Chateau de Clarens, ascending thro
woods of chesnut & seeing the valley, or rather the little plain of Clarens with
its scattered houses & fertile vineyards below. There was a tessellated pavement near which L. B. agreed with me in aspiring to visit. We sailed hence to
Vevai. a most beautiful Town—more beautiful in its simplicity than any
I have seen. Its market place is a spacious square ^opening to the lake^ interspersed with trees & looks directly upon the mountains of Savoie & La Valais,
the lake & the valley of the Rhone. You remember what Rousseau says of
Vevai in ~~less~~ les Confessions. From Vevai we came to Ouches a village near
Lausanne. The coasts of the pays de Vaud full of Villages & vineyards presents an aspect of tranquil & peculiar beauty well compensating the solitude
& wildness which I am accustomed to admire. The hills are very high &
rocky. Waterfalls echo from the cliffs & shine afar. As we approached ^Ouchy^
~~Lausanne~~ ^the^ spires of Lausanne shone behind.

Day 6. We are detained here by a day of violent wind & rain, we spend in
visiting Gibbons house. ~~the~~ We see the decayed summer house where he
finished his history & the terrace overlooking the lake, & the aciacias which
overshadow it. I walked on the pier of Ouchy when we returned. In an
interval of sunshine the rainbow spanned the lake resting one extremity of
its arch upon the water & the other at the foot of the mountains of Savoie.
Some white houses I know not if they were those of Mellerie shone indistinctly through the yellow fire. The waves broke over the pier.

Day 7. Still detained at Ouchy.

Day 8. Go from Ouchy to Rolles—no event, & enter the plain

Day 9. Arrive at home.—So much for our journey to Vevai: –

Affairs are here rather in a desperate condition. The magistrates of Geneva
have prohibited the making of white bread.—all ranks of people are in the
greatest distress.—I earnestly hope that England at least will escape.

– Let me speak once more of my destined home.——Of course I need not recommend all the cheapness that is consistent with comfort. If possible make a post obit transaction of it, & if you find that the possessor of the house at all consents to such an accommodation, you can refer him to Longdill, & have a conversation with Longdill on the subject, stating my commission to you respecting this house, & engaging him to occupy himself in the management of it.——At all events make it as permanent a thing as you can.——Let the Bishopgate furniture be sold & take the produce of it to the account of the expenditures it may be necessary for you to incur in the process of your search.—— ~~When you have got the house, if you do not feel inclined to repose the <?> I should like very much that you would proceed to keep the garden in order, to set creeping plants hear the house &c.—— then if you can get them~~ ^it^ ~~cheaply to collect necessary furniture <?&> I would as I should be able to remit you gradually such sums as I could spare for that purpose. <?> the library.~~ Let a surveyor see the house if you think of buying it. And, if I do not trouble you too much, when you have possession set vigorously about the garden being reformed—set creeping plants near the house, & let there be no lack of shrubs elegantly disposed. I will remit you the necessary money. In if possible to buy it by post obit bond—Mary & Clare send their kind remembrances:

Your sincere friend *PBS*. –

Open all letters that come for me.

APPENDIX E

EXTRACT FROM MARY AND PERCY'S
JOURNAL FOR 21–27 JULY 1816

An extract from Mary and Percy's shared journal for 21–27 July 1816, which can be compared with the version published in Letter IV of *HSWT*. The extract covers the visit to Chamonix and the return to Geneva. It also features a passage where MWS notes, on 24 July: 'write my story – Shelley writes part of [a] letter', presumably referring to *Frankenstein* and PBS's letter to Peacock, respectively. The extract also records the inclement weather of the summer of 1816. Italics indicate PBS's hand and regular typeface MWS's. Punctuation and line breaks are shown as in the original holograph. Original spelling has been retained, e.g. for place names such as 'Arveron' [*for* Arveiron], and other words including 'encreased' [*for* increased] and 'viel' [*for* veil]; other errors, such as 'apine' [*for* a pine] have also been retained. Text from Bodleian Library MS. Abinger d. 28. ff. 10r–19r. Transcription created and reproduced with permission of Bodleian Libraries, University of Oxford, with thanks to Stephen Hebron; the transcription has been informed by the version published in *MWS Journals*, pp. 112–21.

1816

Switzerland July 21st [x] – Sunday

Switzerland—St. Martin

> *[We commenced our intended journey*
> *to Chamouni at ½ after 8. having*
> *taken horses beforehand. We pass*
> *thro the champaign country which*
> *is extend ed from Mount Saleir to*
> *the base of the higher Alps. The*
> *Country is sufficiently fertile, covered*
> *with corn fields & orchards, &*
> *intersected with sudden acclivities*
> *with flat summits. The day is was*
> *cloudless & exceedingly hot, the Alps*
> *are perpetually in sight, & as*
> *we advance, the mountains which*
> *form Their outskirts closed in around*
> *us. We passed a bridge over a*
> *river which discharges itself into the*

*Arve. The Arve itself much
swollen by the rains, flows cons
tantly on the right of the road. —
As we approach Bonneville thro
an avenue composed of a beautiful*

*species of drooping poplar we
observe that the cornfields on
each side are covered with the
inundation. Bonneville is a
neat little town with no conspicuous peculiarity except the
white towers of the prison,
An extensive building overlooking
the Town. At Bonneville the
Alps commence, one of which
clothed in forests ~~almost~~ rises
almost immediately from the
opposite bank of the Arve.
From Bonneville to Cluses
the road conducts thro a
spacious & fertile plain surrounded
on all sides by mountains;
~~perpetually a~~ covered, like those
of Mellerie with forests of
intermingled pine & chesnut.
At Cluses the route turns suddenly
to the right following the
Arve along the chasm which*

*it seems to have followed among
       perpendicular
the mountains. The scene assumes
here also a more savage &
colossal character. The valley bec
omes narrow affording no more
space than is sufficient for the
river & the road. The pines descend
to the banks, imitating with their
regular spires the pyramidal
crags which lift themselves far
above the regions of forest. The
scene, at the distance of half*

a mile from Cluses differs
from that of Matlock in little else
than the immensity of its propor
tions & in its untameable, ina
ccessible solitudes. We now saw
many goats browsing on the
rocks – Near Maglans, within
a league of each other We saw
two waterfalls. They were no
more than mountain rivulets, but
the height from which they

fell, at least 200 feet made
them assume a character incons
istent with the smallness of their
stream.   The first fell in two
parts; – & struck first on an
enormous rock resembling precisely
                some
those a colossal Egyptian statue
of a female deity. It struck
the head of the visionary Image
& gracefully dividing then
fell in folds of foam, more
like cloud than water, imitating
a viel of the most exquisite
woof: – It united then, concealing
the lower part of the statue, &
              hiding
concealing itself in a wind ing
of its channel burst into the
a deeper fall, & crossed our route
in its path towards the Arve.
The other water fall was more
continuous, & larger. The violence
with which it fell, made it
look rather like the app some
shape which an ixhalation

had assumed – than like water – for
it fell beyond the mountain; which
appeared dark behind it as it
might have appeared behind an

evanescent cloud. — The character
of the scenery continues the same until
We arrived at St. Martin,. fi Clouds
had overspread the evening & hid
the summit of Mont Blance – Its
base was visible from the Balcony
of the Inn.]
Chamounix *July 22. Monday*
We leave St. Martin on mules at
[x]ven O'clock - the road for a league
lay through a plain at the end of
                    we
which were taken to see the
Cascade - The water here falls 250
feet dashing & casting a ~~spray~~
spay which formed a mist around
it - When we approached near to it
the rain of the spray reached us and our
                              falling
clothes were wetted with the quick but
                         ^

minute particles of water. This cata

July – 1816 Switzerland
_____

ract fell into the Arve which dashed
against it banks like a wild animal
who is furious in constraint. As we
continued our route to Cerveaux
the mountains encreased in height
& beauty - the summits of the highest
were hid in Clouds but they sometimes
peeped out into the blue sky higher
one would think than the safety of
God would permit since it is well
known that the tower of Babel did
not nearly equal them in immensity
Our route also lay by les chutes d'
Arve which is neither so high or
grand as the catar[x]act among
the mountains but there is som-
thing so divine in all this scenery
that you love & admire it even

magnificent
when its features are less than
                    ^
usu[a]ll.

    From Cerveaux we continued
on a mountainous & rocky path

& passed an apine bridge over the Arve
This is one of the loveliest scenes in
the world – The white & foamy river
broke ~~br~~ proudly through the
rocks that opposed its progress—
Immense pines covered the
bases of the mountains that
closed around it & a rock covered
with woods & seemingly detached
from the rest stood at the
End & closed the ravine—
    As we mounted still higher this
appeared the most beautiful
part of our journey – the river
foamed far below & the rocks
& glaciers towered above – The
mighty pines filled the vale
& sometimes obstructed our view.
We then entered the valley of
Chamounix which was much
wider than that we had just
left & ~~conseq~~ gave room for
cultivated fields & cottages – the
mountains assumed a more
formitable appearance & the

Glaciers approach nearer to the
Road – Le Glace de Buisson has
the appearance at a distance of
a foaming cataract – & on a
reare approach the ~~ey~~ ice seems
to have taken the forms of pyra
mids & s[xx]actalites – In one village
they offered us for sale a poor
squirrel which they had caught
three days before – we bought

it but no sooner had I got it
in my hand Than he bit my
finger & forced me to let ~~me~~
it go - We caught it however
again & Shelley carried it some
time it appeared at length
~~resig~~ resigned to its fate when
we put it on a railing where
it paused an instant won-
dering where it ~~walk~~ was &
then scampered up its native

trees –
　　　　as we went along we heard
a sound like the rolling of ~~thunder~~
distant thunder & beheld an
　　　　　　　a
avelanche rush down ~~the~~ ravine
of the rocks it stopped mid way
　　　　[x] course
but in its ~~course~~ forced a
　　　　　　^　　bed
torrent from its ~~course~~ which
now fell to the base of the
mountain.
　　　　had
　　　　We passed the torrent ~~mo~~
　　　^
here in the morning - The torrents
had torn away the road [x] and it
was with difficulty we crossed –
Clare went on her mule – S. walked
& I was carried.
　　　　~~Late & f~~ Fatigued to death
we arrived at seven oclock
at ~~the~~ Chamounix.
　　　　At the in at servreaux among
other laws of the same nature there
was an edict [x] of the King of

Sardinia's prohibiting his subjects
from holding private assemblies
on pain of a fine of 12 francs

& in default of payment impri
sonment – Here also we saw
some stones picked up in the
mountains & made some pur
chases.

Tuesday 23rd Chamounix
In the morning after breakfast
we mount our mules to see the
source of the arveron – when
we had gone about three parts of
the way we descended & continued
our route on foot over loose
stones many of which were of an
enormous size – We came to
the sourse which lies like a
stage surrounded on the three
sides by mountains & glaciers
we st sat on a rock, which

formed the fourth gazing on the
scene before us – An immense
Glacier was on our left which
continually rolled stones to its foot–
it is very dangerous to go directly
under this – Our Guide told us a
story of two Hollanders who went
without any guide into a cavern
of the Glacier & fired a pistol
there which drew down a large
piece on them – We see seve
ral Avelanches some very smalls
others of great magnitude
                    e
which roard & smoaked – over
                ^
whelming every thing as it
passed along & precipitating
great peas peices of ice into
the valley below – This Glacier
is encreasing every day a foot
closing up the valley – on We

July 1816

———

drink some water of the
arveron & return – After dinner
think it will rain & Shelley
goes alone to the Glacier of
Boison – I stay at home – read
several Tales of Voltaire – in
the evening I copy S.'s letter to Peacock.

———

Wednesday 24th

Today is rainy ~~but m~~ therefore
we cannot go to Col du Baume –
About ten the weather apears
clearing up Shelley and I begin
our journey to Montanverd – nothing
can be more desolate than the
                    this
ascent of mountain – the trees in
                ^

many places have been torn away
by avelanches and some half
leaning over others intermin
gled with stones present the

appearance of vast & dreadful
desolation – It began to rain
almost as soon as we ~~of~~ left our
inn – when we had mounted consi
derably we turned to look on the
scene a ~~vast~~ dense white mist
covered the vale & tops of the
scatered pines peeping above
were the ~~ol~~ only objects that
presented themselves – The rain
continued in torrents –We were
wetted to the skin so that
when has ascended more than
half way we res olved to turn
back – As we descended Shelley
went before and tripping he
fell upon his knee – this added
to the weakness occasioned by a

blow on his ascent he fainted &
　　　some
was for minutes incapacitated
　　　^
from continueing his route.
　　　We ~~des~~ arrived wet to the
skin – I read nouvelle nouvelles

and write my story – Shelley writes
part of letter.
　　　Thursday 25th
This day promises to be fine & we
set out at nine for Montanvert
with
<u>Beaucoup de Monde</u> go also We get
^
to the top at twelve and behold
<u>le mer de Glace</u>. This is the most
desolate place in the world – iced
mountains surround it no ~~sighn~~
g sign of vegetation appears except
on the place from which view the
scene – we went on the ice – it
is traversed by irregular crevices
~~the~~ whose sides of ice appear blue
while the surface is of a dirty
White. We dine on the mountain –
the air is very cold yet many flowers
grow here & among other the <u>r</u>hodo
<u>dendron</u> or <u>Rose des Alps</u> in great
profusion – We descend leisurely
Shelley goes to see the mine of Amianthe
but finds nothing worth seeing.

　　　July 1816
　　　————
We arrive at the inn at six
fatigued by our day s journey but
pleased and astonished by the world of
ice that was opened to our view ——
　　　Friday ~~Wednesday~~ 26.
We determined to return, today as it
rained and we could not possibly

go to Col de Balme as we intended. We
            by which we
return the same way ~~that~~ had before
                     ^

come but the valley through which
we passed appeared to me a thousand
times more beautiful tha~~t~~n before
The hills of the vale of Cervoz are
covered with pines in termixed by
culti vated lawns – On one mountain
that stands in the middle there
are the ruins of a castle – We saw
also the mountain which fell
some years ago and destroyed many
<u>men and cows</u> / <u>des hommes et des</u>
<u>vaches</u> – as our guide expressed it
some of the rocks reached to the
vale ~~w~~ through which we rode –

                              t

         ~~I~~ I talked with the Guide abou
                                   ^

       July 1816
       ———

the manner of living in the coun
try – the women do almost all the
work such as reaping making hay &c.
The men serve for guides in the
summer which is lucrative as
they are able sometimes to put ~~by~~
bye about 20 louis for winter
exigences – in the autumn they
hunt the Chamois – an occupation
they delight in – They think them
selves lucky if they kill three
in the season which they are
glad to sell for 4 or 5 & 20 ~~louis~~
francs – and if they cannot they
eat it themselves – in the winter
They hunt hares, foxes, marmots
& wolves – these last they gain
more by than by any other animal
they can sell the skins for 12 francs

and the ~~goverm~~ government has
set a price on their heads - 12 for a

July 1816
_____

small one 15 for a large one & 18 for
a female big with young.
    They have the custom here of
marrying very early – Ducrèe married
at 18 a girl of 16 - this was partly
~~adn~~ introduced by the conscription
which allowed immunities for
the fathers of families. In the
winter many of the men go to Paris
and hire themselves as porters at
hotels &c. for the winter here is
a starving kind of thing - they
can gain little or no money du
ring the whole course of it –They
enjoy however the benifit here
of cheap firing which in this cold
place ~~be~~ must in estimable -
what indeed could they do if
joined to their poor fare they had
to struggle with the severi ties
of the seasons. Napoleon was
no great favourite here & they
                any
are very indifferent about Government.
                       ^

July –1816
_____

~~Saturday~~ 27th Saturday
             day
It is a most beautiful ~~one~~ with
out a cloud - We set off at 12. the
day is hot yet there is a fine
breeze - we pass by the great
Waterfall which presents an as
pect of singular beauty – the wind
carries it away from the rock
and on Towards the north and the

fine spray into which it is en
tirely disolved passes before the
mountain like a mist –

The ~~eve~~ other cascade has very
little water & is consequently not
so beautiful as before. the evening
of the day is calm & beautiful
– evening is the only time that I
enjoy travelling – the horses went
fast & the plain opened before us
We saw Jura & the Lake like old
friends – I longed to see my pretty

July –1816
_____

babe – at nine after ~~to~~ much enqui
ring and stupidity we find the road
& alight at Diodati – we converse
with Lord Byron till ~~tu~~ twelve &
then go down to Chapuis. kiss
our babe & go to bed.

APPENDIX F

LORD BYRON'S NOTE TO LINE 927 OF *CHILDE HAROLD'S PILGRIMAGE*, CANTO III

Byron's Note (22) to *Childe Harold's Pilgrimage: Canto the Third*, stanza xcix, line 927: 'And sun-set into rose-hues sees them wrought':

Rousseau's Heloise, Letter 17, part 4, note. 'Ces montagnes sont si hautes qu'une demi-heure apres le soleil couche, leure sommets sont encore eclaires de ses rayons; dont le rouge forme sur ces cimes blanches *une belle couleur de rose* qu'on apperçoit de fort loin.'

This applies more particularly to the heights over Meillerie. "J'allais à Vevay loger à la Clef, et pendant deux jours que j'y restai sans voir personne, je pris pour cette ville un amour qui m'a suivi dans tous mes voyages, et qui m'y a fait établir enfin les héros de mon roman. Je dirois volontiers à ceux qui ont du goût et qui sont sensibles: allez a Vevai—visitez le pays, examinez les sites, promenez-vous sur le lac, et dites si la Nature n'a pas fait ce beau pays pour une Julie, por une Claire et pour un St. Preux; mais ne les y cherchez pas." Les Confessions, livre iv. Page 306. Lyons ed. 1796.

In July, 1816, I made a voyage round the Lake of Geneva; and, as far as my own observations have led me in a not uninterested nor inattentive survey of all the scenes most celebrated by Rousseau in his 'Heloise,' I can safely say, that in this there is no exaggeration. It would be difficult to see Clarens (with the scenes around it, Vevay, Chillon, Bôveret, St. Gingo, Meillerie, Evian, and the entrances of the Rhone), without being forcibly struck with it's peculiar adaptation to the persons and events with which it has been peopled. But this is not all; the feeling with which all around Clarens, and the opposite rocks of Meillerie is invested, is of a still higher and more comprehensive order than the mere sympathy with individual passion; it is a sense of the existence of love in its most extended and sublime capacity, and of our own participation of its good and of its glory: it is the great principle of the universe, which is there more condensed, but not less manifested; and of which, though knowing ourselves a part, we lose our individuality, and mingle in the beauty of the whole.

If Rousseau had never written, nor lived, the same associations would not less have belonged to such scenes. He has added to the interest of his works by their adoption; he has shewn his sense of their beauty by the selection; but they have done that for him which no human being could do for them.

I had the fortune (good or evil as it might be) to sail from Meillerie (where we landed for some time), to St. Gingo during a lake storm, which added to the magnificence of all around, although occasionally accompanied by danger to the boat, which was small and overloaded. It was over this very part of the lake that Rousseau has driven the boat of St. Preux and Madame Wolmar to Meillerie for shelter during a tempest.

On gaining the shore at St. Gingo, we found that the wind had been sufficiently strong to blow down some fine old chesnut trees on the lower part of the mountains. On the height is a seat called the Chateau de Clarens. The hills are covered with vineyards, and interspersed with some small beautiful woods; one of these was named the 'Bosquet de Julie,' and it is remarkable that, though long ago cut down by the brutal selfishness of the monks of St. Bernard, (to whom the land appertained), that the ground might be inclosed into a vineyard for the miserable drones of an execrable superstition, the inhabitants of Clarens still point out the spot where its trees stood, calling it by the name which consecrated and survived them.

Rousseau has not been particularly fortunate in the preservation of the 'local habitations' he has given to 'airy nothings.' The Prior of Great St. Bernard has cut down some of his woods for the sake of a few casks of wine, and Buonaparte has levelled part of the rocks of Meillerie in improving the road to the Simplon. The road is an excellent one, but I cannot quite agree with a remark which I heard made, that 'La route vaut mieux que les souvenirs.'

Quoted from George Gordon, Lord Byron, *Childe Harold's Pilgrimage. Canto the Third* (London, 1816), 76–8.

APPENDIX G

LORD BYRON'S NOTE TO LINE 111
OF *THE PRISONER OF CHILLON*

Byron's Note (3) to line 111 of *The Prisoner of Chillon* (1816): 'From Chillon's snow-white battlement':

The Chateau de Chillon is situated between Clarens and Villeneuve, which last is at one extremity of the Lake of Geneva. On the left are the entrances of the Rhone, and opposite are the Heights of Melleirie and the range of the Alps above Boveret and St. Gingo.

Near it, on a hill behind, is a torrent; below it, washing its walls, the lake has been fathomed to the depth of 800 feet (French measure); within it are a range of dungeons, in which the early reformers, and subsequently prisoners of state, were confined. Across one of the vaults is a beam black with age, on which we were informed that the condemned were formerly executed. In the cells are seven pillars, or, rather, eight, one being half merged in the wall; in some of these are rings for the fetters and the fettered: in the pavement the steps of Bonnivard have left their traces—he was confined here several years.

It is by this castle that Rousseau has fixed the catastrophe of his Heloise, in the rescue of one of her children by Julie from the water; the shock of which, and the illness produced by the immersion, is the cause of her death.

The chateau is large, and seen along the lake for a great distance. The walls are white.

Quoted from George Gordon, Lord Byron, *The Prisoner of Chillon, and Other Poems*, 2 vols. (London, 1816), 58–9.

APPENDIX H

PERCY SHELLEY'S DRAFT OF 'MONT BLANC' IN THE SCROPE DAVIES NOTEBOOK

Before Percy, Mary, and Claire returned to England at the end of August 1816, PBS left a notebook containing a number of writings from the summer of 1816 with Lord Byron at Geneva, perhaps for safe-keeping or perhaps simply by mistake. Byron's friend Scrope Berdmore Davies (1782–1852), for whom the notebook is now named, subsequently took it back to London, but, for some reason, never returned it to Percy. When Davies left Britain again in 1820, he deposited the notebook (*SDN*), in a trunk containing various other documents, with his London bankers, Ransom & Co., managed by Douglas Kinnaird (1788–1830), another mutual friend of Byron. And there it remained until 1976, in what was by then the Pall Mall branch of Barclays, which had absorbed Ransom & Co. in 1888. When the trunk was opened, it was found to contain, in addition to *SDN*, a notebook containing Byron's first fair copy of *Childe Harold's Pilgrimage, Canto the Third* (1816), which he had presumably intended Davies to deliver to his publisher, John Murray (1778–1843), and another notebook containing a transcript of Byron's poem *The Prisoner of Chillon* (1816) copied out by MWS and annotated by Byron.

Only fourteen of the forty-four pages of *SDN* are used. They contain transcripts by Mary of two previously unknown poems by Percy, the sonnets 'Upon the wandering winds' and 'To Laughter', and of a first version of 'Hymn to Intellectual Beauty' (1817). The final poem in *SDN*, written in Percy's hand and entitled 'Scene—Pont Pellisier in the Vale of Servox', is an earlier version of 'Mont Blanc. Lines Written in the Vale of Chamonix', which was first published in *HSWT*. For more detail about the composition of 'Scene' and its relation to 'Mont Blanc', see our headnote to that poem. For more on the finding and contents of *SDN*, see Judith Chernaik and Timothy Burnett, 'The Byron and Shelley Notebooks in the Scrope Davies Find', *Review of English Studies*, February 1978, new series, vol. 29, no. 113, pp. 36–49. Text from British Library Loan 70/8, pp. 7–13. Transcription created and reproduced with permission of the British Library; the transcription has been informed by those published in *CPPBS*, *PoS*, and *SPP*.

'Scene—Pont Pellisier in the vale of Servox'

In day the eternal universe of things
Flows through the mind, & rolls its rapid waves

Now dark, now glittering; now reflecting gloom
Now lending splendour, where, from secret springs
The source of human thought its tribute brings   5
Of waters, with a sound not all it's own:
Such as a feeble brook will oft assume
In the wild woods among the mountains lone
Where waterfalls around it leap forever
Where wind & woods content, & a vast river   10
Over its rocks ceaselessly bursts and raves

Thus thou Ravine of Arve, dark deep ravine,
Thou many coloured, many voiced vale!
Over whose rocks & pines & caverns sail
Fast cloud shadows & sunbeams—awful scene   15
Where Power in likeness of the Arve comes down
From the ice gulphs that gird his secret throne
Bursting through these dark mountains like the flame
Of lightning thro the tempest—thou doest lie
Thy giant brood of pines around thee clinging   20
Children of elder time, in whose devotion
The charmed winds still come, & ever came
To drink thier odours, & thier mighty swinging
To hear, an old and solemn harmony;
Thine earthly rainbows stretched across the sweep   25
Of the aerial waterfall, whose veil
Robes some unsculptured image; even the sleep
The sudden pause that does inhabit thee
Which when the voices of the desart fail
And its hues wane, doth blend them all & steep   30
Thier periods in its own eternity;
Thy caverns echoing to the Arve's commotion
A loud lone sound no other sound can tame:
Thou art pervaded with such ceaseless motion
Thou art the path of that unresting sound   35
Ravine of Arve! & when I gaze on thee
I seem as in a vision deep & strange
To muse on my own various phantasy
My own, my human mind . . . which passively
Now renders & recieves fast influencings   40
Holding an unforeseeing interchange
With the clear universe of things around:
A legion of swift thoughts, whose wandering wings
Now float above they darkness, & now rest
Near the still cave of the witch Poesy   45

Seeking among that shadows that pass by,
Ghosts of the things that are, some form like thee,
Some spectre, some faint image; till the breast
From which they fled recalls them—thou art there

Some say that gleams of a remoter world   50
Visit the soul in sleep—that death is slumber
And that its shapes the busy thoughts outnumber
Of those who wake & live. I look on high
Has some unknown omnipotence unfurled
The vail of life & death? Or do I lie   55
In dream, & does the mightier world of sleep
Spread far and around, & inaccessibly
Its circles?—for the very spirit fails
Driven like a homeless cloud from steep to steep
That vanishes among the viewless gales.—   60
Far, far above, piercing the infinite sky
Mont Blanc appears, still, snowy & serene,
Its subject mountains thier unearthly forms
Pile round it—ice & rock—broad chasms between
Of frozen waves, unfathomable deeps   65
Blue as the overhanging Heaven, that spread
And wind among the accumulated steeps,
Vast desarts, peopled by the storms alone
Save when the eagle brings some hunter's bone
And the wolf watches her—how hideously   70
Its rocks are heaped around, rude bare & high
Ghastly & scarred & riven!—is this the scene
Where the old Earthquake demon taught her young
Ruin? were these thier toys? or did a sea
Of fire envelope once this silent snow?   75
None can reply—all seems eternal now.
This wilderness has a mysterious tongue
Which teaches awful doubt, or faith so mild
So simple, so serene that man may be
In such a faith with Nature reconciled   80
Ye have a doctrine Mountains to repeal
Large codes of fraud & woe—not understood
By all, but which the wise & great & good
Interpret, or make felt, or deeply feel.
The fields, the lakes, the forests & the streams   85
Ocean, & all the living things that dwell
Within the dædal Earth, lightning & rain,
Earthquake & lava flood & hurricane—

The torpor of the year, when feeble dreams
Visit the hidden buds, or dreamless sleep   90
Holds every future leaf & flower—the bound
With which from that detested trance they leap;
The works & ways of man, thier death & birth
And that of him, & all that his may be,
All things that move & breathe with toil & sound   95
Are born & die, resolve subside & swell—
Power dwells apart in deep tranquillity,
Remote, sublime & inaccessible.
And this, the naked countenance of Earth
On which I gaze—even these primæval mountains   100
Teach the adverting mind.—the Glaciers creep
Like snakes that watch thier prey, from thier far fountains
Slow rolling on:—there, many a precipice
Frost & the Sun in scorn of human power
Have piled: dome, pyramid & pinnacle   105
A city of death, distinct with many a tower
And wall impregnable of shining ice . . .
A city's phantom . . . but a flood of ruin
Is there, that from the boundaries of the sky
Rolls its eternal stream . . . vast pines are strewing   110
Its destined path, or in the mangled soil
Branchless & shattered stand—the rocks drawn down
From yon remotest waste have overthrown
The limits of the dead & living world
Never to be reclaimed—the dwelling place   115
Of insects beasts & birds becomes its spoil,
Thier food & thier retreat for ever gone
So much of life & joy is lost—the race
Of man flies far in dread. his work & dwelling
Vanish like smoke before the tempests stream   120
And thier place is not known:—below, vast caves
Shine in the gushing torrents' restless gleam
Which from those secret chasms in tumult welling
Meet in the vale—& one majestic river
The breath & blood of distant lands, forever   125
Rolls its loud waters to the Ocean waves
Breathes its swift vapours to the circling air.

Mont Blanc yet gleams on high—the Power is there
The still & solemn Power of many sights
And many sounds, & much of life & death.   130
In the calm darkness of the moonless nights

Or the lone light of day the snows descend
Upon that mountain—none beholds them there—
Nor when the sunset wraps thier flakes in fire
Or the starbeams dart thro them—winds contend   135
Silently there, & heap the snows, with breath
Blasting & swift—but silently—its home
The voiceless lightning in these solitudes
Keeps innocently, & like vapour broods
Over the snow. the secret strength of things   140
Which governs thought, & to the infinite dome
Of Heaven is as a collumn, rests on thee,
And what were thou & Earth & Stars & Sea
If to the human minds imaginings
Silence and solitude were Vacancy?   145

APPENDIX I

EXTRACT FROM MARY SHELLEY'S NOVEL *THE LAST MAN*

In her novel *The Last Man* (1826), Mary sets the burial of the last victim of the plague which has been ravaging humanity, leaving only four survivors, at the Source of the Arveiron. The imagery and vocabulary of the passage echo both Letter IV of *HSWT* and 'Mont Blanc':

This solemn harmony of event and situation regulated our feelings, and gave as it were fitting costume to our last act. Majestic gloom and tragic pomp attended the decease of wretched humanity. The funeral procession of monarchs of old, was transcended by our splendid shews. Near the sources of the Arveiron we performed the rites for, four only excepted, the last of the species. Adrian and I, leaving Clara and Evelyn wrapt in peaceful unobserving slumber, carried the body to this desolate spot, and placed it in those caves of ice beneath the glacier, which rive and split with the slightest sound, and bring destruction on those within the clefts—no bird or beast of prey could here profane the frozen form. So, with hushed steps and in silence, we placed the dead on a bier of ice, and then, departing, stood on the rocky platform beside the river springs. All hushed as we had been, the very striking of the air with our persons had sufficed to disturb the repose of this thawless region; and we had hardly left the cavern, before vast blocks of ice, detaching themselves from the roof, fell, and covered the human image we had deposited within. We had chosen a fair moonlight night, but our journey thither had been long, and the crescent sank behind the western heights by the time we had accomplished our purpose. The snowy mountains and blue glaciers shone in their own light. The rugged and abrupt ravine, which formed one side of Mont Anvert, was opposite to us, the glacier at our side; at our feet Arveiron, white and foaming, dashed over the pointed rocks that jutted into it, and, with whirring spray and ceaseless roar, disturbed the stilly night. Yellow lightnings played around the vast dome of Mont Blanc, silent as the snow-clad rock they illuminated; all was bare, wild, and sublime, while the singing of the pines in melodious murmurings added a gentle interest to the rough magnificence. Now the riving and fall of icy rocks clave the air; now the thunder of the avalanche burst on our ears. In countries whose features are of less magnitude, nature betrays her living powers in the foliage of the trees, in the growth of herbage, in the soft purling of meandering streams; here, endowed with giant attributes, the torrent, the thunder-storm, and the flow of massive waters, display her activity. Such the church-yard, such the requiem, such the eternal congregation, that waited on our companion's funeral!

Quoted from Mary Shelley, *The Last Man* (1826), vol. 3, pp. 250–3.

EXPLANATORY NOTES

*History of a Six Weeks' Tour through a part of France,
Switzerland, Germany, and Holland.*

3 *Preface*: Although it is written from MWS's point of view, the Preface,
like the rest of *HSWT*, was presumably a collaborative composition (see
Introduction).

the swallow . . . world: the swallow, a migratory bird, is a recurring image
in PBS's poetry. Compare the 'Spirit of BEAUTY' in his 'Hymn to
Intellectual Beauty' (line 13), which MWS says (*PW1839*, vol. 3, p. 35)
was 'conceived during his voyage around the lake [Geneva] with Lord
Byron' in June 1816, i.e. the voyage described in Letter III. *Beckford* comments: 'happy those who pursue [. . .]!' and copies out some phrases.

author . . . sister: MWS and PBS were married by the time *HSWT* was
published in 1817, but not during the 1814 and 1816 travels which it
describes; CC was actually MWS's stepsister.

diviner nature: meaning *Childe Harold's Pilgrimage: Canto The Third*, by
Lord Byron (1788–1824), which was written during the spring and summer
of 1816 and published later that year.

classic . . . past: for more on the phrase 'classic ground' and its significance
in *HSWT*, see Introduction. John William Polidori (1795–1821), who
travelled with Byron to Switzerland in 1816, also uses the phrase: 'We saw
Mont Blanc in the distance; ethereal in appearance, mingling with the
clouds; it is more than 60 miles from where we saw it. It is a classic ground
we go over' (*Polidori*, p. 97). MWS and PBS refer in particular, here, to
Jean-Jacques Rousseau's *Julie* (see Introduction); in his original letter of
17 July 1816, PBS told Thomas Love Peacock (1785–1866) that the book
'ought to be read amongst its own scenes which it has so wonderfully
peopled' (see Appendix D).

perhaps . . . one: a rhetorical sleight-of-hand, asserting the originality of
HSWT, and distinguishing it from other travel writing, by presenting it as
a first-person conversation rather than a second-hand narrative. First-hand
address is not uncommon in Romantic-period travel writing, but the feigned
immediacy here may also echo the conversational structure of Samuel
Taylor Coleridge's (1772–1834) 'Rime of the Ancyent Marinere' (1798).

The Poem: MWS included the final paragraph of the Preface in her edition
of *HSWT* in *Essays*, but not 'Mont Blanc' itself, which she had already
published in *PP1824*; both paragraph and poem were removed in her
1845 edition.

undisciplined . . . soul: compare William Wordsworth's (1770–1850) defin-
ition of poetry, in his Preface to *Lyrical Ballads* (1800), as 'the spontaneous

overflow of powerful feelings: it takes its origin from emotion recollected in tranquillity' (vol. 1, p. xxxiii).

4 *sea-bath*: since the mid eighteenth century, sea-bathing had been recommended for health reasons; by 1816, it had become popular and fashionable as a leisure pursuit.

the packet: a medium-sized boat, transporting post and other goods as well as passengers.

The . . . much: this sentence is based on PBS's journal entry for 28 July.

dreadfully sea-sick: MWS had twice made the return sail from London to Dundee (in 1812 and 1813), but in 1814, early pregnancy may have made her sickness worse. By the time *HSWT* was published in 1817, she had undertaken three more sea voyages to and from mainland Europe. It is interesting that *HSWT* reveals her experience as a traveller here, but not her experience as someone carrying an unborn child. For Mary Wollstonecraft's influence on *HSWT*, see Introduction. Compare also MWS's account of her travel sickness in *Rambles*: 'Several years before I had been a bad traveller; and, even in a comfortable English travelling chariot, suffered great fatigue, and even illness' (p. 79).

awaking . . . half way: compare similar imagery in MWS's 'Introduction' to *F1831*: '*Have you thought of a story?* I was asked each morning, and each morning I was forced to reply with a mortifying negative' (ix; original emphasis).

They promised: the remainder of this section is based on PBS's original journal entry for 28 July.

reefing the sail: reducing the amount of a sail exposed to the wind by taking it in, rolling it up, or, in an emergency, tearing it.

5 *coiffures*: the French term can mean hairstyle but here signifies 'head-dresses'.

temples or cheeks: against the backdrop of the French Revolution and the Napoleonic Wars, differences in style, custom, and social etiquette became part of the wider political discourse, as evidenced by contemporary prints such as 'French Liberty, British Slavery' (1792) by the influential political cartoonist James Gillray (1756–1815). But unflattering comparisons between, for example, clothing fashions on either side of the English Channel had long been a commonplace of travel writing.

national . . . English: referring to the Hundred Years' War (1337–1453) and the Siege of Calais (1346–7) by Edward III of England (1312–77). Calais was won back by France in 1558. *Moskal* comments: 'It is unclear whether Mary Shelley herself endorses the "national reflection", "national" having the dual sense of "patriotic" and "nationalistic" [. . .] the apparent sense is that the English (unfortunately) cannot claim that the pleasant citizens of Calais, culturally French for nearly three centuries, display *English* manners [original emphasis]' (p. 16).

the English custom-house: where duties were levied and collected and other official documents (including passports) processed. In her review of *The English in Italy* (1826), MWS recalls that

> in those early days of migration, in the summer of 1814, every inconvenience was hailed as a new chapter in the romance of our travels; the worst annoyance of all, the Custom-house, was amusing as a novelty. ('The English in Italy', *The Westminster Review* (1826), vi, pp. 325–41 (p. 325))

There is no record of where the party stayed in Calais, but various suggestions have been made; most recently, *Bieri* proposes Dessein's Hotel (vol. 1, p. 324).

cabriolet . . . horses: carriage; an English cabriolet was a much smaller, two-wheeled vehicle, drawn by a single horse.

spruce . . . post-boy: an express, four-wheeled travelling carriage with a boy carrying and/or delivering the post and changing horses. Spruce = smart, well-ordered.

craquèed: presumably a playfully anglicized past-tense of the French verb 'craquer' meaning to crack; possibly a coinage, though *Koszul* suggests that the 'curious' word might have been 'a current hybrid', i.e. in wider use (p. 61). The word is incorrectly accented in the original.

femme de chambre: chambermaid (French).

6 *the whole post*: 'post' here refers to stages along post-roads; 'postmen' were tasked variously with riding these stages with letters and dispatches, and with providing fresh horses for express messengers as they arrived. By ordering their horses too far in advance, the Shelleys and CC are accused of disrupting this chain and are therefore forced to pay a premium.

Ah . . . sommeil: 'Oh! Madame. Think about it; it is to compensate the poor horses for losing their sweet sleep' (French).

plentiful harvest: like other earlier accounts, *HSWT* contrasts the abundant crops in France with the state of affairs in England, where parliament had expanded the enclosure of common land in order to maximize agricultural efficiency during the Napoleonic Wars, thereby denying rural populations access to the land they formerly used to raise crops and animals. *Moskal* (p. 17) compares Laurence Sterne's (1713–68) earlier observation on food security in the opening paragraph of *A Sentimental Journey* (1768): 'They order, said I, this matter better in France'.

obliged . . . week: they took rooms at the Hotel de Vienne from 2 to 8 August. MWS's journal records that they visited the Louvre and Notre Dame; at the Louvre they saw Nicolas Poussin's (1594–1665) painting *Winter, or The Flood* (1644), which PBS found 'terribly impressive. It was the only remarkable picture which we had time to observe' (see *MWS Journals*, p. 10); the same painting may have inspired Byron's poem 'Darkness', which he composed at Geneva during the summer of 1816. PBS records that during their stay, they 'looked over' a 'box' containing

MWS's 'own writings, letters from her father & her friends, and [PBS's] letters' (see *MWS Journals*, p. 8). They left this box in Paris and, despite many attempts, never managed to recover it. Compare also MWS's account of her return visit to Paris in 1840: 'The gravel of the Tuilleries and the Champs Elysées is not half so inviting as the sward of Hyde Park; yet there is an air of cheerfulness and lightsomeness about Paris, which seems to take the burthen from your spirits, which *will* weigh so heavily on the other side of the Channel' (*Rambles*, p. 78, original emphasis).

6 *gardens of the Thuilleries*: Les Jardin des Tuileries, formal gardens between the Louvre and the Place de la Concorde in Paris.

I . . . trees: The Boulevards, a series of broad, interconnecting avenues dating from the eighteenth century, are a key feature of central Paris. Here, the Boulevard de Bonne Nouvelle, which leads on to the Boulevard St Denis.

superb cascade: probably the Fontaine du Vert Bois, also known as the Fontaine Saint-Martin, which was constructed in 1712.

St Denis: a triumphal arch in Paris, built in 1671–4 to commemorate the military victories of Louis XIV (1638–1715). As a monument, it is similar in appearance to the more famous Arc de Triomphe de l'Étoile. As *Murray* notes, 'the Porte-St Denis was the traditional entry for ceremonial processions into the city' (p. 435).

Gothic barbarism: written from the perspective of 1817 rather than 1814, the fate of Paris after the defeat of Napoleon Bonaparte (1769–1821) at the Battle of Waterloo (1815) is compared with the sack of Rome by the Goths in CE 410. As *Moskal* notes, 'spoils of Napoleon' refers to the 'paintings and sculptures looted by him from Italy' (p. 18). *Murray* observes that 'there is no evidence that the depredations Mary feared in 1817 had occurred' (p. 335). In his celebrated account of the 'Imperial Mount' in *Childe Harold's Pilgrimage: Canto the Fourth* (1818), Byron draws a similar analogy between the history of Rome and the course of the Napoleonic Wars (see stanzas 107–8).

impotent: 'powerless'; *Murray* glosses as 'unrestrained' (p. 435).

romance: 'charm'.

7 *walk through France*: an enterprise already undertaken by William Wordsworth and recounted, in part, in his *Descriptive Sketches* (1793).

portmanteau: luggage (French).

Early . . . departure: parts of this section are taken directly from PBS's journal entry for 8 August.

Madame L'Hôte: literally, 'Madame the Host' (French), the Housekeeper at the Hotel de Vienne. When she revised *HSWT* in 1839 and 1845, MWS amended the masculine form 'l'hôte' to the correct, feminine form 'Madame l'hôtesse'. *Koszul* (p. 61) suggests that the original error was due to CC (the only member of the group who had any French) acting as their translator.

large army . . . disbanded: the remains of Napoleon's Grande Armée.

les Dames . . . enlevèes: 'The ladies would certainly be carried off' (French). *Moskal* suggests that 'enlever' connotes rape (p. 19). The word is incorrectly accented in the original.

diligence: public coach.

fiacre: private hire coach.

the leagues short: Romantic-period units of measurement are quite difficult to define exactly, not least because definitions also varied at the time and between countries. Broadly speaking, a league on land corresponded to a little less than 5 kilometres. Here of course the term is used more generally to mean 'the distance'.

Charenton: for Charenton-Le-Port.

C*** . . . scene: CC's record of the journey begins on 14 August 1814 and so we do not have her version of these events. MWS and CC had a notoriously turbulent relationship, at times close, at times hostile. On the other hand, CC's response as represented here is also typical of contemporary travel narratives; her repeated expressions of delight connote the youthfulness of the whole party and also speak to the occasionally tongue-in-cheek tone of *HSWT*.

ten Napoleons: 'A napoleon was a twenty-franc gold piece worth slightly less than a pound' (*Moskal*, p. 20).

clad . . . silk: very expensive clothing, often associated with mourning. *SC* (vol. 3, p. 364) implies that their intention may have been to mark the end of the war and lament the defeat of France, a demonstration of respect designed to keep them, as English tourists, safe.

Gros Bois: for Château de Grosbois.

Don Quixote and Sancho: alluding to the main characters in Miguel de Cervantes Saavedra's (1547–1616) novel *Don Quixote* (1605, 1615), who often dine outdoors.

8 *Guignes . . . his Generals*: Guignes-Rabutin, and Hotel St Barbe, which Napoleon visited 14–17 February 1814. PBS's original journal entry for 9 August includes the phrase 'Napoleon and some of his Generals' (see *MWS Journals*, p. 11).

Empress Josephine and Marie Louise: Josephine de Beauharnais (1763–1814), Napoleon's first wife (m. 1796–1810), and Marie Louise (1791–1847), Napoleon's second wife (m. 1810–21). PBS also refers to Marie Louise in Letter III.

After: this sentence is based on PBS's journal entry for 10 August.

the cathedral: Église Sainte-Croix de Provins.

a scene . . . painting: the 'picturesque' is a term that was frequently used to describe landscape in the late eighteenth century, together with 'sublimity' and 'beauty'.

8 *our fare*: food.

Nogent: for *Nogent-sur-Seine*.

desolated . . . Cossacs: this sentence is drawn in part from PBS's journal entry for 11 August. Cossack is the denominator for a people whose historical roots are in Ukraine and western Russia. During the Napoleonic Wars, Cossack units were amongst the most feared in the Russian army; according to a perhaps apocryphal story, Napoleon claimed he could subdue the world if he had them in his army. In their editorial commentary on MWS's journals, Feldman and Scott-Kilvert note that 'the war ruined towns in [MWS's] novel *The Fortunes of Perkin Warbeck* (1830), II, 300–2, are described in similar terms' (see *MWS Journals*, p. 12 n. 1).

Moscow . . . villages: referring to the French invasion of Russia in 1812, during which Napoleon's armies reached Moscow, from where, five weeks later, they began a disastrous retreat. In 1812, St Petersburg was the capital city of Russia; Moscow only became so in 1918.

About: this and the following sentence are based on PBS's journal entry for 11 August.

9 *Trois Maisons*: for *Ossey-les-Trois-Maisons*. In the original journal entry for 11 August, MWS records them arriving at 9 pm rather than 10 pm. At this point in the journey, PBS wrote to his wife Harriet to invite her to join them in Europe (*Bieri*, vol. 1, p. 327).

considerably advanced: HSWT omits some of the grim details of the group's travels recorded in MWS's original journal entries for 11–12 August, which describe 'unmeaning laughter' from locals, a 'wretched apartment' with 'inhabitants [who] were not in the habit of washing themselves either when they rose or went to bed'; CC is unable to sleep due to 'the rats who as she said put their cold paws on her face – she however rested on our bed which her four footed enemies dared not invade perhaps having overheard the threat that Shelley terrified the man with who said he would sleep with her' (see *MWS Journals*, pp. 11–12).

S*** . . . ancle: in her journal entry for 12 August, MWS recorded that 'Shelley having sprained his leg was obliged to ride [on the mule] all day' (*MWS Journals*, p. 13) but she does not record how this injury occurred.

cabarêt: restaurant.

to dress: carve and season.

use of passports: permission was needed to travel between the various regions of France.

Napoleon . . . deposed: Napoleon abdicated on 6 April 1814, and in August of that year he was exiled on the island of Elba. He returned to power for a short time afterwards but was defeated at Waterloo in June 1815. By the time *HSWT* was published, Napoleon had been in a second exile on the island of St Helena for two years.

Echemine: for Échemines.

most disgusting place: in her original journal entry for 12 August, MWS dismisses Échemines with the comment that 'the Cabaret we rested at was not equalled by any description I have heard of an Irish Cabin in filth & certainly the dirtiest Scotch cottage I ever entered was exquisitely clean beside it – we could hardly swallow their food' (*MWS Journals*, p. 13).

10 *Pavilion*: for *Le Pavillon-Ste-Julie*.

sands of Lybia: alluding, as *Moskal* notes (p. 23 n.a), to Lucan's (CE 39–65) description in *Pharsalia* (first century CE), IX. 438–50, 511–30. *Moskal* further notes that *Pharsalia* 'may be among the otherwise unrecorded' Latin works that MWS was reading in the summer of 1816, as noted in Letter I of *HSWT*. She was continuing her study in December 1816 (see *MWS Letters*, vol. 1, p. 22).

We rested: this paragraph is based on journal entries for 13 August by both PBS and MWS.

voiture: 'carriage' or 'coach' (French).

five Napoleons: five was the smallest denomination of this coin.

Neufchâtel: for *Neuchâtel*, in Switzerland.

I remained . . . writing: PBS's original journal entry for 13 August records: 'Mary is alone and writes to Mrs. [?B].', possibly Isabel Booth, née Baxter (1795–1863), her childhood friend (see *MWS Journals*, p. 14). PBS also records how he and CC arranged their transportation and visited the cathedral. Several biographers have read the fact that PBS and CC sometimes spent time together away from MWS as evidence that they were romantically involved, but there is no actual evidence of an affair.

voiturier: driver (French).

Vandeuvres: for *Vendeuvre*. This paragraph is based on PBS's journal entry for 14 August, which notes that the grounds where they walked and rested belonged to the famous Château de Vendeuvre.

11 *the highest of these*: probably Colline Sainte-Germaine (349 m).

It was evening: based on PBS's journal entry for 14 August. *Murray* notes that CC's revised journal 'quotes S's original reaction to this meteorological phenomenon: "S– said, Look there how the Sun in parting, has bequeathed a lingering look to the Heaven, he has left desolate"' (436; quoting *SC*, vol. 3, p. 342). PBS's remark seemed to inspire CC's first ever journal entry: she considered it 'a most beautiful thought' (*Bieri*, vol. 1, p. 327; quoting *SC*, vol. 3, p. 342).

frowning mountains: *Beckford* highlights this 'evening scene'.

Chaumont: for *Chamount-en-Bassigny*.

Langres: *Elton* notes that 'This town is now a very strong fortress; but at the time of their visit there were only remains of old and scanty works of defence. From a point at the edge of this plateau it is possible to see Mont Blanc, about a hundred and eighty miles away. Looking towards the Jura about sunset, the head of the mountain shows like a star above the purple ridges on the horizon' (pp. 26–7).

11 *Champlitte*: for *Champlitte-et-le-Prélot*.

unprepared for the scene: expressing surprise at mountainous landscapes was a commonplace of Romantic-period travel writing.

a pleasant river: the Doubs.

delight: a term long associated with the experience of the sublime in works of philosophical aesthetics. In his *Philosophical Enquiry into the Origin of our Ideas of the Sublime and the Beautiful* (1757), for instance, Edmund Burke (1729–93) identifies 'delightful horror' as the 'truest test of the sublime', with 'delight' being the emotion produced by the vicarious experience of 'terror', i.e. when no actual danger is present (Part II, Section VII and Part II, Section VIII).

12 *lost his reason*: *Elton* comments:

> The man appears to have been both sulky and perverse: but we need not attribute his dark moods to anything like lunacy. The idea may have been an after-thought, suggested by Shelley's feelings when he stood under the pinnacles of Mont Blanc [see Letter IV, entry for 22 July 1816], and felt his spirit breathless before 'the harmony of nature' [. . .] Goethe made a remark of much the same kind when Eckermann complained of the 'uncomfortable feeling' produced by the gloomy sublimity of the Alps upon one who was born in the plains. (pp. 28–9)

Mort: for *Morre*. In her original journal entry for 17 August, MWS notes: 'We go out on the rocks & Shelley & I read part of Mary a fiction', meaning *Mary, A Fiction* (1788) by Mary Wollstonecraft. In his entry for 31 August, PBS records they were reading *Mary* again (see *MWS Journals*, pp. 15, 22).

Je ne puis pas: 'I can't do [it]' or 'I can't go any further' (French). *Koszul* comments:

> it seems as if, probably for its shortness and picturesqueness, the worse road had been chosen: not the one *via* Ornans, which was rather circuitous [. . .] but an old road [. . .] the gradient of which was not improved before the thirties; and this no doubt accounts for the unwillingness of the *voiturier*, of which we hear so much. (p. 62)

Beckford remarks: 'a very disagreeable sort of Voiturier in the worst possible humour with his passengers & they with him [. . .] Our Travellers frequently abandoned by this Brute'—but also that the scenery provided some compensation.

From the top: This paragraph is adapted from PBS's journal entry for 18 August. Compare similar imagery in PBS's 'Lines written among the Euganean Hills' (1818), lines 66–89, and *Prometheus Unbound* (1820), Act II, Scene III, lines 17–27, 43–50 (*Elton* and *Murray* also note these parallels).

While he waited: this and the following paragraphs are based on PBS's journal entry for 18 August.

13 *Maison Neuve . . . auberge*: it is not clear where exactly this 'auberge' (French = 'inn') was located. Several passages from the following paragraph are adapted from PBS's journal entry for 18 August; draft revisions made when preparing *HSWT* survive in the Bodleian Library (see *MWS Journals*, p. 15 n. 4).

Pontalier: for *Pontarlier*: the party actually crossed the border at Les Verrières (see *MWS Journals*, p. 16 n. 2). In her revised journal, CC describes a discussion arising from their driver's discontent:

> it was all our faults he said – and after thinking a while, Shelley remarked that the driver was right and it was his dissertation upon the perfectibility of man that had put us into such difficulties. Mary laughed and said Men always were the sources of a thousand difficulties – then Shelley asked her why she of sudden looked so sad – and she answered I was thinking of my father – and wondering what he was now feeling. He then said, "Do you mean that as a reproach to me–" and she answered "Oh! No! Don't let us think more about it." But I think something or other had brought her flight into her mind and the sorrow her father must feel—and she loves him so much. (quoted from *SC*, vol. 3, pp. 346–8)

Moskal (p. 26) suggests that 'the Godwinian theme of human perfectibility may have prompted Mary Shelley's reflection on her father', William Godwin (1756–1836).

the horned moon: MWS adopted the moon as a significant symbol in her journal (see entries for 5 and 10 October 1822, following PBS's death; and discussion by Feldman and Scott-Kilvert in *MWS Journals*, pp. 579–81). It has been suggested that she is the 'cold chaste moon' in line 281 of PBS's *Epipsychidion* (1821).

Swiss . . . contrast: compare CC's journal entry for 19 August: 'The Cottages & people [(as) if by magic) became almost instantaneously clean & hospitable'; whereas in France 'it is almost impossible to see a woman that looks under fifty', in Switzerland 'you see cheerful content & smiling healthy faces' (*CC Journals*, pp. 27–8).

14 *The scenery*: this sentence is based on PBS's journal entry for 19 August.

St. Sulpice: for *Saint-Sulpice*, now a commune in the Haute-Saône area of eastern France, close to the Swiss border.

The man . . . Swiss: in her revised journal, CC describes how the party were bored by this man's account of his travels and his enthusiasm for the Swiss pastures, recalling that he 'spoiled the associations with mountains' to such an extent that PBS left the carriage 'to be with his own thought' (quoted from *SC*, vol. 3, p. 348–9).

The . . . beautiful: this sentence is based on PBS's journal entry for 19 August.

iron chain: used to mark the border between the two countries.

14 *Two leagues*: the remainder of this paragraph is based on PBS's journal
    entry for 19 August. Compare CC's account for the same day: 'oh then
    come the terrific Alp[s] I thought they were white flaky cloud[s] what was
    my surprize when after a long & steady examination I found them really to
    be the snowy Alps – yes, they were really the Alps' (*CC Journals*, p. 27). In
    his diary, Polidori recorded a similar situation: 'All the way had debates
    about whether clouds were mountains, or mountains clouds' (*Polidori*,
    p. 213). Compare also PBS's account of the mountains around Chamonix
    in Letter IV (entry for 25 July 1816). In *F1818* (volume 2, chapter 1),
    MWS described the Alps 'as belonging to another earth, the habitations
    of another race of beings' (p. 13).

    its immense lake: the Lake of Bienne near Neuchâtel, mentioned by Jean-
    Jacques Rousseau in the Fifth Walk of his *Rêveries du Promeneur Solitaire*
    (1783). PBS asked CC to translate this work on 20 August (*Moskal*, p. 28).
    In Neuchâtel, the Shelleys and CC stayed at the Hotel du Faucon, in the
    Rue de l'Hôpital; the building still stands but is no longer an inn (see *SC*,
    vol. 3, p. 362).

15 *upon discount*: at a reduced rate.

    lake of Uri: Lake Lucerne, which also features in the novel *Fleetwood; or,
    the New Man of Feeling* (1805), by MWS's father William Godwin.
    Newman Ivey White suggests that they had intended to follow in the foot-
    steps of the hero of that novel (*Shelley*, 2 vols., New York: A.A. Knopf,
    1940, vol. 1, pp. 352–3). See also *F1818* (volume 3, chapter 1): 'I have
    visited the lakes of Lucerne and Uri, where the snowy mountains descend
    almost perpendicularly to the water, casting black and impenetrable
    shades, which would cause a gloomy and mournful appearance, were it not
    for the most verdant islands that relieve the eye by their gay appearance;
    I have seen this lake agitated by a tempest, when the wind tore up whirl-
    winds of water, and gave you an idea of what the water-spout must be on
    the great ocean' (pp. 15–16).

    A Swiss . . . postoffice: some words from the beginning of this paragraph are
    taken from PBS's journal entry for 20 August. Compare CC's extended
    account of the episode in her revised journal:

    > Our new Swiss friend whose name we do not know, but who seems
    > a perfect Gentleman, got into the carriage and drove out of the town
    > with us. Going along he told us, he was much struck yesterday, when he
    > met them at the Bureau des Postes, by seeing two such very young
    > people as Shelley and Mary wandering in search of a carriage, and
    > speaking ~~the~~ french so imperfectly they could scarcely make them-
    > selves understood, he wondered how they got into a strange town and
    > a distant country and felt interest in them, and thought he would see
    > more of them and serve them. He said from the first moment I took you
    > for Lovers, and supposed you might have run away from your parents
    > and meant to give you good advice. Then he asked if indeed they ~~were~~
    > had escaped from England, on account of Love, and they said Yes – He

then begged them to return to England, rather than proceed further –
but they refused. Next he asked if I had also run away for the sake of
Love and I answered Oh! dear No – I came to speak french. He seemed
puzzled and yet amused by our Youth and Simplicity, and left us just
outside the Gate of the Town, expressing his hearty wishes for our
safety and happiness. (Quoted from *SC*, vol. 3, p. 351)

more than two days: MWS's journal provides more detail, including stops
at Soleure, Zoflingen, and Sursee on the night of 22 August. Other details
omitted from *HSWT* include a dislike of a cathedral ('modern & stupid'),
MWS's sickness, PBS's 'jocosely horrible mood', 'magnificent mountains',
and discussion of CC's 'character' (see *MWS Journals*, p. 18). CC supposedly defaced her own journal at this point (21–22 August) to remove
a negative comment PBS made about her (see *CC Journals*, p. 29).

The country . . . interest us: Compare *Hamlet* 1. 2. 136–8: 'O God, God, |
How weary, stale, flat and unprofitable | Seem to me all the uses of this
world!'

we hired a boat: MWS's journal entry for 23 August records that on this
journey they read 'part of' Clifford's English translation of Abbé Augustin
Barruel's (1741–1820) *Memoirs illustrating the History of Jacobinism*
(1797–8), which may have given PBS the idea for his short story, 'The
Assassins', which he began to write the following day (see *MWS Journals*,
p. 18). The copy they read survives in the Berg Collection of the New York
Public Library.

Altorf: for *Altdorf*, on the southern shore of the lake, famous as the place
where, according to legend, William Tell shot an apple from his son's head
(see note to p. 16).

S***'s health: in the summer of 1814, PBS was generally healthy, but by
the time that the Shelleys were preparing *HSWT* for the press in 1817, he
had been (mis)diagnosed as consumptive, which informed his decision to
leave England for Italy in 1818. He called it his 'constitutional disease'
(*PBS Letters*, vol. 1, p. 547) and complained of a cough and chest pain. He
consulted the physician William Lawrence (1783–1867) in 1815 and 1817,
who prescribed relocation to a warmer climate and also that PBS stop
writing poetry, which latter suggestion MWS fiercely dismissed (see *Bieri*,
vol. 1, pp. 381, 384–5).

16 *Brunen*: for *Brunnen*: before leaving, PBS began dictating to MWS his
short story 'The Assassins', which is mentioned in journal entries for
25 and 26 August (see *MWS Journals*, pp. 19–20). In their editorial commentary on MWS's journal, Feldman and Scott-Kilvert suggest that the
party stayed at the Gasthof zum Alder on the shores of the lake, one of two
inns at Brunnen at that time (see *MWS Journals*, p. 19 n.1).

a priest . . . mistress: compare *F1818* (volume 3, chapter 1) on 'the base
of the mountain, where the priest and his mistress were overwhelmed by
an avalanche, and where their dying voices are still said to be heard amid
the pauses of the nightly wind' (p. 16). We have not identified any source

for this story; perhaps it was simply a local legend which MWS heard at Brunnen.

16 *the chapel of Tell*: *Travels* provides a description of this chapel as part of a longer account of the legendary William Tell, the 'glorious deliverer' of the Swiss from 'the tyranny' of the equally legendary Albrecht Gessler, who had his fortress at Altdorf; *Travels* also recounts the incident with the apple (vol. 1, pp. 275–8).

heroic deeds: the notion of a causal relationship between Switzerland's dramatic Alpine scenery and democratic polity had been a commonplace of European writing since at least Jean-Jacques Rousseau's account of the Upper Valais in Part 1, Letter 23 of *Julie*. It became an especially visible trope of British Romantic writing following the French invasion of Switzerland in 1798; see, for instance, Samuel Taylor Coleridge's *France: an Ode* (1798), lines 64–77 on 'the bloodless freedom of the mountaineer' (77).

vent d'Italie: 'wind from Italy' (French).

Siege . . . Tacitus: referring to the account of the Roman assault on the city in CE 70 given by Cornelius Tacitus (*c*. CE 55–120) in his *Histories* (CE 100–10), V. i–xiii. This sentence is based on PBS's journal entry for 24 August.

an ugly . . . Chateau: *SC*, noting that 'nothing is now known of any house with such a name', speculates on the basis of topographical details from CC's journal entry: 'the only place where there is a hill in front of the lake is at the southern end of the village of Brunnen, where the Grand Hotel Brunnen now stands. A house on this hill can be seen in contemporary prints and must have been Shelley's abode' (vol. 3, p. 368).

17 *until . . . December*: when PBS would receive his next quarterly allowance of £250 from his father, Sir Timothy Shelley (1753–1844).

Thus . . . England: this sentence is based on PBS's journal entry for 26 August.

*S*** only knew*: CC's journal entry for 27 August suggests that she was not aware of their financial difficulties: 'Bustle toil & trouble – Most laughable to think of our going to England the second day after we entered a new house for six months – All because the stove doesn't suit' (*CC Journals*, p. 31). MWS, however, may have known a little more than she implies here, through the journal she shared with PBS, in which he had written, on 24 August 1814: 'We consult our situation. We cannot procure a house; we are in despair' (*MWS Journals*, p. 19).

diligence par-eau: public transport by boat (French).

Loffenburgh: for *Laufenberg*.

18 *The Reuss . . . rapid*: the Reuss, a river in south central Switzerland, which flows through Lake Lucerne. MWS later suggested that this 'river navigation' through 'magnificent scenes' influenced PBS's extended account of a journey by boat in *Alastor; or, The Spirit of Solitude* (1815), lines 305–514 (see *PW1839*, vol. 2, p. 267).

deep green: this comparison was added when *HSWT* was being compiled for the press; the Shelleys had not seen the Rhone in 1814.

Sleeping . . . Mumph: for *Mumpf*. This sentence is based on PBS's journal entry for 29 August.

Dettingen: for *Döttingen*.

Indian appellation: in eighteenth-century usage, 'Indian' could signify 'primitive' rather than indicate any specific geographical or cultural origin. *Elton* comments that these boats were 'narrow punts [. . .] alarmingly unsafe' (p. 39).

We . . . foot: this sentence is based on PBS's journal entry for 29 August. The landing spot at Mumpf was close to the Hotel Sonne, where the Shelleys may have procured their carriage (see *SC*, vol. 3, p. 363).

Rheinfelden: a town straddling the Swiss–German border, on either side of the Rhine (the 'swift river' mentioned a few lines later).

Basle: for Basel.

Mayence: for *Mainz*.

19 *Letters from Norway*: meaning *Letters Written During a Short Residence in Sweden, Norway, and Denmark* (1796), by Mary Wollstonecraft. Compare CC's journal entry for 30 August: 'Shelley reads aloud the Letters from Norway – This is one of my very favourite Books – the language is so very flowing & Eloquent & it is altogether a beautiful Poem' (*CC Journals*, p. 33). For the influence of *Short Residence* on *HSWT*, see Introduction.

passed . . . delightfully: MWS turned 17 on 30 August 1814. Compare PBS's journal entry for 30 August: 'It is Marys birth day. we do not solemnize this day in comfort. We expect to be not happier but more at ease before the year passes' (*MWS Journals*, p. 21).

Suddenly: the remainder of this and the beginning of the next paragraph is based on PBS's journal entry for 31 August.

Strasburgh: for *Strasbourg*.

three of these were students: the names Schwitz, Hoff, and Schneider are found in PBS's journal entry for 1 September; the observations about their appearance and character were added when *HSWT* was being prepared for the press. CC's description in her journal entry for the same day is equally unflattering: 'One of our Passengers the name of Hoff very odious – The Second was neither one thing or the other [. . .] the third was an ideot' (*CC Journals*, p. 34). *Beckford* also notes these travelling companions, copying out some observations.

Manheim: for *Mannheim*. 'A usual form of the name in the early nineteenth century' (*Koszul*, p. 61).

20 *batalier*: for *batelier* = boatman (French).

C'est . . . noyès: the literal translation from French would be 'It is only a boat, which was only overturned, and all the people are only drowned'. It is not clear what the *batelier* intended by the repetition of *seulement* ('only'), though he presumably meant to add (perhaps ironic) emphasis to his account rather than to dismiss the events as described as routine or inconsequential.

20 *the bombardment . . . war*: On 21 October 1792, following the defeat of Austria and Prussia at the Battle of Valmy on 20 September, the army of the French Republic entered Mainz. In March 1793, the Republic of Mainz was proclaimed. On 22 July, Austrian and Prussian forces retook the city, having destroyed much of it in the process, and abolished the short-lived Republic, which had counted amongst its leaders the naturalist Georg Foster (1754–94), who had sailed with James Cook (1728–79) on his second expedition in 1772–5; the German intellectual Caroline Michaelis (1763–1809), future wife of August Schlegel (1767–1845), was briefly imprisoned during the reprisals against the former Republic. Napoleon's army reoccupied the city in 1797. Hence CC's observation in her journal entry for 3 September: 'The Inhabitants of Mayntz do not know to whom they belong – They are without a government at present & have been for some months – The town is kept in a state of strong defence & the soldiers parade the streets [. . .] Napoleon had made it the strongest fortified town in all Europe – it is large & clean' (*CC Journals*, pp. 35–6).

We took our place . . . Cologne: this passage is based on PBS's journal entry for 3 September.

mercantile: commercial.

like a steam-boat: travel by steamboat was increasingly popular in the early nineteenth century. In his verse 'Letter to Maria Gisborne' (1820), PBS describes the steamboat which his friend Maria's (1770–1836) son, the engineer Henry Willey Reveley (1788–1875), was planning to design, with financial support from PBS, to sail between Livorno and Genoa.

kissed one another: *Beckford* copies out the 'horribly disgusting' behaviour of the Germans, describing the narrator as very much in the guise of a 'picturesque Tourist'.

Byron . . . Harold: an allusion to the group having read *Childe Harold, Canto the Third* after its publication in 1816; as *Moskal* explains, 'The insertion of "have since" before "read" would make this clearer' (p. 36). Compare MWS's journal entry for 28 May 1817:

> I am melancholy with reading the 3rd Canto of Childe Harold. Do you not remember, Shelley when you first read it to me? One evening after returning from Diodati. It was in our little room at Chapius – the lake was before us and the mighty Jura. That time is past and this will also pass when I may weep to read these words and again moralize on the flight of time. (*MWS Journals*, p. 171)

21 *these scenes*: during this voyage along the Rhine, MWS, PBS, and CC would have passed the 'Frankenstein Castle', Burg Frankenstein, which can be seen from the river: the ruin sits on a hill overlooking Darmstadt. Scholars have debated whether the castle has any links to Mary's novel: most think it unlikely since she never refers to it in her writing. It is interesting,

though, that a local myth tells of a student-alchemist who lived in the castle in the seventeenth century: Konrad Dippel (1673–1734), who conducted experiments with prussic acid to try to find the secret to longevity and, supposedly, died after testing an elixir on himself.

these borderers: Murray glosses with: 'those who lived along the Rhine' (p. 438).

appearance of extreme delicacy: compare CC's journal for 4 September: 'See the only beautiful girl <I> we have seen since we [p]arted from Paris' (*CC Journals*, p. 37). Comments on the physical appearance of the locals are commonplace in late eighteenth- and early nineteenth-century travel writing.

Clêves: on the border between Prussia and Holland. The Battle of Cleves, a major victory for the French in the Napoleonic Wars, took place in July 1805.

22 *post . . . way*: to complete the journey using the mail coach.

flying . . . Montague: Mary Wortley Montagu (1689–1762) was an English travel-writer and poet. The reference is to the account of Nimegen in her influential, posthumously-published *Letters* (1763):

> I must not forget to take notice of the bridge, which appeared very surprising to me. It is large enough to hold hundreds of men, with horses and carriages. They give the value of an English two-pence to get upon it, and then away they go, bridge and all, to the other side of the river, with so slow a motion, one is hardly sensible of any at all. (See *Letters of Lady Mary Wortley Montague* (Paris, 1800), Letter III, 13 August 1716, p. 8)

In her journal for 8 September, CC also mentions crossing 'a Branch of the Rhine over a flying Bridge' (*CC Journals*, p. 38).

Triel: for *Driel*.

During . . . day: Moskal (p. 39) notes that this and the next paragraph is 'a re-writing of an excised passage in Mary Shelley's *Frankenstein* manuscript'. *Beckford* plays up the jeopardy here, noting 'narrow escape from the sweep of a windmill'.

the flax: also known as linseed (*Linum usitatissimum*), a plant often used to make textiles.

23 *man . . . condition*: presumably one of the many displaced and driven into poverty by the Revolutionary and Napoleonic Wars.

August: error for September.

Marsluys: for *Maassluis*. Based on PBS's Journal entry for 9 September. PBS wrote more of *The Assassins* and MWS began a short story (now lost) entitled 'Hate'. CC also began some fiction, entitled 'Ideot', also lost (see *Bieri*, vol. 1, p. 331).

brilliant shews of earth and sky: compare William Wordsworth's sonnet, 'Composed upon Westminster Bridge, September 3, 1802': 'Earth has not anything to show more fair . . . Ships, towers, domes, theatres, and temples lie | Open unto the fields, and to the sky' (lines 1, 6–7).

23 *a king's pilot*: an official title for the most highly qualified or experienced rank of navigator.

The bar of the Rhine: a part of the river where sediments have built up, making it difficult and potentially dangerous to navigate.

24 *Marsluys*: in her original journal entry for 12 September 1814, which describes the crossing from The Netherlands to England, MWS records: 'We dispute with one man about the Slave trade' (*MWS Journals*, p. 24). The trade in enslaved people was prohibited in British territories in 1807 but slavery itself was not abolished until 1833. PBS's father had supported an earlier anti-slavery bill in parliament in 1790 and his constituency, Horsham, was in favour of abolition.

Letters written During a Residence of Three Months in the Environs of Geneva, in the Summer of the Year 1816

27 *Hôtel de Secheron*: Sécheron is a district of Geneva, north of the city centre and directly across the lake from Cologny and the Villa Diodati, where the Shelleys and Byron later lived (see Letter II). The hotel in which the Shelleys stayed (the *old* Hotel d'Angleterre, established in 1777 by Antoine-Jérémie Dejean), is no longer standing, but was adjacent to what is now the Hôtel de la Paix, on the Quai du Mont Blanc. Byron and Polidori arrived at the same hotel the following week, on 25 May, and PBS and Byron met for the first time in the garden on 27 May. Polidori notes: 'We arrived at Sécheron . . . L[ord] B[yron] . . . put his age down as 100' (*Polidori*, p. 97).

Lavalette: Antoine Marie Chamans, the Comte de Lavalette (1769–1830), occupied a number of important posts in Napoleon's army and government. He was imprisoned when the French monarchy was restored after Napoleon's defeat in 1814 and sentenced to death in 1815. He escaped to England, with British help, after exchanging clothing with his wife during a prison visit. *Rouhette* suggests that the story might have inspired MWS's 'The False Rhyme', published in *The Keepsake* in 1829.

The manners of the French: compare this passage with PBS's letter to Thomas Love Peacock (1785–1866) of 15 May 1816:

> The manners of the French are interesting, altho less attractive at least to an Englishman than before. The discontent & sullenness of their minds perpetually betrays itself. I despise this nation so much the less, enslaved & well fit for slavery as it is because it has not learned to wear its chains with smiles of sycophantic gratitude. The best thing would be that they should love & practice true liberty,—but it is well that the vilest servitude can extract one murmur. (*PBS Letters*, vol. 1, p. 474)

the last . . . Allies: under the Treaty of Paris (20 November 1815), 150,000 troops from the coalition of countries which had defeated Napoleon at the

Battle of Waterloo (18 June 1815) were stationed around France and at French expense. The Treaty provided for an occupation of five years, but most of the troops were withdrawn after three. The 'detested' Bourbon 'dynasty', overthrown by the French Revolution, was restored with Allied support and Louis XVIII installed as monarch. For the impact of the previous 'invasion', see 'France' in the first part of *HSWT*. *Moskal* (p. 41) directs the reader to Sydney Owenson, Lady Morgan's (1781–1859) study *France* (1817) for a detailed, contemporary account of the state of the country following the defeat of Napoleon and the restoration of the monarchy; Morgan's novel *The Wild Irish Girl* (1806) was a favourite of PBS.

28 *Neufchâtel*: for *Neuchâtel*.

Dôle: for *Dole*. *Elton* comments: 'They passed Dole without waiting for a view of Mont Blanc, which is visible from the hills though a hundred miles away' (p. 46).

the foot of Jura: the Jura Mountains run along the French–Swiss border, from Basel to Geneva.

Champagnolles: for *Champagnole*, in the Jura.

inaccessible expanse: the idea of the *inaccessible* forms an important part of the Shelleys' response to the Alps in 1816, as it does of contemporary travel writing about the Alps more generally. Cf. 'Mont Blanc', lines 96–7. The trope persists today: the ski-lift and cable-car passes sold by the Compagnie du Mont Blanc at Chamonix carry the marketing slogan *l'Exceptionnel Accessible* ('the exceptional accessible').

The spring . . . excessive: another notice of the 'unusually' cold weather conditions during the so-called 'year without a summer' (see Introduction).

29 *Nion*: for *Nyon*, on the shore of Lake Geneva.

our passport: *Moskal* comments: 'British travellers were required to determine their itineraries before departing, as regulations required that the ambassadors in London of the countries to be visited must sign the passports before the traveller's departure' (p. 43 n.).

difficulty . . . overcome: compare PBS's account of the journey to Geneva in his letter to Thomas Love Peacock of 15 May 1816: 'to come to Geneva, we have crossed the Jura branch of the Alps. The mere difficulties of horses & high hills & postillions, & cheating lying aubergistes you can easily conceive' (*PBS Letters*, vol. 1, p. 475).

the picturesque . . . sublime: Romantic-period travel writing routinely uses the terms 'picturesque', 'beautiful', and 'sublime', which have their origins in eighteenth-century philosophy, not only to describe different kinds of landscape but also to account for the effects of those landscapes on the viewer. Developed by William Gilpin (1724–1804) in a series of works starting with *Observations on the River Wye* (1770), 'picturesque' came to denote a landscape which shared the kind of compositional features associated with the landscape painting of Poussin (1594–1665) and Claude Lorrain (1604–82). Dorothy Wordsworth (1771–1855) records that Samuel

Taylor Coleridge (1772–1834), on a visit to the Falls of Clyde in 1803, was outraged at the lack of precision with which other tourists used these terms—but by 1816, they were often interchangeable. See Dorothy Wordsworth, *Recollections of a Tour Made in Scotland*, ed. J. C. Sharp (Edinburgh: James Thin, 1874), p. 37.

29 *natural . . . desert*: Cf. 'Mont Blanc' on 'the accumulated steeps' of the mountain as 'a desart peopled by the storms alone | Save when the eagle brings some hunter's bone, | And the wolf tracts her there' (lines 66–9). In his *Descriptive Sketches* (1793), William Wordsworth (1770–1850) frequently uses the term 'desert' to describe high Alpine landscapes. This whole passage closely parallels PBS's account of crossing the Jura in his letter to Peacock of 15 May 1816:

> The mountains of Jura are a very h{igh} ridge of the Alps. They exhibit scenery of wonderful su{blimity.} Pine forests of impenetrable thickness & untrodden, nay, inaccessible expanse spread on every side. Sometimes descending they follow the route into the vallies clothing the precipitous rocks & struggling with knotted roots between the most barren clefts. Sometimes the route winds on high into the region of frost, & there these forests become scantier & are loaded with snow. The trees in these regions are incredibly large, but stand in scattered clumps in the white wilderness. Never was scene more awfully desolate as that which we passed in one evening of our last days journey. The natural silence of that uninhabited desert contrasted strangely with the voices of the people who conducted us. (*PBS Letters*, vol. 1, pp. 475–6)

patois: 'local dialect' (a stock term of Romantic-period travel writing).

Gentlemens' seats: aristocratic homes.

queen of all: in representing Mont Blanc as female, *HSWT* departs pointedly from the conventions of contemporary travel writing which routinely referred to the mountain as a male 'monarch'; cf. Byron, *Manfred* (1817): 'Mont Blanc is the monarch of mountains: | They crowned him long ago' (Act I, scene 1, line 60). PBS, in 'Mont Blanc', consciously avoids any such personification. Thomas Medwin (1788–1869), quoting this passage in *Life of Shelley* (1847), notes that the Hotel d'Angleterre was, in 1816, 'the best hotel' in Geneva 'in a position equalled by none, for it lies immediately under the eye of Mont Blanc' (vol. 2, p. 236). Compare Byron's note to *Childe Harold's Pilgrimage* III. lxvii. 8: 'This is written in the eye of Mont Blanc (June 3d, 1816) which even at this distance dazzles mine'.

deep seclusion: perhaps an echo of William Wordsworth, 'Tintern Abbey' (1798), lines 4–7.

30 *that sickness*: for MWS's seasickness on the crossings to France in 1814 and 1816, see the preamble to *HSWT*.

Latin and Italian: the Shelleys often read together, or aloud to each other; a number of works in Latin and Italian feature on their reading lists for 1816. See *MWS Journal*, pp. 93–8. Although not mentioned on those lists, references in *HSWT* suggest the Shelleys also read or at least discussed the *Odes* of Horace and the *Annals* of Tacitus. MWS was certainly reading Tacitus in August–October 1817, while she was compiling *HSWT* (see *MWS Journal*, pp. 178–83).

cockchaffers: large flying beetles, more usually known in England as 'Maybugs' or 'doodlebugs', and popular in European folklore since Classical antiquity; presumably MWS means turning over those which had fallen on their backs. *Elton* comments: 'It is curious to observe how closely the writer of the Journal noticed insects and reptiles' (p. 43).

the garden: *Beckford* glossed this passage 'innocent pleasures'.

M: in the versions of *HSWT* published in *Essays*, MWS amended this signature to 'M.S.' (see Introduction).

31 *Coligny*: for *Cologny*, then a small settlement east of Geneva on the southern shore of the lake. Byron took the Villa Diodati, in Cologny. The 'little cottage' taken by the Shelleys and CC, a short walk away in Montalègre, was called Maison Chappuis, though it is not known whether they rented the main house or a side-annex. See *Bieri*, vol. 1, p. 375; and H. W. Häusermann, *The Genevese Background* (London: Folcroft, 1952), pp. 1–8. *Campagne ****** = 'the Chappuis estate'. MWS passed through Cologny again in October 1840, describing, in *Rambles*, how the familiarity of the scene made her painfully aware of the many changes in her own life (see Part 1, Letter XII, 4 October).

snowy aiguilles: as a number of contemporary guidebooks observe, *aiguille* (the French word for *needle*) is the term used to describe exposed rocky summits, especially, though not exclusively, in the Mont Blanc massif (e.g. *Travels*, vol. 1, p. 311 n.; *Traveller's Guide*, p. 40). The expression *snowy aiguilles* is therefore something of a contradiction, especially in summer, but the term was often used loosely by travellers.

that glowing . . . hue: *Rouhette* compares Rousseau, *Julie*, Part 4, Letter 17, note 1: 'These mountains are so high that a half-hour after sunset their crests are still lit by the sun's rays, the red of which covers these white peaks with a lovely rose colour that can be seen a long way off' (p. 424).

excursions on the water: *Moskal* comments 'At this point there is apparently a break in the continuity of the letter. The rain and thunderstorm mentioned below were a prominent feature of the period 8–13 June, according to Polidori's diary, but not before' (p. 45 n.).

we enjoyed a finer storm: the emphasis presumably signals the combined senses of 'experienced' and 'took pleasure in'. Both MWS's *F1818* and Byron's *Childe Harold's Pilgrimage: Canto the Third* (1816) feature Alpine thunderstorms; a number of commentators have suggested that MWS drew on this experience when describing the thunderstorm that occurs when Victor arrives back in Geneva from Ingolstadt in *F1818* volume 1, chapter 7.

32 *Plainpalais*: properly, the Plaine de Plainpalais (Plainpalais being the name of the boulevard which leads to the 'grassy plain'). In volume 1, chapter 7,

of *F1818*, Victor's brother William is killed by the Creature on the Plaine de Plainpalais.

32 *Here . . . vain*: Rousseau, born in Geneva in 1712, was exiled from the city in 1762 after the publication of his treatise *Émile, ou l'Éducation* (1762), which was banned (and burned) in Geneva and Paris. In the early nineteenth century, Voltaire (1694–1778) and Rousseau were considered the major intellectual and cultural architects of the French Revolution, though both had died before it began. Political unrest, inspired by the Revolution, affected Geneva between 1792 and 1794, when the former magistrates of the city were condemned to death, on 25 July, by a Revolutionary Tribunal, the members of which apparently carried out the sentence themselves: an event condemned even by contemporary supporters of the French Revolution, such as the controversial writer and traveller Helen Maria Williams (1759–1827). The long-term view of the French Revolution offered in this passage of *HSWT*—i.e. that despite the apparent catastrophes of the Terror, the Napoleonic Wars, and the attempted restoration of the Ancien Régime, the long-term effects would be positive—finds full expression in the 'Preface' and main text of PBS's *Laon and Cythna* (1817). See headnote to 'Mont Blanc' and compare also 'Mont Blanc' (lines 85–125) for a similarly 'anti-catastrophist' account of glaciation. In his diary entry for 28 May 1816, Polidori records: 'Saw the bust of Jean Jacques erected upon the spot where the Geneva magistrates were shot. L[ord] B[yron] said it was probably built of some of the stones with which they pelted him' (*Polidori*, p. 106). *Traveller's Guide* also records that 'the house in which the immortal Jean Jacques Rousseau drew his first breath stands at the entrance to this street [i.e. Plainpalais], and is distinguished by an inscription consecrated by the government and the nation' (p. 12). The statue of Rousseau currently standing on the Plaine de Plainpalais dates from 1834.

Mont Salêve: Salève (1379 m), in France, is approximately 20 kilometres south of Geneva. In volume 1, chapter 7 of *F1818*, Victor encounters his Creature during a stormy night on the Plaine de Plainpalais and becomes convinced that it was he who had killed William. 'I thought of pursuing the devil,' Victor says, 'but it would have been in vain, for another flash discovered him to me hanging among the rocks of the nearly perpendicular ascent of Mont Salêve, a hill that bounds Plainpalais on the south. He soon reached the summit, and disappeared' (p. 148). Given the actual distance between Salève and the Plaine de Plainpalais, one could wonder about the accuracy of both MWS's geography and Victor's eyesight. But compare *Traveller's Guide* on the Plaine de Plainpalais:

> This square is remarkable on account of a deception of the sight which takes place here; for that part of the city which is actually on the other side of the river, appears exactly as if it were really at the foot of Mont Saleve, though the latter is more than a French league distant. (p. 13)

Arve: the river Arve, which rises on the Tête de Balme and flows through the valley of Chamonix, joins the Rhône at Geneva.

equality . . . England: cf. Mary Wollstonecraft, *Letters Written During a Short Residence in Sweden, Norway, and Denmark* (1796): 'the treatment of servants in most countries, I grant, is very unjust; and in England, that boasted land of freedom, it is often extremely tyrannical' (p. 28). *Rouhette* compares Rousseau's remarks about social equality in Switzerland in *Julie*, Part 1, Letter 23, and Part 4, Letter 10.

inapt: 'lacking in aptitude', i.e. without agricultural knowledge. *Moskal* comments: 'Perhaps she had originally learned the months from the French Revolutionary Calendar [based on prevailing weather conditions], which was adopted for a time in Switzerland during the period of the Helvetic republic [1798–1803]' (p. 46 n.).

Genevese . . . puritanism: 'puritanism' here is a reference to Calvinism, the reformed version of Protestantism established by John Calvin (1509–64) at Geneva in 1541–9. Compare *Tour* on Calvin's legacy in Geneva after the French Revolution:

> It is not unworthy of observation, that the great religious Reformer of Geneva [. . .] should have rivetted the chains of religious despotism, while he became, by his political institutions, the father of civil liberty in Europe. These spots in the constitution of Geneva will perhaps vanish after a few years of independence, provided it can maintain the due balance between attractive and repulsive forces, when placed within the orbit of so mighty a planet as the French Republic. (vol. 2, pp. 175–6)

French . . . abolished: Geneva was annexed by France on 13 December 1798 and made capital of the newly created Department of Léman, first under the French Republic and then under the French Empire; the local Swiss government was restored on 13 December 1813 and Geneva joined the alliance against Napoleon.

33 *M*: in her 1845 edition of *Essays*, MWS changed this signature to 'M.S.', having possibly forgotten to do so in 1839.

34 *T. P. Esq.*: the original letters by PBS on which Letters III and IV of *HSWT* are based are addressed to his friend Thomas Love Peacock. See Introduction.

Mellterie . . . Lausanne: Meillerie, Clarens, Chillon, Vevey, and Lausanne are towns and villages on the eastern shores of Lake Geneva, many of them featured in Rousseau's celebrated epistolary novel *Julie* (1761); for the importance of *Julie*, and of Part 4, Letter 17 in particular, to *HSWT*, see Introduction. Various different spellings of *Meillerie*, on the French shore of the lake, were current in 1816. For the (incorrect) theory about the origins of the name, see note to p. 37.

Montalegre: for *Montalègre*; a former estate now swallowed up by the Cologny municipality; all that survives of the name is a bus stop near the Villa Diodati.

34 *July 12th*: in the original letter by PBS on which Letter III is based, the date is given as 'July 17, 1816' (see Appendix D). For more on the implications of the different dates, see Introduction.

Julie: possibly a reference to the heroine of Rousseau's eponymous novel, but more likely to the novel itself.

It is inconceivable . . . arises: this is the first of a number of passages in this part of *HSWT* in which the cultural impact of Rousseau's *Julie* on the landscapes where that novel is set prompts reflection on the ability of literary texts to influence our perception of the world. In 'Mont Blanc', PBS returns again to the idea of a reciprocal relationship between the perceiving mind and the landscape perceived (see especially lines 1–8, 36–40). But the refrain was a commonplace of travel writing about the region, long before the Shelleys visited. See, for example, *Travels*, vol. 1, p. 437; and *Tour*:

> It would be hopeless to attempt a new sketch of these enchanting regions after the glowing description of Rousseau, which has already been so often detailed by the hundred sentimental pilgrims, who with Heloise [i.e. *Julie*] in hand, run over the rocks and mountains to catch the lover's inspiration. All in nature is still romantic, wild, and graceful, as Rousseau has painted it. (vol. 2, pp. 179–80)

In his *Confessions* (1782), Rousseau himself not only emphasizes the connection between the landscape and his novel but also seems to anticipate the kind of tourism *Travels* and *Tour* describe. 'I would say to any one who has taste and feeling', Rousseau writes:

> go to Vevay, visit the surrounding country, examine the prospects, go on the lake, and then say, whether nature has not designed this country for a Julia, a Clara, and a St. Preux; but do not seek them there. (Quoted from *The Confessions of J. J. Rousseau*, 3rd edition, 2 vols. (London, 1796), vol. 1, p. 279)

For Byron's response to the local legacy of *Julie* in his third canto of *Childe Harold's Pilgrimage* (1816), see Appendix F.

23d of June: in fact, PBS and Byron began their trip on Saturday, 22 June (see *SC*, vol. 4, pp. 690–701).

a ruined tower: still standing today, the ruined tower is all that remains of the castle actually built in the thirteenth century by Aymon II de Faucigny (d. 1253), who also founded the village. PBS's original letter to Peacock (see Appendix D) comments that 'the marks of Cæsar's liberticide legions yet remain on the walls'. The passage seems to conflate Caesar's campaign against the Helvetii (a Swiss tribe), which began the Gallic Wars (58–50 BCE), with the last major battle of those wars, when Caesar laid siege to the city of Alesia (nowhere near Hermance) in 52 BCE by building a wall around it.

in 1560: Geneva, which had been Protestant since the 1530s, was involved in an ongoing conflict with the Catholic Duchy of Savoy.

a Queen of Burgundy: the Kingdom of Burgundy, which was incorporated into the Holy Roman Empire in 1033, stretched along the borders of France, Switzerland, and Italy, from Lake Geneva to the Mediterranean. PBS's history seems a little confused here: the *queen* whom he has in mind is probably Béatrice of Savoy, Dame De Faucigny (*c.*1237–1310), granddaughter of Aymon II, the founder of Hermance; she was forced to cede the castle of Hermance to her aunt in 1269 following an inheritance dispute. She never bore the title *Queen of Burgundy*.

inhabitants of Berne: Bern, now the capital of Switzerland, expanded its territorial possessions considerably in the fourteenth and fifteenth centuries, becoming by 1536 the largest city-state north of the Alps. See *Travels*, vol. 2, pp. 63–4.

Nerni: for *Nernier*, a village further along the shore from Hermance.

"beached margin": quoting *A Midsummer Night's Dream*, 2. 1. 85.

35 *like ninepins*: presumably *kegel*, the German variant of skittles (or ninepin bowling), which was popular across central Europe in the early nineteenth century.

The children . . . throats: the poor mental and physical health of the local inhabitants was often noted by travellers and formed a sharp contrast to the idyllic portrait of high Alpine communities given by Rousseau in *Julie*. See, for example, *Tour*:

> I have often admired the charming picture which Rousseau traces of the inhabitants of those regions; but [. . .] a number of the inhabitants are afflicted by the most humiliating of all the visitations of heaven, Idiotism [. . .] Another spectacle of disgust which this country presents, is the excrescence on the neck, known by the name of Goitres, and which is often associated with Idiotism. (vol. 2, pp. 188–9)

In his original letter to Peacock, PBS specifies that 'this is Savoy, the King of Sardinia's dominion' (see Appendix D), which ties the condition of the inhabitants to the oppression of monarchy.

mien: demeanour; mannerisms.

which his education . . . crime: the remark recalls Rousseau's ideas about the corrupting influence of institutional education in his *Émile, ou De L'Éducation* (1762).

My companion: in reality, Byron, with whom PBS was touring the environs of Lake Geneva, although this is never made explicit in *HSWT*. PBS's original letter makes no mention of Byron's gift, but records that 'Lord Byron, a new convert to Wordsworth, reminded me of the Highland Girl' (see Appendix D). The reference is presumably to Wordsworth's poem 'The Solitary Reaper' (1807). It was PBS who had 'converted' Byron, albeit temporarily, to Wordsworth, whose influence on *Childe Harold's Pilgrimage: Canto the Third* (1816) has often been noticed. In his *Conversations of Lord Byron* (1832), Medwin records Byron telling him that 'Shelley, when I was in Switzerland, used to dose me with Wordsworth physic even to nausea;

and I do remember then reading some things of his with pleasure. He once had a feeling of Nature, which he carried almost to a deification of it: – that's why Shelley liked his poetry' (pp. 24–5). In his original letter to Peacock, PBS remarked that Byron

> is an exceedingly generous person, & as such, is it not to be regretted that he is a slave to the vilest & most vulgar prejudices, & mad as the winds [. . .] he has shewn me great kindness, & [. . .] I had some hope that an intercourse with me would operate to weaken those superstitions of rank & wealth & revenge & servility to opinion with which he, in common with other men, is so poisonously imbued. (*SC*, vol. 7, p. 28)

35 *All . . . be*: 'It is hard to believe this actually happened.' Another passage reflecting on the ability of the 'imagination' to influence the perception of reality. The sentence is not in PBS's original letter of 17 July (see Appendix D).

five years . . . beds: the comparison was not intended to be complimentary, as the phrasing of PBS's original letter ('as bad as those of Greece') makes clear (see Appendix D). Byron was in Greece from July 1810 until April 1811 and his recollection of Greek beds may have been coloured by his having been confined to one for five days with a fever, which he describes in verse in a letter to his friend John Cam Hobhouse (1786–1869) dated Patras, 25 September 1810: 'On a cold room's floor, within a bed | Of iron, with three coverlids like lead' (quoted from *BLJ*, vol. 2, p. 15).

the river Drance: a number of rivers in the Alps have this or a very similar name. The reference here is to the *Dranse (Haute-Savoie)* which forms a delta (the 'plain near the lake') where it flows into Lake Geneva, between Evian-les-Bains and Thonon-les-Bains.

36 *besolets*: probably black-headed gulls, but possibly black or common terns, all of which frequent the lake—precise identification can be difficult and the French word covers a variety of birds. Cf. Rousseau, *Julie*, Part 4, Letter 17, in which St Preux describes a boating expedition on Lake Geneva with Julie: 'I had brought along a rifle to shoot besolets; but she shamed me for killing birds wantonly and for the sole pleasure of doing harm'; Rousseau appends a note glossing *besolets* as 'a migratory bird on Lake Geneva [. . .] not good to eat' (p. 422 and n.). The same letter narrates one of the most celebrated incidents in the novel, when the rowing boat carrying St Preux and Julie almost sinks in a storm (see note to p. 37).

Diespiter . . . egit equos: adapting Horace, *Odes* 1. 34, lines 5–8: 'namque Diespiter, | igni corusco nubila dividens | plerumque, per purum tonantis | egit equos volucremque currum' [For Jupiter, who normally splits the clouds with his flashing fire, drove his thundering horses and flying chariot across a clear sky] (transl. Niall Rudd; Loeb Classics edition). Horace's speaker credits this phenomenon with restoring his belief in God, which had lapsed under the influence of 'mad philosophy' [insanientis dum sapientiae consultus erro]. 'Some [of] Horace's odes' are on MWS's reading list for 1816, but do not have the 'x' marked next to their entry which usually indicates '[PBS] has read also' (see *MWS Journals*, pp. 85, 97).

the King of Sardinia: in 1816, Victor Emmanuel I (1759–1824) ruled the composite state of Savoy-Sardinia, as duke of the former and king of the latter. In her journal entry for 22 July 1816, written at Chamonix, MWS notes that in the inn where they ate in Servoz 'among other laws of the same nature there was an edict of the king of Sardinia's prohibiting subjects from holding private assemblies on pain of a fine of 12 francs & in default of payment imprisonment' (see Appendix E).

eaux savonneuses: 'cleansing waters' (French). 'They' include the Swiss mountaineer and scientist Marc-Théodore Bourrit (1739–1819), who uses the expression when describing Evian in his widely-read *Itinéraire de Genève, des glaciers de Chamouni, du Valais, et du canton de Vaud* (1808), p. 260. Cf. *Traveller's Guide* on the 'Salutary Baths in Different Parts of Switzerland': 'there are ferruginous waters, that are much used in summer-time' (p. 23).

the syndic: local governance in Swiss towns and cities usually consisted of a number of counsellors and civil magistrates (syndics), who had responsibility for different functions; the reference in this case is presumably to the Syndic of the Guard.

Maria Louisa: Marie Louise of Austria (1791–1847) married Napoleon on 11 March 1810, thereby becoming Empress of France. She visited Switzerland in 1814, after Napoleon's abdication; in a letter dated 8 September 1814, Byron's friend, the poet Samuel Rogers (1763–1855), reports seeing her in the park at Sécheron, in Geneva. See P. W. Clayden, *Rogers and His Contemporaries*, 2 vols. (London, 1889), vol. 1, p. 165.

37 *remembrance of St. Preux*: in Part 4, Letter 17, of Rousseau's *Julie*, one of the most celebrated sections of the novel, St Preux describes how, having rowed with Julie across Lake Geneva to Meillerie, he leads her to 'a wild and forsaken nook [. . .] filled with those sorts of beauties that are pleasing only to sensible souls'—and where, ten years earlier, he had spent 'sad and delightful days thinking of nothing but her' (p. 424).

A Bourbon . . . Rousseau: the House of Bourbon was a French dynasty which produced a number of European monarchs, including Louis XVI of France (1754–93), Charles IV of Spain (1748–1819), and Ferdinand IV (1751–1825) of the Kingdom of the Two Sicilies (Sicily and Naples), all of whom were dethroned during the Revolutionary and Napoleonic Wars. Rousseau's political and literary writings were understood by many conservative and radical thinkers to have had a profound influence on the emergence of revolutionary ideas in France, even more so than those of Voltaire and Diderot (1713–1814), and hence 'a Bourbon' would not respect his legacy. The Bourbon monarchy was restored in France following the Battle of Waterloo (1815).

that democracracy . . . earth: PBS shared with many European Romantic-period writers this assessment of Napoleon, the overthrower of kings turned emperor himself, as at once the defender and the betrayer of the democratic ideals of the French Revolution. PBS wrote three poems addressing Napoleon's paradoxical character: 'To the Emperors of Russia and Austria' (1810–11), 'Feelings of a Republican on the Fall of Bonaparte' (1815), and 'Written on hearing the news of the death of Napoleon' (1821). Napoleon (and Rousseau) also play a central role in PBS's unfinished poem 'The Triumph of Life' (1822).

37 *the . . . fragrant*: *Beckford* transcribed this description.

Probably . . . production: travellers often praised the quality of Alpine honey (e.g. *Voyages*, vol. 2, pp. 134–6); this theory about the name of the village is presumably based on *miele*, the French word for honey, but the etymology is faulty: the name is derived from an older word meaning *rocks*.

St. Preux's visionary exile: that is, where he had wandered alone amongst the rocks, longing for Julie. In his original letter of 17 July, PBS remarked that 'I had not yet read enough of Julie to enjoy the scene as I do by retrospect' (see Appendix D). The omission of this remark from *HSWT* is further evidence of how the text was prepared for publication and of the, at least partial, disingenuity of the claims to immediacy and authenticity made in the Preface.

The lake . . . Mellerie: Both PBS (in his original letter) and Byron (in letters and conversation) record that the incident described in this paragraph took place in the same part of the lake as two comparable occurrences in Rousseau's *Julie*. In his *Conversations of Lord Byron* (1832), Medwin says that Byron told him 'it would have been classical to have been lost there, but not so agreeable' (p. 15). Byron mentions the incident in a letter to his publisher, John Murray, of 27 June 1816 (see *BLJ*, vol. 5, p. 82); see also Thomas Moore, *Life of Lord Byron*, new edition (London, 1847), p. 320. PBS's account of the incident in his original letter of 17 July is more matter-of-fact than *HSWT*:

> We went from Mellerie to St Gingoux [for *Saint-Gingolph*], & were overtaken by a tremendous storm which made the waves at least 15 feet high. We all prepared for swamp as it was impossible to keep the smallest sail & the water began to break over the head. Contrary to all chances we arrived safe at St Gingoux, all the inhabitants of which town were watching on the shore to see who had ventured in so perilous a sea & who exchanged looks looks of wonder & congratulation with our conductors (see Appendix D).

Byron was an excellent swimmer; PBS could not swim.

38 *Roche de St. Julien*: not mentioned in PBS's original letter of 17 July, this may well be Les Cornettes de Bise. Alternatively a misprision of (or an older, local name for?) Les Jumelles [The Twins] a distinctive, double rocky peak near Saint-Gingolph. Describing Saint-Gingolph, *Traveller's Guide* mentions 'a rock on the side of the lake, crowned with verdure, which will give the traveller *some idea* of the obstacles which nature offered

in the construction of the road' around the lake (pp. 59–60). Le Dent D'Oche, which a number of contemporary travel guides mention, is another possibility. Saint-Julien is a district of Geneva.

stalactites: mineral deposits resembling icicles.

chesnut . . . overthrown: compare Byron's note to *Childe Harold's Pilgrimage: Canto the Third*, 94, line 927 (see Appendix F).

La Valais: the third largest, and the highest, canton in Switzerland, bordering the south-eastern extremity of Lake Geneva. In Part 1, Letter 23 of *Julie*, Rousseau offers an extended account of the 'enchantment' of the Alpine scenery and the 'yet sweeter enchantment in the frequentation of the inhabitants', characterizing the region as a republican utopia amidst the mountains (p. 65). Rousseau's description often caused dismay amongst travellers when confronted with the realities of poverty and hardship in the area.

La Tour de Bouverie: all that today remains of this building in Le Bouveret is the restaurant *La Tour*, which features a tower as its logo.

39 *my companion rises late*: compare PBS's letter of 10 August 1821 to MWS, sent from Ravenna, where he was staying with Byron: 'L[ord]. B[yron]. gets up at two – breakfasts – we talk read &c. until six then we ride, & dine at eight, & after dinner sit talking until four or five in the morning' (*PBS Letters*, vol. 2, p. 322).

the river: La Morge.

a succession . . . sound: compare the waterfall imagery in 'Mont Blanc', lines 27–31.

nosegay: small bunch. As PBS later observes, he was also collecting the seeds of Alpine plants for his garden in England.

castle of Chillon: starting with *Travels*, most guidebooks describe the Château de Chillon and its dungeon, which, by 1816, had become a standard stop on the tour of Lake Geneva. The dungeon inspired Byron's poem *The Prisoner of Chillon* (1816), which tells the story of François Bonivard (1493–1570), a Genevan nobleman, who was incarcerated there from 1532 to 1536; *Travels* also briefly recounts Bonivard's fate (vol. 2, p. 440). Compare Byron's note to line 111 of *The Prisoner of Chillon*: 'it is by this castle that Rousseau has fixed the catastrophe of his Heloise, in the rescue of one of her children, by Julie, from the water; the shock of which, and the illness produced by the immersion, is the cause of her death' (p. 32; see Appendix G). The incident is described in Part 6, Letter 9, of *Julie*. The name 'Byron' has been carved into the dungeon wall at Chillon, but when, and by whom, remains a matter of controversy.

See . . . Part 4: presumably referring to the passage from Letter 17 when St Preux and Julie reach 'the middle' of Lake Geneva on their way to Meillerie:

There [i.e. from the middle of the lake] I explained to Julie all the parts of the superb horizon around us. I showed her in the distance the mouths of the Rhône whose rushing current stops after a quarter of a league, and seems hesitant to soil with its muddy waters the azure crystal of the lake. (p. 422)

It is shortly after this incident that their boat almost capsizes in a squall.

39 *They . . . reality*: another passage in which the legacy of Rousseau's *Julie* occasions reflection on the ability of imaginative works to transform our perceptions of the world—and, by extension, to query what 'reality' means. Cf. PBS's 'A Defence of Poetry' (1821): 'Poets are the unacknowledged legislators of the World' (quoted from *SPP*, p. 678). In PBS's original letter of 17 July, this sentence is preceded by a more extended discussion which, as Benjamin Colbert has noted, anticipates the imagery of 'Mont Blanc' (lines 1–48):

> I read Julie all day. I forgot its prejudices – it is an overflowing of sublimest genius & more than mortal sensibility. – It ought to be read amongst its own scenes which it has so wonderfully peopled. Mellerie, Chillon Clarens the mountains of La Valais & Savoy are monuments of the being of Rousseau. like the valley path of a might river– whose waters are indeed exhausted but which has made a chasm among the mountains that will endure forever. The feelings excited by this Romance have suited by creed, which strongly inclines to immaterialism. (See Appendix D; and Benjamin Colbert, *Shelley's Eye: Travel Writing and Aesthetic Vision* (Farnham: Ashgate, 2005), pp. 110–12.)

seven columns: cf. Byron, *The Prisoner of Chillon*, lines 27–39: 'There are seven pillars of Gothic mould, | In Chillon's dungeons deep and old, | There are seven columns, massy and grey'. Byron's Note (2) to line 111 of the poem covers many of the details given in *HSWT*'s account of Chillon (see Appendix G).

40 *pernicies . . . Tacitus*: the Latin phrase means 'destruction of the human race'. But it is not quite an accurate recollection of Tacitus, *Annals* XV. 44, which recounts how Nero, looking to apportion blame for the Great Fire of Rome (CE 64), condemned Christianity as teaching 'odio humani generis' [hatred of the human race]. The *Annals* are on PBS's reading list for 1816 (see *MWS Journals*, p. 97).

irrefragable: 'undeniable', 'irrefutable'.

gendarme: guard; literally 'man-at-arms' (French).

le bosquet de Julie: 'Julie's wood.' In Part 1, Letter 14 of Rousseau's novel, Julie and St Preux kiss in an 'enchanting' 'bower' near the house where she is staying at Clarens (pp. 50–2).

At least . . . existence: *Erkelenz* (p. 95) suggests that the 'language' of *ideas* and *impressions* recall's David Hume's (1711–76) *Treatise of Human Nature* (1740). The comparison is valid, though in fairness such terminology had, by 1816, become commonplace in British and European philosophy.

the spot: for St Preux and Julie being 'nearly overset', see note to p. 36. The second incident from the novel to which *HSWT* refers here is described at the end of Part 4, Letter 17, when St Preux and Julie are returning across Lake Geneva after their visit to Meillerie. St Preux says:

> in a transport it makes me shudder to think about, I was violently tempted to hurl her with me into the waves, and there in her arms put an end to my life and my long torments. This horrible temptation finally became so strong that I was obliged to let go her hand suddenly and gain the bow of the boat. (*Julie*, p. 428)

Since it is not possible, from the novel, 'precisely' to identify the 'spot' where either incident occurred, there is presumably some degree of artistic licence in *HSWT*'s account.

41 *this brutal folly*: perhaps combining the two senses of *folly* as 'ignorance' and (ironically) 'architectural extravagance'. Cf. Byron's remark in his note to *Childe Harold's Pilgrimage: Canto the Third* (1816), stanza 99, line 927, where he discusses 'the scenes most celebrated by Rousseau in his "Heloise"':

> Rousseau has not been particularly fortunate in the preservation of the 'local habitations' he has given to 'airy nothings'. The Prior of Great St. Bernard has cut down some of his woods for the sake of a few casks of wine, and Buonaparte has levelled part of the rocks of Meillerie in improving the road to the Simplon. The road is an excellent one, but I cannot quite agree with a remark which I heard made, that 'La route vaut mieux que les souvenirs' [the road is more useful than memories].

It was at Vevai: Rousseau's lover Françoise-Louise de Warens (1699–1762) was born at Vevey and *Julie* draws, in part, on their relationship. In his *Confessions*, Rousseau recalls that he 'conceived a love for that city, which had followed me through all my travels, and was finally the cause that I fixed on this spot in the novel I afterwards wrote, for the residence of my hero and heroines (vol. 1, pp. 278–9). The connection was also routinely made in travel writing, e.g. *Travels*: 'Rousseau himself passed some time at different parts on the borders of the lake [. . .] about that period of his life when he may be supposed to have written his Eloise' (vol. 1, p. 437).

Pays de Vaud: the Swiss canton of Vaud runs along the northern shore of Lake Geneva.

Gibbon's house: from September 1783 until August 1787, Edward Gibbon (1737–94) stayed at the mansion of his friend Jacques Georges Deyverdun (1734–89) at Lausanne on the shore of Lake Geneva and it was there that he completed his *History of the Decline and Fall of the Roman Empire* (1776–89). In his posthumously-published *Memoirs of my Life and Writings* (1796), Gibbon gives the following account of the property, which was demolished in 1896:

> Instead of a small house between a street and a stable-yard, I began to occupy a spacious and convenient mansion, connected on the north side with the city, and open on the south to a beautiful and boundless horizon. A garden of four acres had been laid out by the taste of

Mr. Deyverdun: from the garden a rich scenery of meadows and vine-yards descends to the Leman Lake, and the prospect far beyond the Lake is crowned by the stupendous mountains of Savoy. (Quoted from *The Miscellaneous Works of Edward Gibbon*, 5 vols. (London, 1814), vol. 1, pp. 250–1)

Many of the details of this passage of *HSWT* are taken from Gibbon's own account of the completion of *Decline and Fall* in his *Memoirs*:

> I shall now commemorate the hour of my final deliverance. It was on the day, or rather night, of the 27th of June, 1787, between the hours of eleven and twelve, that I wrote the last lines of the last page, in a summer house in my garden. After laying down my pen, I took several turns in a berceau, or covered walk of acacias, which commands a prospect of the country, the lake, and the mountains. The air was temperate, the sky was serene, the silver orb of the moon was reflected from the waters, and all nature was silent. I will not dissemble the first emotions of joy on the recovery of my freedom, and, perhaps, the establishment of my fame. But my pride was soon humbled, and a sober melancholy was spread over my mind, by the idea that I had taken an everlasting leave of an old and agreeable companion, and that whatsoever might be the future fate of my History, the life of the historian must be short and precarious. (*Miscellaneous Works*, vol. 1, p. 255)

In his original letter of 17 July, PBS remarks only that 'we see the decayed summer house where [Gibbon] finished his history & the terrace overlooking the lake, & the aciacias which overshadowed it' (see Appendix D). The reflection on Gibbon's character which follows was introduced in *HSWT*. Note that Gibbon does not mention Mont Blanc by name although it is visible from the spot and neither does PBS in his original letter of 17 July: that detail was introduced in *HSWT*.

41 *It . . . Capitol*: Cf. Gibbon, *Memoirs* on the genesis of his *Decline and Fall*:

> It was at Rome, on the 15th of October 1764, as I sat musing amidst the ruins of the Capitol, while the bare-footed fryars were singing vespers in the temple of Jupiter, that the idea of writing the decline and fall of the city first started to my mind. (*Miscellaneous Works*, vol. 1, p. 198)

42 *acacia leaves*: that is, leaves from the same trees which Gibbon mentions in his account of the completion of his *History*. On 27 June 1816, Byron wrote to his publisher John Murray (1778–1843) sending 'a sprig of *Gibbon's Acacia* and some rose-leaves from his garden, which, with part of his house, I have just seen' (*BLJ*, vol. 5, p. 81).

a cold and unimpassioned spirit: this assertion contrasts sharply with the remark only a few lines earlier on the 'grand' and 'touching' nature of Gibbon's 'regret' on completing his *History*. But it is easy to see how PBS might have been provoked by some of Gibbon's observations about his time in Lausanne: for instance:

Our importance in society is less a positive than a relative weight: in London I was lost in the crowd; I ranked with the first families of Lausanne, and my style of prudent expence enabled me to maintain a fair balance of reciprocal civilities. (*Miscellaneous Works*, vol. 1, p. 250)

yellow fire. in his original journal of the tour around Lake Geneva (see Appendix D), PBS adds at this point: 'a dog followed us from Lausanne, & slept all night at my door' (see *Geneva Nbk*, pp. 106–7). *Elton* (p. 67) compares this paragraph with PBS's 'The Cloud' (1820), lines 63–70.

Saturday the 30th of June: 30 June 1816 was a Sunday; PBS and Byron actually left Ouchy on Saturday, 29 June, stopping at Rolle that night, and returning home on Sunday, 30 June (see *SC*, vol. 4, pp. 690–701).

on Sunday evening: in PBS's original letter of 17 July, he continues: 'Affairs are here rather in a desperate condition. The magistrates of Geneva have prohibited the making of white bread [on account of a shortage of wheat, triggered by the bad weather of the year without a summer]. – all ranks of people are in the greatest distress. – I earnestly hope that England at least will escape' (see Appendix D). This observation was of course no longer relevant in 1817.

43 *St. Martin*: an alternative name for the village of Sallanches, as is later explained. In the account of this journey which PBS entered in MWS's journal there is an additional sentence not in *HSWT*: 'Clouds had over-spread the evening & hid the summit of Mont Blanc – Its base was visible from the Balcony of the Inn' (see Appendix E). Based on correspondence and reported conversations of Byron and his travelling companions, *De Beer* argues that on 26 July, on the return journey from Chamonix to Geneva, PBS entered the word 'atheist', in Greek, after his name in the guest book at the inn in Sallanches, prompting another traveller to write 'fool', also in Greek; Byron claimed to have erased PBS's inscription (see Introduction, and *De Beer*, pp. 4–6, 11). For the possibility that the Shelleys met the man, Ducrée, who would be their guide in Chamonix at Sallanches, see note to p. 47.

Hôtel de Londres: PBS, MWS, and CC stayed at the Hôtel de Ville de Londres which had been established by the Tairraz brothers *c*.1785 at what is now 30–36 Rue des Moulins, in Chamonix. The original hotel building was demolished in 1920, but some adjacent buildings dating from 1846, when the hotel was expanded, still survive (we are indebted to Laure Decomble, at the Musée Alpin Chamonix, for this information). When Byron arrived at Chamonix later in the summer, he stayed at the nearby Hôtel d'Angleterre. The names of both establishments speak to the nationality of most visitors to Chamonix in the late eighteenth and early nineteenth centuries. On 23 July, PBS entered the names Percy Bysshe Shelley, M[ary] W[ollstonecraft] G[odwin], and J[ane] C[lairmont] in the visitors' book at the Hôtel de Ville de Londres, citing their destination as 'L'Enfer' [French = *hell*] and writing alongside, in Greek, 'I am a lover of mankind, a democrat and an atheist'. The page from the hotel register on which PBS wrote survives in Trinity College Library, Cambridge. *De Beer* argues that PBS made a similar inscription in the visitors' book at the Hôtel d'Angleterre, describing himself (again, in Greek) as 'democrat, great lover of mankind, and atheist'. For more on both these inscriptions, the context for them, and contemporary responses to them, see Introduction, and *De Beer*, pp. 8–11. For an interesting account of the rivalry between the two hotels, see *Elton*, pp. 89–90.

43 *a home for us*: in his letter of 17 July, PBS had asked Peacock, then living in Marlow in Buckinghamshire, to find 'an unfurnished house, with as good a garden as may be, near Windsor Forest, & to take a lease of it for 14 or 21 years. The house must not be too small'; the journal portion of the original letter provided additional instructions about size, furniture, and garden (see Appendix D). Peacock was still looking when the Shelleys returned to England, and so they went to Bath; they moved into Albion House, in Marlow, in March 1817.

to exhaust the epithets: the idea that sublime mountain scenery defied description was a frequent refrain of both eighteenth-century philosophical aesthetics and Romantic-period travel writing. By 1816, however, the attempt to avoid the clichéd phrases of writing about Chamonix by describing the landscape as *indescribable* had itself become a cliché.

champain country: flat, open landscape.

Bonneville: Bonneville, in Haute-Savoie, is approximately halfway between Geneva and Chamonix-Mont Blanc.

44 *Matlock*: a town in Derbyshire, in the English Peak District, popular for its warm baths and dramatic surroundings, which include a number of curious geological features. In Jane Austen's *Pride and Prejudice* (1813), the heroine, Elizabeth Bennet, visits its 'celebrated beauties' (vol. 2, ch. 19).

Maglans: for *Magland*.

two waterfalls: the Nant d'Arpenaz and the Cascade de Doran.

some . . . deity: probably recalling Isis, the Egyptian goddess of nature. PBS's interest in classical Egyptian statuary also informs his well-known sonnet 'Ozymandias' (1818). Compare this passage of *HSWT* with the 'ethereal waterfall' and 'unsculptured image' in 'Mont Blanc', lines 25–7.

woof: fabric.

45 *a cascade*: La Cascade de Chedde (alternatively known as Le Cascade du Coeur). An entry made by MWS in the notebook that PBS kept during the summer of 1816 (see Introduction) comments: 'we mount the hill to see the cascade [replacing *chute*, which MWS deleted] du Chede - - this cataract falls 240 feet & spreads a round it a most beautiful spray- it falls on various projections of the rock & the mass is divided & unites again in a thousand places' (see *Geneva Nbk*, pp. 98–9). *Elton* (pp. 79–80) remarks on the fact that neither MWS nor PBS mention the 'lake' and 'grassy lawns' which 'all travellers' were 'expected' to see as part of their excursion to the Cascade but suggests that PBS may have recalled them in his

unfinished short story 'The Coliseum' (1819), which compares the over-grown ruins of the amphitheatre with 'the lawny dells of soft short grass' of 'the Alps of Savoy' (quoted from *Prose*, p. 226).

the vast . . . Arve: in 'Mont Blanc' (lines 1–11), PBS uses the mutually-shaping relationship between the Arve and the ravine in which it flows as a metaphor for the relationship between objective reality ('the everlasting universe of things') and the subjective, perceiving mind ('human thought'). Compare also the imagery in *F1818* volume 2, chapters 1 and 2.

a cabinet . . . Bethgelert: purpose-built museums, accessible to the general public, were not yet widespread in the early nineteenth century; hence, local scientific and cultural 'curiosities' tended rather to be gathered in display cabinets, in stately homes or other semi-private buildings—a process which reflected the eighteenth-century practice of amateur collection more than the scientific idea of curated (public) exhibition—or else offered for sale in shops or inns, in more heavily-touristed areas; the singular *cabinet* could (and often did) also refer to a location containing a number of individual displays. Éric Asselborn confirms that PBS refers here to Joseph Deschamps' shop in Servoz; Deschamps also owned the inn (see Éric Asselborn, *Mont Blanc: La Conquête Naturaliste* (Les Houches: Éditions du Mont Blanc, 2019), p. 215). *Bethgelert* = Beddgelert, a village in Snowdonia, Wales; from September 1812 until February 1813, PBS and his first wife Harriet Westbrook (1795–1816) lived in Tremadog, approximately 12 kilometres away. They stayed briefly in Keswick, in the English Lake District, in the winter of 1811–12, where PBS met the poet Robert Southey (1774–1843). Victor Frankenstein makes a similar comparison between the cabinets at Matlock and those at Servoz and Chamonix (see *F1818*, vol. 3, ch. 2, p. 29).

chamois' horns: a species of mountain goat, common in the Alps and widely hunted; *Voyages* (vol. 2, pp. 124–7) describes the dangerous life of the chamois hunter, a stock figure of Alpine travel writing; see also Act 1, scene 2, of Byron's *Manfred* (1817), where a chamois hunter intervenes as the protagonist contemplates throwing himself from a precipice on the Jungfrau.

bouquetin: the Alpine ibex, a species of mountain goat which had been hunted to near extinction by the end of the eighteenth century. *Travels* (vol. 1, p. 402) provides an extended description and illustration of the 'extremely rare' animal, Coxe having seen the 'head and horns' of a male and 'stuffed specimens of a female and a young one' in Chamonix.

46 *Pinnacles . . . on high*: cf. MWS's journal entry for 22 July: 'As we continued our route to Cerveaux [Servoz] the mountains encreased in height & beauty – the summits of the highest were hid in Clouds but they sometimes peeped out into the blue sky higher one would think than the safety of God would permit since it is well known that the tower of Babel did not nearly equal them in immensity' (see Appendix E).

The immensity . . . madness: again, a commonplace of both eighteenth-century philosophical aesthetics and Romantic-period travel writing about the Alps in general and about Chamonix in particular. Compare, for example, Bourrit's *Relation of a Journey to the Glaciers of Savoy* (1775) on the 'prodigious' summits 'shooting up to an immeasurable height': 'such is the engrossing nature of these objects, that they seem to efface every other idea. We are no longer our own masters; and it is next to impossible to stop the impulse of our inclinations' (p. 114). *Beckford* transcribed this sentence, underlining 'not unallied to madness' for emphasis.

46 *all was . . . our own*: a complex phrase, the exact sense of which is elusive: for commentary, compare 'Mont Blanc', lines 35–40 and editorial note.

Nature was the poet: compare the 'sublime expression' which PBS attributes to the Italian poet Torquato Tasso (1554–95) in a letter of 16 August 1818 to Peacock from Bagni di Lucca and subsequently cites in his essays 'On Life' (1819) and 'A Defence of Poetry' (1820): 'Non c'è in mondo chi merita nome di creatore, che Dio ed il Poeta' [There is no one in the world who deserves the name of creator, except God and the Poet] (quoted from *PBS Letters*, vol. 2, p. 30). Polidori records reading Tasso with MWS at Villa Diodati in 1816 (see *Polidori*, pp. 116, 119).

aiguilles: a range of rocky summits running along the south side of the Chamonix valley between the Mer de Glace and the Glacier de Bossons, including the Aiguille du Midi (3842 m), Aiguille du Plan (3673 m), and Aiguille des Pélerins (3318 m). *Aiguille* is the French word for needle.

Glacier de Boisson: after the Mer de Glace and the source of the Arveyron (see notes to pp. 47, 49), the Glacier des Bossons was the most popular tourist attraction in early nineteenth-century Chamonix, partly on account of its easy accessibility (various spellings of the name were in use). Today, the glacier has receded considerably farther than 'a few minutes' walk' from the old road and is only reachable after a lengthy ascent.

pyramidical crystalizations: the area adjacent to the Bossons glacier is still known as the Plateau des Pyramids.

47 *source . . . Arveiron*: in 1816, the Arveyron river, a tributary of the Arve, emerged from spectacular ice caves at the snout of the Mer de Glace glacier, just outside Chamonix. After the view of the Mer de Glace itself from Montenvers (then sometimes called 'Montanvert'; see note to p. 49), the source was the most popular tourist attraction in the area; it is described in detail by most contemporary travel accounts and frequently illustrated, as, for instance, in Carl Ludwig Hackert's (1740–96) *Vue de la source de l'Arveron* (1780), one of his series of influential paintings of the Chamonix valley. In her journal entry for 23 July, MWS records that during their visit to the source their 'Guide told us a story of two Hollanders who went without any guide into the cavern of the Glacier & fired a pistol there which drew down a large piece upon them' (see Appendix E). In volume 3, chapter 8, of MWS's novel *The Last Man* (1826), the final victim of the mysterious disease which kills all but four of the human race is buried by the survivors near the source (see Appendix I). Today, the Mer de

Glace has retreated far up the valley and the sublime scene visited by the Shelleys no longer exists.

the immense . . . Montanvert: the Mer de Glace. See note to p. 49.

Ducrée: Éric Asselborn suggests that PBS, MWS, and CC met Ducrée at Saint Martin (see Asselborn, *Mont-Blanc*, p. 215); in private correspondence with the editors, Laure Decomble, of the Musée Alpin Chamonix, supports this suggestion, noting that Ducrée is not a common name in Chamonix. *Elton* (p. 88) suggests that in the local 'patois' the surname might actually have been 'Ducroz', which raises the possibility that their guide was actually Joseph Ducroz, one of a number of important guides to carry that name, who had close connections with the individuals involved in the earliest ascents of Mont Blanc (see headnote to 'Mont Blanc'). In her journal entry for 26 July, MWS records that Ducrée told her 'about the manner of living in the country – the women do almost all the work such as reaping making hay &c' whilst the men guide in summer and hunt in winter; she also notes that 'they have a custom here of marrying very early – Ducrée married at 18 a girl of 16 – this was partly introduced by the conscription which allowed immunities for the father of families. In winter many of the men go to Paris and hire themselves as porters at hotels &c– for the winter here is a kind of starving thing' (see Appendix E).

river . . . irretrievably: compare PBS's long, descriptive letter to Thomas Love Peacock of 17/18 December 1818, in which he reflects on the volcanic landscapes around Naples: 'Vesuvius is, after the glaciers the most impressive expression of the energies of nature I ever saw [. . .] The lava like the glacier creeps on perpetually with a crackling sound' (*PBS Letters*, vol. 2, pp. 62–3).

48 *Saussure . . . probable*: *Voyages*, by the celebrated Swiss explorer and natural philosopher Horace Bénédict de Saussure (1740–99), remained, in 1816, the most comprehensive natural history of the region. Saussure discusses the behaviour of the glaciers at Chamonix in the first volume of *Voyages* (pp. 385–6). Contemporary guidebooks and travel writing often included excerpts or partial translations from *Voyages*, especially Saussure's account of his successful ascent of Mont Blanc in 1787 (see headnote to 'Mont Blanc'). Given that Saussure's ideas were in wide circulation, this reference is not in itself evidence that MWS and PBS had read *Voyages*.

Buffon's . . . theory: in the seventh section of his *Époques de la Nature* (1779), Georges-Louis Leclerc, Comte de Buffon (1707–88), an early theorist of evolution, speculated that polar and alpine ice would increase as part of the gradual but inevitable cooling of the earth ('refroidissement successif de la Terre'), which he believed was losing its heat after having been ejected from the sun by the impact of a comet. See Buffon, *Histoire Naturelle*, vol. 12, pp. 312–13. PBS offers a more meliorative account of glaciation in 'Mont Blanc', lines 120–6.

Do you . . . Ahriman: Ahriman is the evil deity of the Zoroastrian religion, the cosmic opponent of the benevolent deity, Ahura Mazda. Peacock had recently begun work on an epic poem entitled *Ahrimanes*, though he never made much progress with it; *Murray* (p. 446 n. 221) refers the reader to the 'excellent account of Peacock's unfinished poem on the subject and its relation to S and his works' in *SC*, vol. 3, pp. 226–44. The opening of PBS's sentence ('Do you') suggests a question, but the absence of a question mark and the final clause suggest, rather, that he is making a recommendation, i.e. that Peacock should do this. 'Arimanes' also plays a key role in Act II, scenes iii–iv of Byron's *Manfred*, where he is identified as semi-Alpine 'Prince of Earth and Air', whose hall can be accessed from the summit of the Jungfrau (IV. iii. 1).

48 *adamantine . . . necessity*: the term *necessity*, an idea prominent in PBS's work since *Queen Mab* (1813), broadly speaking names the inevitable (*adamantine* = unbreakable) chain of causes and effects which determines all the operations of the universe, humans included (i.e. 'natural law'). But the concept has a complex history in eighteenth-century British and French philosophy, science, and political theory, and PBS's understanding of it responds to an array of sources, including William Godwin's (1756–1836) *Enquiry Concerning Political Justice* (1793) and Thomas Malthus's (1766–1834) *Essay on the Principle of Population* (1798). See also headnote to 'Mont Blanc'.

49 *glacier of Montanvert*: first described and brought to widespread notice by William Windham's (1716–61) *Account of a Journey to the Glacieres or Ice Alps of Savoy* (1744), by 1816, the Mer de Glace glacier had become the premier tourist attraction in Chamonix and a mainstay of contemporary travel-writing and painting. The standard route, taken by the Shelleys, brought tourists to view the glacier from the shoulder of the adjacent Montenvers. In volume 2, chapter 2, of *F1818*, the Mer de Glace is made the scene of the first confrontation between Victor and his Creature, when a distressed Victor decides to revisit scenes familiar from his youth. As noted above, the ice has retreated substantially since 1816 and the scenery visible then no longer exists today. *Beckford* transcribed several phrases from this description of the glacier.

950 . . . feet: estimates in eighteenth- and early nineteenth-century travel writing of the elevation of key Alpine locations do not always agree, partly because of the different units of measurement involved. *Toises* were in use in both France and Switzerland in 1816, but signalled slightly different lengths (approximately 2 metres); French *feet* also differed from English.

We have . . . wonder: in her journal entry for 25 July, MWS records that they began their ascent at nine in the morning, with 'Beaucoup de Monde' (i.e. lots of other people), and reached 'the top at twelve [. . .] we went on the ice [. . .] we dine on the mountain' (see Appendix E).

cabin of Montanvert: the 'Temple of Nature', built in 1795 to replace an earlier refuge constructed by Charles Blair in 1779 which had gradually fallen into disrepair (Blair's refuge is the 'hut' where Victor and the Creature converse in volume 2, chapter 2, of *F1818*). For a more detailed account of both sites, see Patrick Vincent, 'Le Temple de la Nature, Chamonix' on the *Rêve (Romantic Europe: Virtual Exhibition)* website (https://www.euromanticism.org/virtual-exhibition/). As Vincent points out, the 'Temple' was intended not only to replace the dilapidated earlier building but also 'to honour both natural religion and revolutionary politics'. During their visit to the 'cabin' on 25 July, PBS entered his name in the visitors' book as 'Mr. Percy Bysshe Shelley', MWS as 'Madam son Epouse' [*French* = 'Madam his wife'], and CC as 'Theossteique la soeur'. *De Beer* explains 'Theossteique' as 'a gallicized version of θεοστυγη meaning "hated of god" or "god hating"' (p. 5; cf. MWS's playful gallicism *craquèed* earlier in *HSWT*; 'la soeur' = *French*: 'the sister'). For more on this notorious inscription, which was seen by a number of subsequent visitors to Montenvers, including Robert Southey, and contemporary responses to it, see Introduction and *De Beer*, pp. 2–8, 11.

a mauvais pas: a difficult or dangerous part of a mountain route (from the French = 'bad step'). Whilst the expression was in general use, however, it is also worth noting that, in 1816, both a specific section of the original (*ancien*) route up Mont Blanc and the track along the side of the Mer de Glace, where PBS fell, were called Le Mauvais Pas (a small road in the hamlet of Le Lavancher, below the Mer de Glace, still bears the name today). Cf. MWS's journal entry for 24 July: 'As we descended Shelley went before and tripping he fell upon his knee – this added to the weakness occasioned by a blow on his ascent – he fainted and was for some minutes incapacitated from continueing his route' (see Appendix E).

50 *It exhibits . . . torrent*: the description, a commonplace of travel writing by 1816, finds its earliest incarnation in Windham's *Account of a Journey*.

In . . . motion: compare 'Mont Blanc' on the same scene: 'all seems eternal now' (line 75).

it breaks . . . for ever: compare 'Mont Blanc' on the Arve: 'a vast river | Over its rocks ceaselessly bursts and raves' (lines 10–11).

the god . . . Stoics: the entry for Zeno of Elea (*c*.495–430 BCE) in John Lemprière's (1765–1824) *Classical Dictionary* (4th edition; 1801) notes that 'he acknowledged only one God, the soul of the universe, which [i.e. 'the universe'] he conceived to be the body, and therefore he believed that those two united, the soul and the body, formed one perfect animal, which was the god of the stoics'. In other words, the Stoics understood god as the active principle of the material universe, an understanding broadly consistent with PBS's idea of 'Necessity' (see headnote to 'Mont Blanc'). In PBS's *Refutation of Deism* (1814), one of the interlocutors, Eusebes, asserts that 'the God of the rational Theosophist is a vast and wise animal' (quoted from *Murray*, vol. 1, p. 121).

M***, C****: MWS and CC.

Pont Pelissier: for *Pont Pélissier*, a bridge (= *pont*) across the Arve around halfway between Servoz and Les Houches; a concrete road bridge now stands adjacent to the site of the original wooden bridge which the Shelleys crossed in 1816. The scene was often illustrated by Romantic-period painters and engravers. In her journal entry for 22 July, MWS records crossing this 'alpine bridge' on the way *towards* Chamonix (see Appendix E). See headnote to 'Mont Blanc'.

50 *the chateau . . . Michel*: built in the late thirteenth century by Béatrice of Savoy, to guard the approach to the valley of Chamonix and its priory. It was abandoned in 1435 and gradually fell into ruin.

one of which . . . valley: part of the Rochers de Fiz, near the Pointe d'Anterne, which collapsed in 1751. *Elton* says that 'the King of Sardinia at once despatched Vitaliano Donati, a famous Venetian naturalist, to report on the disaster' (p. 71) and the episode is also described in *Voyages*. MWS's journal entry for 26 July records: 'we saw also the mountain which fell some years ago and destroyed many men and cows (des hommes et des vaches – as our guide expressed it – some of the rocks reached to the vale through which we rode' (see Appendix E).

51 *cabinet . . . Chamouni*: Asselborn identifies this as the shop run by the Carrier family on Place de l'Église in Chamonix (Asselborn, *Mont-Blanc*, p. 215). Neither the business nor the building survives today. Joseph and Michel Carrier also made and sold relief models of the Mont Blanc massif (Asselborn, *Mont-Blanc*, p. 122). *Elton* (pp. 90–1) mentions some of the other purveyors and the pressure to buy exerted on travellers by their guides.

Clifton: presumably the suburb of Bristol (England) where MWS and PBS spent time together in the summer of 1815 after visiting the fossil-rich Devon coast (see *MWS Letters*, vol. 1, p. 15); but at least two other villages in the north of England share the name.

aubergistes: innkeepers; from the French *auberge*, meaning 'hostel'.

the sick: *Beckford* transcribed this sentence.

the Celandine . . . poet: Peacock sent a lesser celandine (*Ranunculus ficaria*), which flowers throughout spring, in one of his letters to PBS, who commemorated its arrival in July with his 'Verses written on receiving a Celandine in a letter from England'. The reference to the flower in *HSWT* is a thinly-veiled critique of William Wordsworth (the 'vernal poet'), whom MWS and PBS, like Byron, believed to have betrayed the political and artistic radicalism ('daring') of *Lyrical Ballads* (1798) in more recent poems like *The Excursion* (1815): Wordsworth had published three poems on the celandine in his *Poems, in Two Volumes* (1807), where he identifies himself and his poetry with the flower. The critique of Wordsworth is more explicit in 'Verses written'; compare also PBS's 1815 sonnet 'To Wordsworth'.

troops of wolves: in her journal entry for 26 July, MWS records Ducrée telling her that 'in the winter' (when there are no tourists), the guides 'hunt hares, foxes, marmots & wolves – these last they gain more by than by any other animal – they can sell the skins for 12 francs and the government has set a price on their heads – 12 for a small one – 15 for a large one & 18 for a female big with young' (see Appendix E). Whilst the comparison with dogs is obvious, MWS and PBS presumably knew the well-known anecdote, told by Thomas Gray (1716–71) in a letter to his mother of 7 November 1739, of how Horace Walpole's (1717–97) spaniel was killed by a wolf on Mont Cenis (see *The Works of Thomas Gray*, 3rd edition, ed. W. Mason, 2 vols. (London, 1807), vol. 1, pp. 207–8). Cf. 'Mont Blanc', lines 68–9. *Beckford*'s gloss on this passage is particularly scathing:

> No, you did not; but had you told me there were troops of wild <u>Bores</u> & yourself their Captain, as raving <u>mad</u> about Mountains as Hares in March about Love, I should have believed you – your prose most pompously picturesque Sir is high flown enough, God knows but your poetry [ ] is overwhelming, an avalanche of nonsense.

Mont Blanc. Lines Written in the Vale of Chamouni.

PBS made a rough draft of this poem in the notebook that he used during the summer of 1816 (hereafter *Geneva Nbk*), some of which survives in the Bodleian Library, probably beginning on 22 or 23 July 1816, shortly after he arrived in Chamonix. Parts of this draft are in pencil, which has led a number of commentators to suggest that they were composed outdoors. PBS later wrote out a complete, first version of the entire poem in what has become known as the Scrope Davies Notebook (*SDN*; see Appendix H). This must have been done by 29 August, when PBS returned to England, leaving *SDN* with Byron at Geneva. The poem was first published in *HSWT* where it is dated '23 June, 1816'; this is obviously an error, since PBS did not arrive in Chamonix until 22 July, but MWS nevertheless retained the June date in all her collected editions of PBS's work. Because PBS no longer had access to *SDN* whilst *HSWT* was being prepared for the press, he presumably used the draft in *Geneva Nbk* as the basis for the text published there, which may date from mid September 1817 (see Introduction and *MWS Journals*, p. 180).

'Mont Blanc. Lines Written in the Vale of Chamouni' is one line shorter than the *SDN* text and differs appreciably from it in a number of places. The first and most obvious of these differences is the title itself. The *SDN* text is headed 'Scene—Pont Pellisier in the Vale of Servox': Pont Pélissier was the bridge over the river Arve which most tourists crossed on their way to and from Chamonix; the view from it was often described and illustrated (today a modern road bridge has replaced a variety of earlier, wooden crossings, remnants of which can still be seen). The *SDN* title is consistent with MWS's claim, in her 'Note on the Poems of 1816', that PBS 'was inspired by a view of that mountain and its surrounding peaks and valleys, as he lingered on the Bridge of Arve on his way through the Valley of Chamouni' (*PW1839*, vol. 3, p. 35). But as *Erkelenz* notes, the *HSWT* title is more appropriate to a poem 'which describes not a single scene viewed from Pont Pelissier or multiple scenes fancifully compressed into one, but the entire Chamonix excursion as presented in Letter IV [of *HSWT*]' (p. 82). And there may be another, more mundane reason for the change in title. Letter IV records that the Shelleys and CC did not see the summit of Mont Blanc as they crossed Pont Pélissier on the way to Chamonix: 'Mont Blanc was before us, but it was covered with cloud [. . .] Pinnacles of snow intolerably bright, part of the chain connected with Mont Blanc, shone through the clouds at intervals on high.' Nor could they have seen it on their way from Chamonix either, because the summit is not actually visible from Pont Pélissier even in clear weather: perhaps PBS, like many other tourists before and since, initially mistook the adjacent Dôme du Goûter (4,303 m) for Mont Blanc. *CPPBS* (p. 499) suggests that the overcast weather of 'the year without a summer' might have prevented PBS from seeing the summit of Mont Blanc at all during his stay in Chamonix. Interesting, in this respect, is the fact that neither of the sketches of mountain scenery in *Geneva Nbk*, which seem to have been made at Chamonix, show the Mont Blanc massif. Further significant differences between the *SDN* and *HSWT* texts of the poem are discussed in our notes.

Mont Blanc (4808 m), the highest mountain in Western Europe, was first summited on 8 August 1786, by Jacques Balmat (1762–1834), a local guide, and Michel Gabriel Paccard (1757–1827), a local doctor. The following year, on 3 August 1787, the famous Swiss explorer and scientist Horace-Bénédict de Saussure (1740–99) reached the summit with a small group, led by Balmat, and remained there for a number of hours conducting experiments—whilst Saussure's wife and sisters-in-law looked on through a telescope in Chamonix and a flag was raised in his honour. Both ascents were celebrated around Europe and widely reported in popular and scientific publications, including Saussure's own *Relation Abrégée d'un Voyage à la Cime du Mont Blanc en Août 1787*, which was immediately translated into a range of languages and later included in *Voyages*. By the time MWS, PBS, and CC arrived at Chamonix in July 1816, Mont Blanc had been summited at least seven times, including the first ascent by a woman, Marie Paradis, on 14 July 1808 (also guided by Balmat).

The various attempts to climb Mont Blanc in the latter part of the eighteenth century helped to cement the status of Chamonix as *the* destination for mountain tourism in Europe, a status which had increased year-on-year following William Windham's description of the spectacular Alpine landscape in his widely-read *Account of the Glacieres or Ice Alps in Savoy* (1744). Accessible again to tourists following the end of the Revolutionary and Napoleonic Wars in 1815, travel to Chamonix burgeoned. This Alpine travel industry is made an object of critique in Letter IV of *HSWT*, but MWS's journal reveals the extent to which she, PBS, and CC were themselves tourists, following well-established and popular itineraries: for example, visiting the Mer de Glace in company with 'Beaucoup du Monde' and picnicking on the Montenvers belvedere overlooking the ice (see Appendix E). This tourist industry and its impact on the landscape are almost entirely absent from 'Mont Blanc', however, beyond the fact that the poem took its place in an already long line of topographical poems about the area, as is tacitly acknowledged in the Preface to *HSWT* which, echoing the poem itself, seeks to distinguish PBS's work as

> composed under the immediate impression of the deep and powerful feelings excited by the objects which it attempts to describe; and as an undisciplined overflowing of the soul, rests its claim to approbation on an attempt to imitate the untameable wildness and inaccessible solemnity from which those feelings sprang.

In reality, PBS would seldom, if ever, have been alone amidst this increasingly less 'untameable wildness and inaccessible solemnity'.

By the summer of 1816, however, the cultural significance of Chamonix extended well beyond commercial tourism. The study of Mont Blanc and its surrounding glaciers continued to play a key role in the development of various branches of the earth sciences and, consequently, the area remained a major focal point for wider ideological debates about how such landscapes should be interpreted. One common position was to see the 'sublime' Alps as evidence for the existence of the creator–God described by the Christian tradition, both as the remains of a once Edenic world destroyed by flood and as leading, through the awe which they inspired, to an intuition and appreciation of divine power. Much of Chamonix's tourist industry was predicated around this view of the landscape and PBS reacted angrily against it in the notorious inscriptions which he left at various tourist sites and hotels around the valley, describing himself, MWS, and CC as atheists, democrats, and philanthropists (for more about these inscriptions, see Introduction). PBS extends this critique in 'Mont Blanc', which, as commentators have long recognized, is at least in part a response to the 'Hymn Before Sun-Rise, in the Vale of Chamouni' (1802) of Samuel Taylor Coleridge, a semi-plagiarized poem which reads the Alpine landscape, unequivocally, as evidence of divine power (see notes to lines 76–9 and 80–1); Coleridge himself had never been to Chamonix.

Religious responses to Mont Blanc were not merely a matter of personal faith, however: as PBS's atheist inscriptions make clear, reading the Alpine landscape as evidence by design for the existence of a creator God bore directly on questions of civil society and political justice since the prevailing legal and social systems of most European countries were still predicated upon a Christian theology. Against this idea of a divinely ordained creation, 'Mont Blanc' reads the landscape instead as evidence of systematic *natural* processes governing both the physical and the moral universe, processes which have no special regard for or exclusive relation to human life. Throughout 'Mont Blanc', PBS uses the term 'Power' to describe these processes operating over enormous geological timespans (see notes to lines 16, 76–9, and 96–100). In so doing, he challenges the conventional explanation for the overwhelming affective impact of the landscape on the viewer: the source of the Alpine sublime is not divine grandeur but the power of nature, made visible (even if unrecognized) in the landscape.

PBS's challenge to conventional, religious responses to the Alpine sublime in 'Mont Blanc' is informed by his engagement with contemporary speculation in the earth sciences, both about the wider, long-term dynamics of geomorphic change and about the more local actions and effects of glaciation. One of the major geological controversies of PBS's day was whether water or volcanic activity was the primary agent of geomorphic change, the so-called 'Neptunist' and 'Plutonist' positions. PBS hedges his bets on that point in 'Mont Blanc' (see note to lines 71–5). But his treatment of glaciation, which should be compared with his more negative discussion in Letter IV of *HSWT*, is unambiguous. Lines 85–125 make clear that whilst the mountain's glaciers have an overwhelmingly destructive effect in their immediate vicinity, they are also, as a source of mineral-rich water carried downstream, 'the breath and blood of distant lands'. When this anti-catastrophist understanding of natural history as ultimately meliorative is read in the wider context of *HSWT*, an analogy between natural and political history also becomes visible: seemingly disastrous events like the French Revolution—the defining political trauma of the early nineteenth century—may yet have, in the long term, a beneficial outcome (see commentary on Letter II). Today, the glaciers surrounding Mont Blanc have receded dramatically and continue to decrease year-on-year: in a very real sense, the landscape seen by PBS, MWS, and CC in 1816 no longer exists and catastrophe on an altogether different scale has become apparent.

In addition to PBS's engagement with contemporary religious and scientific responses to Mont Blanc, commentators have also identified an array of literary influences on the poem, notably including various works by Coleridge and William Wordsworth; the *De Rerum Natura* (first century BCE) of Lucretius (*c.*99–*c.*55 BCE); and Canto 3 of *Childe Harold's Pilgrimage* (1816), on which Lord Byron was working whilst he and PBS made the journey along the eastern side of Lake Geneva described in Letter III. Donald Reiman argues that *HSWT* was 'carefully conceived to culminate' with 'Mont Blanc' and that the poem, which has often been read in isolation, 'should be studied [. . .] in terms of the ideas and attitudes that precede it' in the book (*SC*, vol. 7, p. 41). Doing so reveals the extent to which the poem is informed by PBS's response to Jean-Jacques Rousseau's (1712–78) influential novel *Julie, ou la Nouvelle Héloïse* (1762), a major theme of and influence on Letter III. Benjamin Colbert notes not only that the Preface to *HSWT* 'implicitly draws a parallel between' *Julie* and 'Mont Blanc', but also that 'the poem repeatedly points towards' the power of Rousseau's imagination to 'cast a shade of falsehood', as PBS puts it in Letter III, on 'the records that are called reality' (Benjamin Colbert, *Shelley's Eye: Travel Writing and Aesthetic Vision* (London: Ashgate, 2005), p. 110). Rousseau's novel, Colbert argues, exemplified for PBS how 'poetic language' can 'work to the betterment of mankind' (p. 109). *Erkelenz*, for whom Rousseau 'haunts the entire' *HSWT*, similarly argues that PBS learned from *Julie* how imaginative works can 'offer radical alternatives to oppressive morality and politics [and] can also lend those alternatives the force of truth' (pp. 89, 90). It seems reasonable to think that PBS was trying to do for Mont Blanc what he understood Rousseau's *Julie* to have done for the landscapes where it is set: to challenge what PBS saw as the prevailing, reactionary cultural values inscribed upon the mountain and to replace them with more scientifically astute and politically progressive 'imaginings', to re-imagine Europe's most celebrated peak for his own generation. See also Notes to lines 6–11, 80–1, and 142–5 for further discussion of Rousseau's influence on 'Mont Blanc'.

Contemporary responses to 'Mont Blanc' seem to have been few and those few which are known often form part of wider commentary on *HSWT* (see Introduction). Both *The Eclectic Review* (vol. 9, May 1818, pp. 470–4) and *The Monthly Review* (vol. 88, January 1819, pp. 97–8) were dismissive, with the former quoting the opening lines and wondering if the 'reader . . . can understand them' (p. 473) and the latter noting that *HSWT* 'concludes with a poetical essay on Mont Blanc, which will scarcely rank [PBS] with the Scotts and Byrons of the Age' (p. 98). *Beckford* was also dismissive, describing the poem as 'overwhelming, an avalanche of nonsense—I took it at first for blank verse as blank as an unsuccessful number in the Lottery – til certain uncouth jinglings informed me there were attempts at Rhyme—'. But Beckford nevertheless took the trouble to write out part or all of lines 12, 19–24, 67–8, 71–2, 80–1, and 99–102 of the poem, heading his transcriptions with 'Now for Mont Blanc' and ending them with what looks like an ironic 'ok[e] I am sati[s]f[ied]'. The reviewer of *HSWT* for *Blackwood's Edinburgh Magazine* (vol. 3, July 1818, pp. 412–16) gave a more nuanced appraisal, noting that

> the volume concludes with a little poem by the husband, which, though rather too ambitious, and at times too close an imitation of Coleridge's sublime hymn on the vale of Chamouni, is often very beautiful. In the following passage [quoting lines 50–83] there is some darkness and confusion, as if the writer were grappling with objects above his strength, but there is grandeur both of thought and expression,—indubitable indications of a truly poetical mind. (p. 416)

The review of *Posthumous Poems of Percy Bysshe Shelley* (1824) in *The Edinburgh Review* (vol. 81, July 1824, pp. 494–514) is similarly nuanced, affirming that '*Mont Blanc* is full of beauties and of defects; but is akin to its subject and presents a wild and gloomy desolation' (p. 508). In 1831, John Aitken published 'Mont Blanc' as the first entry in his *The Cabinet, or, The Selected Beauties of Literature* (pp. 1–4).

'Mont Blanc' has been the subject of extensive discussion by scholars and editors of PBS's work and of Romanticism more generally, given the poem's enduring status as one of a number of representative Romantic-period engagements with the mountain sublime and one of the best-known of PBS's works (probably second only to 'Ozymandias' (1818)). For detailed treatments of compositional background, publication, sources, and critical responses, the reader should consult editorial commentary in: *PoS*, pp. 532–48; *CPPBS*, pp. 497–523; see also *SPP*, pp. 718–21. Critical commentaries which read 'Mont Blanc' in relation to *HSWT* include: Colbert, *Shelley's Eye*, pp. 81–115; Cian Duffy, *Shelley and the Revolutionary Sublime* (Cambridge: Cambridge University Press, 2005), 84–122; *Erkelenz*; and Anna Mercer, *The Collaborative Literary Relationship of Percy Bysshe Shelley and Mary Wollstonecraft Shelley* (London: Routledge, 2019), 54–62. The seminal engagement with the scientific contexts for the poem is Nigel Leask, 'Mont Blanc's Mysterious Voice: Shelley and Huttonian Earth Science', in *The Third Culture: Literature and Science*, ed. Elinor S. Shaffer (New York: De Gruyter, 1998), 182–203.

55 *The . . . mind*: *CPPBS* compares William Wordsworth, *Tintern Abbey* (1798) on 'a motion and a spirit, that impels | All thinking things, all objects of all thought, | And rolls through all things' (lines 101–3). *SDN* opens with the potentially more limiting assertion that 'In day the eternal universe of things | Flows through the mind'.

Such . . . raves: Colbert compares the imagery of these lines and stanza II with PBS's account of the legacy of Jean-Jacques Rousseau's *Julie* (1762) in his letter to Thomas Love Peacock of 17 July 1816 (a passage omitted from the version of the letter published in *HSWT*): 'like the path of a might river—whose waters are indeed exhausted but which has made a chasm amon the mountains that will endure forever' (Colbert, *Shelley's Eye*, p. 111; cf. also the account of the approach to Chamonix at the beginning of Letter IV).

Ravine of Arve: from its source on the Tête de Balme, the river Arve runs through the valley of Chamonix, where it is joined by the Arveyron, which rises at the foot of the Mer de Glace. For a discussion of how PBS's wordplay in this section of the poem relates to the poem's epistemological concerns, see Frances Ferguson, 'Shelley's *Mont Blanc*: What the Mountain Said', in *Romanticism and Language*, ed. Arden Reed (Ithaca: Cornell University Press, 1984), 202–14 (206). See also note to lines 16 and 34.

Power . . . Arve: starting with *Queen Mab* (1813), VI. 197–8, PBS often uses the terms 'Power' or 'Necessity' to describe the underlying mechanism of causality governing what he calls, in his Note to *Queen Mab* VI. 198, 'the moral and material universe', i.e. a natural law which governs not just physical but also human nature. 'Mont Blanc' reads the Alpine landscape as visible manifestations of the effects of this law (hence 'Power *in likeness* of the Arve') rather than as the work of a creator God. Shelley's concept of Power/Necessity has roots in an array of eighteenth- and early nineteenth-century philosophical and scientific works, including David Hume's *Enquiry Concerning Human Understanding* (1748) and William Godwin's *Enquiry Concerning Political Justice* (1793). PBS was strongly critical of what he saw as a reactionary appropriation of the idea by Thomas Malthus in his *Essay on the Principle of Population* (1798). See also notes to lines 76–9 and 96–7.

56 *ethereal . . image*: cf. the waterfall imagery in Letter IV.

Dizzy Ravine: at no point is the ravine especially deep, so 'dizzy' presumably refers to the 'ceaseless motion' of the Arve (cf. *OED* 'dizzy' 6: 'whirling with mad rapidity') but perhaps also to the 'dizzying' effect of the scene on the viewer.

I seem . . . around: these lines have been extensively discussed in relation to debates in eighteenth-century and Romantic-period philosophy about the extent to which the mind, and especially the imagination ('phantasy'), plays an active or passive role in perceiving the external world. *SDN* has 'unforeseeing' in place of 'unremitting' (= incessant), in line 39, which suggests that PBS, in revising, wished to increase the sense of the mind's activity. *CPPBS* suggests an echo of Samuel Taylor Coleridge's 'The Eolian Harp' (1796), lines 39–43. The passage recalls the discussion, in Letter III of *HSWT*, of how Rousseau's *Julie* was both influenced by and an influence on the landscapes it describes—and PBS's response to Rousseau's novel may well constitute a more immediate context here than more abstract, philosophical discussions of perception. Compare also Letter IV, describing the first view of the Chamonix valley:

> And remember this was all one scene, it all pressed home to our regard and our imagination [. . .] all was as much our own, as if we had been the creators of such impressions in the minds of others as now occupied our own. Nature was the poet, whose harmony held our spirits more breathless than that of the divinest.

legion . . . thoughts: the image perhaps recalls both Hannibal's (*c.*247–181 BCE) crossing of the Alps into Italy in 218 BCE, en route to attack Rome, and Napoleon's (1769–1821) crossing of the Alps into Italy in 1800, en route to defeat the Austrian army at the Battle of Marengo on 14 June.

the still . . . Poesy: a range of possible influences for this image of the perceiving mind have been proposed, including the allegory of the cave in Plato's (*c.*428–347 BCE) *Republic* (*c.*375 BCE) and the *idola specus* ('idols of the cave') proposed by Francis Bacon (1561–1626) in his *Novum Organon* (1620), often considered a founding work of empiricism, as obstacles to accurate perception. The most topographically immediate influence is, of course, the source of the Arveyron, which PBS visited in Chamonix (see Letter IV). As *Erkelenz* (p. 81) points out, Marc-Théodore Bourrit (1739–1819), in his widely-read *Relation of a Journey to the Glaciers in the Dutchy of Savoy* (London, 1776), describes the source as 'this fairy dwelling, this enchanted residence, or cave of *Fancy*' (p. 130; Bourrit's emphasis).

pass by,: we follow most eds. and *SDN* by adding a comma at the end of this line; *HSWT* has none.

viewless gales: invisible; the *gales* which drive the *homeless cloud from steep to steep*—an echo of William Wordsworth's 'I wandered lonely as a cloud'

(1807)—are amongst those forces shaping the landscape which cannot be perceived directly but only through their visible effects. *CPPBS* comments: 'the word brings into play the notion, central to the poem's close, that what cannot be seen may still exist'.

57 *subject mountains*: monarchist language was a familiar feature of travel writing about Mont Blanc and part of the conventional representation of the mountain as a symbol of divine power. Compare MWS's reference to Mont Blanc as 'queen' in Letter I.

tracts: possibly an error for 'tracks' or 'traces'; *CPPBS* retains 'tracts', citing *OED* (*v.* 2.5): 'to pursue or follow up by the footprints or traces', giving Edmund Spenser, *The Faerie Queene* (1590), II. i. 12 as an example. *Geneva Nbk* and *SDN* read 'and the wolf watches her'.

Is this . . . now: PBS here and in other parts of the poem addresses ongoing contemporary debates, many of them focused on the Alps, about whether volcanic activity or glaciation and flooding were the primary agents of geomorphic change: the so-called 'Plutonist' and 'Neptunist' positions. These lines also evidence the extent to which the language of earth science had not yet fully been dissociated from that of myth and religion ('the old Earthquake-dæmon') as other, competing ways of knowing and describing the world.

The wilderness . . . reconciled: the enigmatic phrase *But for such faith* has made these lines the occasion of a great deal of discussion. *SDN* reads 'In such faith', which is less difficult to interpret. But as *CPPBS* points out, PBS experimented with various formulations in *Geneva Nbk* and it seems likely that the reading in *HSWT* represents his final, deliberate intention, rather than a slip of the pen. Read in conjunction with lines 80–3, the passage seems to imply two possible reactions to the Alpine landscape: a potentially disturbing scepticism ('awful doubt') which sees that landscape as evidence of natural laws ('Power'/Necessity) which have no regard for human interests, or, alternatively, a conventional, religious response to the landscape which sees it as evidence of a benevolent creator-God, the 'faith so mild' exemplified in Samuel Taylor Coleridge's 'Hymn Before Sun-Rise, in the Vale of Chamouni' and a plethora of other contemporary responses to Chamonix, including those which prompted PBS's atheist inscriptions. Although perhaps more comforting than 'awful doubt', this 'faith', in PBS's view, is an error which actually prevents humans from truly understanding (truly being 'reconciled with') nature. The 'mild faith' is a kind of false-consciousness, i.e., 'But for such faith' = 'except for such faith'. *SDN* reads 'This wilderness' rather than 'The wilderness', in line 77; PBS apparently revised to make a point about nature in general rather than about Alpine nature specifically.

Thou . . . woe: correctly understood, the Alpine landscape challenges rather than legitimates political systems predicated upon a conventional, religious belief in the divine origin of natural and social order ('large codes of fraud and woe'). The lines have been compared to the biblical 'voice of one crying in the wilderness' (John 1: 23) and Coleridge's 'Hymn Before Sun-Rise', where the speaker's questions about the origin of the Alpine landscape are answered by a 'Voice' from the 'Torrents', 'Ice plains', 'Pine-groves', and 'Piles of Snow' that says 'GOD!' (see especially lines 55–60). *CPPBS* compares the phrase 'large codes of fraud and woe' with similar expressions in PBS's 'The Daemon of the World' (1816), line 269, and *Epipsychidion* (1821), lines 153–4. Compare also Letter III of *HSWT* on Rousseau's 'powerfully bright' mind which 'cast a shade of falsehood on the records that are called reality'. *SDN* reads 'Ye have a doctrine Mountains'; PBS, in revising, focused the address to Mont Blanc specifically.

the wise . . . good: PBS would presumably have included Rousseau on this list. Compare similar phrases and groupings in 'The Triumph of Life' (1822), lines 128–37 and 208–15.

the dædal earth: meaning the creative power of nature; from the Greek myth of Daedalus, the father of Icarus, who was a skilled inventor and craftsman. Earlier occurrences of the phrase have been proposed in Lucretius, *De Rerum Natura*, I. 1–20 and Spenser, *Faerie Queen*, IV. x. 65: 1; see also Linnaeus on the 'daedal Soil' in *Systema Vegetabilium* (1774), transl. John Anders Murray, 2 vols. (Lichfield, 1783), vol. 1, p. 5. As *SPP* observes, 'the sense has usually been understood passively to mean "intricately fashioned earth"'—but such a reading seems incompatible with the anti-creationist rhetoric of 'Mont Blanc'.

the torpor . . . year: winter: 'torpor' = lethargy or inactivity. *Geneva Nbk* reads 'the sleep of winter'. Cf. MWS's account of winter at Chamonix in her journal (see Appendix E).

58 *Power . . . inaccessible*: whilst the operations of 'Power'/Necessity are visible in the material and moral universe, the principle itself remains 'inaccessible' to human perception, i.e. 'Power' cannot be perceived directly but only intuited through its effects and manifestations.

And this: neither *Geneva Nbk* nor *SDN* emphasizes *this*.

adverting: 'attentive'; but suggesting an element of activity rather than merely passive observation.

Like snakes: cf. William Wordsworth, *Descriptive Sketches* (1793) on the 'five streams of ice' which 'descend' on Chamonix and 'like two enormous serpents, wind | And drag their length of deluge train behind' (lines 680–702). Cf. also CC's account of the Rhine in her journal entry for 30 August 1814: 'the undulating motion of the waves rolling ever one over the other produced the same effect as if snakes were creeping perpetually onwards' (see Appendix B).

dome . . . pinnacle: recalling PBS's engagement with Edward Gibbon in Letter III of *HSWT*, *Erkelenz* remarks that 'the gradual decline' begun in these images of culture and civilization 'ends in a Gibbonian fall, the city becoming, like ancient Rome, "a flood of ruin"' (p. 97). Cf. also Letter IV on the use of 'pyramid' to describe certain forms of glacial ice.

58 *distinct with*: 'distinguished by', i.e. 'in which can be seen'.

their place . . . known: a biblical phrase, reflecting the transience of human experience. Compare Nahum 1: 5–6 and 3: 17, and Psalms 103: 15–16.

Below . . . vale: PBS is presumably thinking, again, of the source of the Arveyron, which joins the Arve outside Chamonix. Compare the 'caverns measureless to man', 'deep romantic chasm', 'sacred river' which 'sank in tumult to a lifeless ocean', and 'caves of ice' from Samuel Taylor Coleridge, 'Kubla Khan' (1816), lines 4, 12, 26, 28, 36. In *HSWT*, line 122 has *torrent's*, but most eds. follow *SDN*, which has *torrents'*, since *Meet* (in line 124) requires a plural form.

one majestic River: the Rhône, one of the principal rivers of France, which flows into the Mediterranean at the Camargue delta; the Arve is a left tributary of the Rhône, which it joins at Geneva.

the power . . . death: these lines register not only the visible manifestations of 'Power' in the Alpine landscape but also the affective power of that landscape on the viewer, i.e. the connection between the manifestations of 'Power' and the experience of the sublime.

59 *voiceless lightning*: the distances and elevation in the Alps make it possible to see lightning at such a distance that the thunder is not audible. Compare *F1818*, volume 2, chapter 1: 'I remained many hours at the window, watching the pallid lightning that played above Mont Blanc, and listening to the rushing of the Arve' (p. 15).

And what . . . vacancy?: these ambiguous and to an extent intractable final lines have been extensively discussed by scholars of PBS's work, who have read them as aligned with an array of philosophical positions, from materialism to idealism and from empiricism to scepticism. To be fair, these various readings probably say as much about the assumptions which an individual critic brings to the text as they do about any identifiable epistemological conclusions which the poem itself might be said to reach. The lines, and particularly the final question, do, however, bear close comparison with PBS's remarks about Rousseau and *Julie* elsewhere in *HSWT* and especially with PBS's understanding of how Rousseau's novel had reshaped for PBS's generation the cultural significance of the locations where it was set. If we read 'Mont Blanc' as an attempt to do for the mountain what PBS believed Rousseau had done for Clarens and Meillerie, then the poem's final question might be read, more or less literally, as implying that it is impossible to know what the mountain would be if we could see it without any preconceived cultural assumptions, i.e. that we cannot see nature for what it *is* but only through the particular way in which we choose to *represent* it. The issue, then, becomes *how* to represent it—and PBS's choice in writing 'Mont Blanc' would seem to have been to try to replace the dominant conservative, religious 'imaginings' with more scientifically-informed and politically-progressive ones.